DANIEL
foreword by Travis J. Vanden Heuve

k

52 MASSES

A Journey to Experience Catholicism Across America

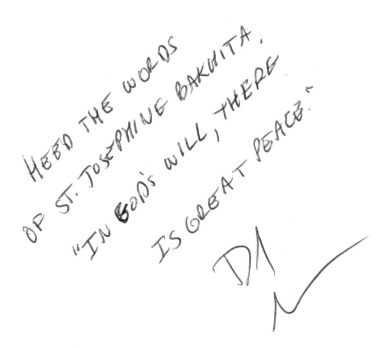

Over two years, author Daniel Markham celebrates the
Eucharist in all fifty states, Washington, D.C., and Puerto Rico.

52Masses.com

Over the course of his journey, author Daniel Markham documented his experiences with photography and blog posts.

We encourage you to engage with this supplementary content, and with Daniel himself, by visiting www.52Masses.com.

52 Masses: A Journey to Experience Catholicism Across America

© Daniel Markham. ALL RIGHTS RESERVED.

Authored by Daniel Markham.

Published by Peregrino Press
De Pere, Wisconsin

No part of this book may be reproduced in any form or by any means, electronic or mechanical, including photocopying, recording, taping, or by any storage and retrieval system, without the written permission of Daniel Markham or Peregrino Press.

Interior design © Peregrino Press
Cover design © Peregrino Press

Publisher's note:
This book, including names, characters, places, and incidents, is based on true events. Some names and identifying details may have been changed for privacy reasons. The authors alone bear responsibility for any remaining errors in the text, which are wholly unintentional.

ISBN (hardcover): 978-1-949042-34-4
ISBN (paperback): 978-1-949042-35-1
This title is also available in electronic and audiobook formats.

PUBLISHER'S CATALOGING-IN-PUBLICATION DATA
Markham, Daniel
52 MASSES / MARKHAM
1st edition. De Pere, WI: Peregrino Press, c2022.

Proudly Printed in the United States of America
10 9 8 7 6 5 4 3 2 1

DEDICATION

This book is dedicated to the women
in my life who made it possible:

My mother, Mary Lou Markham,
and mother-in-law, Mary Lou Marciniak,
both of whom I miss tremendously.

My daughter Kiera.

And, most especially, my wife Kemberly.

ACKNOWLEDGMENTS

When you travel across the country, you meet an awful
lot of people, and a few you already know,
who make your journey a little easier.

Here are just a few of them:

*Sloane, Marliss and Brian McManus; Fathers John Metzinger,
Roger DiBuo, Joseph Christensen; Scott Garrett, Bernard Gorges,
Mateusz Rudzik, Jack Ledwon, Chapin Engler, Charlie Urnick,
Jared McCambridge, Gerald McManus, Neil Pezzulo, Kevin McCarthy; Bishops Donald Hying and Robert McClory; Deacons Jim
Trzinski, Skip Olson, Gene Fadness; Melissa LaCaze; Emily Pickett;
Phil Marciniak; Amanda and Verne Carlson; Gene and the late
Ellen Lois; George and Mary Ellen Porter; Carleton and Lara Cole;
Jim and Sueann Bilello; Robin Vance; Claire Rung; Ken Billinger;
Gabrielle Nolan and Bill Brewer; Dave Hrbacek; Amy VerSteeg;
Linda Petersen; Christopher Gunty; Rob Herbst; Gaby Smith; Gail
Finke and Father Rob Jack; Jay Luzardo; Danny Gallagher;
Marlene Zloza; Francisca Jones; Jacqueline Tetrault;
Tom and (now) Dana Arena; Bryan Hooper and Ann Cook;
Dr. Mary Soha; and the music ministry at
St. Joseph in Dexter, Mich.*

Foreword

IN THIS TIME AND PLACE (UNITED STATES, 2022), IT CAN BE QUITE easy to ask, "Where is God?" Many Americans are fueled by the widespread acceptance of conspiracy theories and an ever-growing lack of trust in the very institutions that have woven the fabric of American society – a nation that has long embodied principles that foster equality, inclusivity, and love of our neighbors. Sadly, some of us have become eager to embrace a populism predicated on fear, division, and hate.

At the same time, the number of Americans practicing Christianity is rapidly declining. A 2022 report by the Pew Research Center and the General Social Survey shows that, since 1990, the number of Americans who self-identify "Christian" has declined by nearly 30 percent, while the number of Americans who don't affiliate with any religion has doubled.

While correlation isn't necessarily causation, these two realities are – at least in part – connected.

As human beings, we all yearn for something. Something more. Something we might embrace and build upon as the foundation of our lives. Without falling prey to the seduction of a nostalgia that rejects criticism, I would point to this correlation as an indicator that where God once served as a cornerstone in our lives, many Americans now turn elsewhere for foundational formation.

Whereas, in the past, we'd invest our time, talents, and treasure in a *greater* good – a *common* good – Americans today seem quick to expend these resources pursuing what benefits and advances their *own* good. Selfishly, more and more people are approaching an altar of materialism, worshiping false idols and counterfeit Gods, and seeking out narratives that validate and foster the worst parts of us.

The result? We – as individuals and as a society - have become more isolated, afraid, and adrift. Maybe without even knowing it, most of us yearn for God and His presence in our lives. But as we turn away from Him and toward the things of this Earth, we position ourselves to feel abandoned and on our own. And in those times, we seek to fill the emptiness with other things – material, Earthly things – only to find that they will never satisfy our spiritual hunger.

This might even raise doubts about God's very presence in our lives and in our world.

We may, at the end of each day, feel alone.

But are we?

Our author assures us we are neither cut off nor abandoned, and in *52 Masses: A Journey to Experience Catholicism Across America*, Daniel Markham shares the stories of parishes and parishioners whose experiences bear witness to the immediate and unquestionably real presence of God in their lives. *52 Masses* resoundingly assures us that we never journey alone.

Every day, across the United States and around the globe, Catholics gather for Mass. As the *Church Universal*, we examine the same readings, recite the same prayers, and enter into the same Mysteries. It is in and through the Mass – the source and summit of our faith - that we are unified. We become one body, in communion not only with God and the people in the room, but with our brothers and sisters united in Christ throughout the world.

Daniel invites his readers to ride sidecar as he embarks on a journey that takes him to all fifty states, the District of Columbia, and Puerto Rico. In each territory, Daniel visits chapels and Cathedrals, Basilicas and makeshift churches. And while God's Church may be visibly embodied in these houses of worship, Daniel reminds us that Church extends beyond brick and mortar, beyond altar and sacristy. God's Church is found, ultimately, in each of us.

Knowing this to be true, Daniel spent months meticulously researching the cities and sites he would visit. In this book, Daniel profiles the people, parishes, and ministries faithfully serving their communities in unique and relevant ways. In the remarkable, true stories in *52 Masses*, we encounter abundant reminders that in our journey through this world, we are never alone. God is always with us and we may encounter His abundant love if we seek His presence by opening our minds and hearts.

Like so many of God's works made manifest in the world, they are brought to light in and through our brothers and sisters in faith here on

Earth. Daniel's work is no exception; as it helps us to appreciate God's capacity to guide, direct, and inspire our thoughts, words, and deeds. In this manner, our thoughts become His thoughts; our words become His words; and our work becomes His work. All of this ultimately brings us closer to one another, and to the Father who created us.

The key to any of this being so, however, hinges upon our recognition that God's love for us is abundant and that His presence in our lives – and in the Mass – is real. For as different as all of the parishes, people, and ministries in *52 Masses* might be, they are knit together by the common thread of God's true presence in our lives. It's my prayer that, through Daniel's stories – and the inspiration, contemplation, and examination they so naturally foster – we can recognize God's hand at work in our lives today, and all days.

Travis J. Vanden Heuvel
Co-Author of the bestselling book, *To Heaven & Back*

Introduction

I CAN REMEMBER, VIVIDLY, THE MOMENT THE IDEA FOR THIS BOOK came to me. I had just dropped off my youngest son, Cormac, at soccer practice before he began his freshman year at Marquette Catholic High School in Michigan City, Indiana. On my way home, I was reminded of a nearby church my oldest son, Ian, and I had attended on a few occasions. St. Ann of the Dunes is a beautiful little church tucked inside the Indiana Dunes National Park. Constructed in 1950 with the help of the many Lithuanian immigrants who lived in the area, the parish still offers the liturgy in Lithuanian every third Sunday. My eldest, a lover of all things worldly, often invited me to tag along as he experienced the Mass in new, to us anyway, tongues.

Within moments of that delightful reminder, the idea for *52 Masses* washed over me. I would attend Mass in all 50 states. And the District of Columbia. And Puerto Rico. Fifty-two Masses. Fifty-two weeks in a year. And I would write about something taking place at each parish.

The idea, then and now, was to write about how we are living as Catholics, both people who have followed the path of religious life and lay people alike. The stories didn't have to be groundbreaking. They were not necessarily tales of heroes or martyrs. I just wanted to write about the many ways our faith comes to life – through evangelism, ministry, education, etc.

I would do so also while shining a light on the diverse nature of our religion. I hoped to visit parishes large and small. Urban, rural and suburban. Parishes made of up various ethnicities and demographics. And Masses that took place in places that weren't even parishes at all.

We are, after all, the universal church.

I targeted 2021 for this mission to begin, timed as it was with the graduation of that youngest child from high school. COVID-19 laughed at such hubris. Instead, I took off when things started to open up in the spring of 2021, my carefully designed plans tossed aside for this new reality. It didn't matter. The coronavirus was no match for the faith.

It took a little more than a year to complete, the trip wrapping up right back where it began in Northwest Indiana. It was an experience I will never forget.

Every parish has a story, I believe, and I was only writing 52 of them. If someone wanted to mirror this endeavor, she could choose 52 different places to visit and come away as blessed as I was, of that I have no doubt. That's the beauty and richness of our shared Church.

I pray the stories that follow adequately convey the wonderful ways the men and women I've met are using their gifts to answer God's call.

And I pray you are as inspired by them as I continue to be.

Cathedral Basilica of St. Augustine
St. Benedict the Moor

St. Augustine, Florida

"Go, therefore, and make disciples of all the nations, Baptize them, in the name of the Father and of the Son and of the Holy Spirit."
Matthew 28:19-20

Ponce de León guided the first successful Spanish expedition to La Florida, the New World land he gave name to in 1513. The popular and persistent and proofless myth was the conquistador was on a quest for the Fountain of Youth.

Yet, the Spanish explorers who followed him stumbled upon a wellspring far more important than any waters promising perpetual adolescence. They landed upon a site that would help deliver eternal life to the men and women of this New World.

"St. Augustine is really the baptismal font for the United States," said Dr. Mary Soha, a resident of the city on Florida's northern Atlantic Coast and the vice-postulator for the canonization cause for The Martyrs of La Florida.

It's not possible to separate the history of St. Augustine, the oldest city in the 50 states, with Cathedral Basilica of St. Augustine, the oldest Catholic parish. Fortunately, no one wants to.

"One of the great parts about being in St. Augustine is the people – not only Catholics but non-Catholics alike – have a real pride of place for the history of our city and the history of this parish," said Rev. Tom Willis, the former pastor at the Cathedral who was also raised in the parish.

The city and parish are intrinsically linked. When Spanish settlers arrived on the north Florida coast in 1565, Father Francisco López de Mendoza Grajales stepped off the boat carrying a cross. Before those settlers even shook off their sea legs, the colonizers were establishing a Catholic presence.

"When you study the founding of many of our nation's, let alone our hemisphere's, towns and cities, we're one of the very few that begins with an overt religious service," said Father Tom.

The site where the party landed, Nombre de Dios (Name of God), is today the home of the Shrine of Our Lady of La Leche. In 2019, the U.S. Conference of Catholic Bishops elevated it to a national shrine.

The Cathedral is similarly venerated. It was placed on the National Register of Historic Places in 1970 and was designated a minor basilica by Pope Paul VI in 1976, further cementing its significance to both Catholic life and U.S. history. In 2021, an image of Our Lady of La Leche was canonically crowned, only the fourth image in the U.S. to hold that distinction.

"To understand American Catholic history, you must understand what happened in St. Augustine," Dr. Soha said.

The Cathedral is located in the heart of downtown St. Augustine, which remains a small metropolis, particularly by Florida standards. But the stable population belies the changes that have occurred in the community in the last half century.

Once a sleepy town with rare bursts of tourism, the community now is invaded by travelers year-round. And given its place in the history of the community, the Cathedral is often a must-visit site on their travel itineraries. On any given weekend, visitors may represent 55-60 percent of the total Mass attendance. Such a steady influx of visitors is obviously good for the collection basket, but the situation is not without its challenges, particularly when those visitors are there for reasons outside the spiritual realm.

Walling itself off to the hordes is not a viable option. Rather, the parish has embraced the situation by creating a department devoted to serving those visitors. Its docents are responsible for serving as ambassadors for the church.

Docents lead tours, answer questions, man the gift shop, and perform other duties to accommodate the thousands of people who enter its halls every year. And it isn't just traveling Catholics, but history buffs of all faiths and school kids with no choice in the matter. As state history is a part of the curriculum for all Florida school students in fourth and seventh grades, the church hosts many public school students, children of varying degrees of experience with the Catholic Church or any kind of faith traditions.

It isn't just the non-Catholics who may need a reminder. St. Augustine has become something of a destination site for weddings, which leads to many hoping to have their nuptials inside the Cathedral. They're welcome to, but only if they're invested in a traditional Catholic wedding. It's a house of worship, not a resort.

It's also not a relic. The challenge for every priest who serves at the Cathedral is to balance the unmatched history of the space with the present-day needs of its existing parishioners.

Margo Pope has been a member of Cathedral Basilica of St. Augustine since her baptism there in 1947. Her three years 75 miles west in Gainesville for university were the only time she's not been a Sunday fixture at Mass. She sees parishioners who would like the church, and the community, to return to its quaint roots, while another group yearns for a more "modern church." She just wants the best one. "It's not the buildings; it's the religion."

Through the years, the Cathedral parish has bled some families to other parishes in the area, the victim of moves away from the crowded downtown. But many still return for special days, feeling a profound kinship to the mother church of Florida, Margo Pope said.

Those special events include the annual church festival, held this past year just before the start of Lent. It takes place near the shrine grounds, upon which sits a statue of Father Grajales, an enormous cross erected in celebration of the 450th anniversary in 2015, and an island with the Our Lady of La Leche chapel, a site described by former President John F. Kennedy as "America's most sacred acre."

Perhaps no group represents St. Augustine's oversized role in the importance of Catholicism in America better than the Martyrs of La Florida. The Martyrs were a group of Native Americans whose ancestors were introduced to the faith by the Spanish settlers and decimated by the British trying to rid the colonies of the Catholic Church. Many of the native survivors of the attacks fled the state for areas more amenable to the religion. Others found a home in the one part of Florida that defied the British and kept its Catholic identity – St. Augustine.

Dr. Mary Soha has been working on their canonization cause, opened in 2015 by Bishop Gregory Parkes, then prelate for the Diocese of Pensacola. Dr. Soha, a medical doctor, previously worked on the successful canonization effort for Kateri Tekakwitha.

She marvels at the incredible faith of the Martyrs, whose number has grown from 10 to 86 to "so many you can't count them all," she said of the extensive study into the Martyrs' past.

"Every time a Christian says the Our Father, and says 'thy Kingdom come,' what they are saying is I am willing to defend you. That's what these people in Florida did. They died saying 'I won't let anyone dilute you. I won't let anyone desecrate you. I will defend you,'" she said.

The Cathedral represents just one church in the larger parish. A few blocks away sits a much more modest structure, though one with a similarly important history. St. Benedict the Moor was the Catholic Church for African Americans in St. Augustine, an unfortunate reality for all longtime churches in the South.

The school property was donated by St. Katherine Drexel, one of many she was instrumental in founding for Blacks and Native Americans. The Sisters of St. Joseph operated a school for decades. Three of those sisters, Mary Thomasine Hehir, Mary Scholastica Sullivan and Mary Beningus Cameron, were arrested for violating a Florida law that prohibited whites from teaching Black children, a law they successfully challenged in court. Nearly 50 years later, the leading voices of the Civil Rights movement arrived in town to further that cause and decamped in the Lincolnville section of the city where St. Benedict is located.

Donna Hughes is a parishioner at St. Benedict, continuing a family tradition that dates back to the parish's founding. She spends each Sunday in the pew donated by her ancestors. In the 1960s, her family hosted Ralph Abernathy, while fellow civil rights leader Dr. Martin Luther King stayed at her cousin's home. The extended Hughes family has had a front row seat, and occasionally a more active role, in many of St. Benedict's dalliances with history, big and small.

She relates the story of the current building's construction, made with help from bricks taken from a building torn down near the beach. Black parishioners, many of them children, hauled the bricks from the beach over dirt roads to Lincolnville in little red wagons, excited at the prospect of their own house of worship. "That's how devoted they were," she said.

That spirit continues to thrive. The church and other buildings on the grounds have been undergoing regular improvements over the past decade, while the now-closed school building is being renovated by the Sisters of St. Joseph for eventual use as a center for unwed mothers.

Parishioner Jess May has been instrumental in many of the efforts at the parish, which she hopes will soon include some structural work to allow the church to once again use the choir loft. The rectory has already been upgraded, which benefits not just the congregation at St. Benedict but also the Cathedral, as the property has space for parking and a working kitchen that are not available downtown.

Money for the projects comes from a variety of fundraising efforts, most notably the annual Blues Festival held on site. A gospel Sunday that brings in all of the Lincolnville churches is also expanding.

But more important than raising funds is growing the faith, particularly among its neighbors in the Lincolnville community, an eclectic mix that includes longtime families and students from nearby Flagler College. "There are many people in Lincolnville we're not serving, absentee Catholics who don't even know what's going on here," said Jess May.

Like Dr. Soha, Jess May is not a native to St. Augustine. Rather, she and her husband were drawn to the city by its rich Catholic roots. On the Sunday I was there, a family planted another seed in the Church, staying after the Mass was complete for their child's baptism.

That child's entrance into the faith was completed in an exact replica of Ponce de Leon's baptismal font, a gift to the Cathedral in 2012 from the explorer's hometown of Santervás de Campo, Spain. It was another reminder that St. Augustine is not just a dot on a timeline, but a living, breathing location that is as much a part of the Church's future as it is its past

"It has history; it continues to make history," Jess May said.

St. Joseph

Dexter, Michigan

"And the king will say to them in reply, 'Amen, I say to you, whatever you did for one of these least brothers of mine, you did for me.'"
Matthew 25:40

They have seen the worst devastation nature can wreak. They have sifted through the wreckage of flood-ravaged lowlands and tornado-throttled plains. They have cried with the men and women who have lost homes, and worse, to unforgiving storms.

And every year, they enthusiastically sign up to experience it again.

Each summer, a few dozen young men and women from St. Joseph parish in Dexter, Mich., shuttle off to the site of a natural disaster to help those communities in the recovery process. It's a ministry that demands exhausting work and a sacrifice of self from the young people of the parish.

St. Joseph is a healthy parish community, so much so that it retains two separate facilities to conduct Mass. Sunday Masses are held at the country church, dedicated in 2008 on the Feast of St. Joseph. The new facility, built on 46 acres, has ample space to operate the annual summer festival and amenities not available in the downtown "Village Church."

But the parish hasn't abandoned the historic older church altogether. Weekday Masses continue to be held at the church building a few miles away, a spectacular older structure complete with a grotto to honor the Virgin Mary.

While the two churches are otherwise different in design, they share a similar steeple, providing continuity between the old and the new.

Though lacking a school, the older one having closed in 1968 when the repair bills got too steep, the parish's efforts at engaging and educating its youth are not lacking. Don Dalgleish, coordinator of youth formation, and Director of Religious Education Michelle Hochrein see to that. When I visited, the two church leaders delivered remarks and showed a video at Mass highlighting the programs available and the value in religious ed.

Of all the activities for the youth of the parish, few have been greeted more enthusiastically than the summer youth trips. The expeditions are organized by Don Dalgleish. For years, until COVID-19 kept them home, he led the team of eager volunteers into the worst-hit areas in the U.S. Since the pandemic began, his cadre of young people have been sidelined, waiting the chance to return to action.

He learned about the ministry at a National Catholic Youth Conference. In its first year participating, St. Joseph paired with another local parish in the diocese. After that, St. Joseph had enough volunteers to go it alone, often filling up more than one charter bus with eager young adults.

Working through the National Relief Network, a team of anywhere from 40 to 60 kids, plus adult chaperones, set off on the third week of July. The group is typically not informed of where it's going until a few weeks prior. On one occasion, in fact, the plans were changed just a few days before the students and parents boarded the charter bus.

Once they've arrived, the students can be faced with any number of responsibilities, depending on the nature of the disaster. A group including Don Dalgleish and other adult volunteers will survey the site ahead of time to determine what the young people can safely accomplish. Downed power lines or unstable houses can keep them from a site, and on another occasion the adults found weapons on the premises and made a quick exit from that location.

But make no mistake; they are all there to work.

In some locations, they will do full home teardowns, a common occurrence when an insurance company will cover the cost of a rebuild, but not the expenses associated with gutting the old one. They've taken down trees, tapping on the young people proficient in the chainsaw arts to do the heavy work.

When one of his groups visited St. Bernard Parish in New Orleans post-Katrina, the kids were tasked with tearing down houses to the studs. These were homes that had been swept up by the floodwaters, forcing quick exits with the homeowners often never returning. The kids had to get rid of old, moldy clothing, dispose of spoiled food in refrigerators, and other stomach-turning duties. But the odiousness of their responsibility was not a deterrent.

"They still talk about it. Most groups take four days to dismantle a house. We did 12 in four days," the youth minister said proudly.

The ministry is not without risks, though the adult leaders take great pains to ensure the kids' safety. But injuries still arise, typically ranging from stepping on nails to getting stung by bees, with one student once needing stitches to repair a cut finger. Fortunately, the group has avoided any major catastrophes, a noteworthy development given the places they can find themselves in.

In West Virginia, Ashlee Root remembered a particular sketchy flood-ravaged home that demanded volunteers put on hazmat suits to engage in the cleanup. "I was like, 'Pick me. I'll do it.'"

The hidden benefits to all this are the skills the young people learn beyond the spiritual and emotional growth that come from selfless work in the service of others. They learn demo work, construction, safety precautions, and the like. "One father asked me, 'What did you to my daughter? She had my chainsaw ripped apart, and then she put it back together and it runs great,'" Don Dalgleish recalled.

Brian Robards knows the values of those skills. A contractor by trade, he has been on several trips, accompanying his three sons over their high school days. Regardless of how much his sons and other children get out of the experience, Brian Robards said it doesn't just benefit them.

"I think every father should do this with their kids," he said. "These other fathers are just missing out on what a what a great experience it is for them and their kids."

The student volunteers range from grades 7 through 12. Many of the kids, such as Ashlee Root, are repeat do-gooders, participating year after year.

"Since I was little, I was raised to help others – going to soup kitchens, helping neighbors. It's something I want to do in the future, making a positive difference and helping people the best I can," she said.

The trips have not just sated Ashlee Root's desire to help, but expanded the limits of what she thought possible. Since participating in her first relief effort, a tornado clean-up in Coal City, Illinois, during her freshman year of high school, she has since gone overseas twice on similar endeavors. Rather than a new car or an elaborate party for her Sweet 16th birthday, Ashlee begged her parents to let her go to the Dominican Republic for a week to build a home for a family. A second, longer, trip to Thailand followed which included work in an elephant sanctuary and a stint teaching English and math to young Thai children.

"The parish trip really lit that fire," said Ashlee, who graduated from Washtenaw Community College with plans to attend the University of Michigan after that. Not surprisingly, a stint in the Peace Corps was on her to-do list.

On the spiritual side, the students attend a weekday Mass wherever they are located. Days include faith sharing and an evening reflection, where the students talk about the day they just experienced.

During those evening events, an odd thing happens on every trip, Don Dalgleish said. The children typically race through the tasks they performed and the hardships they endured. But when it comes time to talk about the people they've met and the friendships they've built, then they can talk all night.

"What the kids talk about is the relationships they've made," Don Dalgleish said.

Ashlee Root made it a point to speak to as many homeowners as she could when she was on her relief trips. "The awful things they've experienced you wouldn't wish on anyone," she explained. However, it also makes the experience that much more enriching. "By talking to them, you really get a feeling of what it's like, and it makes the work you're doing that much more satisfying."

That sentiment is shared by all, from the veteran kids who naturally take the lead to the first-time students who might have approached the process with some hesitation. The experiences touch them in so many ways.

"They make friendships. They get to know people. And some of the kids get really emotional," Don Dalgleish said. And not just the students. Brian Robards vividly recalled an experience in White Sulfur Springs, W.Va. While demolishing homes destroyed by a horrendous flood, he and a young female volunteer came across a man standing beside a tree. They approached the man, who greeted them with a look of anger.

They asked what they could do for the forlorn local gentleman, and he suggested they head over to another tree and pray for his wife, who had perished in the flood while his children and grandchildren looked on helplessly. In an instant, while the West Virginia man was stranded elsewhere, unable to return to the family home, he lost his wife and every material possession he owned.

Brian Robards and the young lady did as they were asked, walking over to the nearby tree, right where the man's wife had died. There, they prayed to God for the woman's soul, and the widower's relief. And they cried.

"This is the biggest thing we teach the kids, and ourselves: you never know someone else's story," Brian Robards said.

Holy Child of Jesus

Canton, Mississippi

Sacred Heart

Camden, Mississippi

"Even if I must suffer greatly, thanks be to God's mercy, I will not lack courage."
Saint Genoveva Torres Morales

IN THE 1980S, THERE WERE FEW THINGS THAT PUT THE FEAR INTO Americans more quickly than the discovery that Mike Wallace and the 60 Minutes cameras had just arrived for an interview. The journalist's reputation for devastating interrogations, sit-downs that left his subjects looking embarrassed at best and prison-bound at worst, preceded him into town.

Yet Wallace, like so many before and after him, was no match for Sister Thea Bowman, FSPA. And when they sat together in a classroom at Holy Child of Jesus in Canton, Mississippi, in 1987, it was the legendary newsman who was put on the spot. At Sister Thea's prodding, the scariest man in news was forced to acknowledge that Black was, indeed, Beautiful.

It was just another encounter for Sister Thea Bowman, a proud African American Franciscan sister who could get schoolchildren and bishops alike on their feet, singing and dancing in praise of the Lord. She was a force of nature and joy and spirituality in equal proportions.

She was born Bertha Bowman in 1937 in Yazoo City, Mississippi, the Jim Crow laws of the day keeping her, and her physician father, out of the Madison County hospitals and into the Black hospital in the neighboring county. Racial segregation was a way of life.

As a child, her mother determined she wasn't getting the quality education she needed in the segregated public school, so she enrolled her at Holy Child of Jesus where she would be educated by the Franciscan Sisters of Perpetual Adoration. But her education included more than just catching up on literature and math. At age 9, the young girl born Bertha soon announced to Theon and Mary Esther Bowman that she was not just intent on becoming Catholic, but determined to follow these sisters into religious life. She would take the name Thea: of God.

Her commitment to living a life of God was evident immediately. During Sister Thea's grade school days, Mary Esther noticed her daughter was coming home hungry from school. Her mother soon realized why; the young girl was sharing her lunch with the other children at the school who had little or nothing to eat. Mother and daughter rectified that by rising early each school day to fix extra lunches for her classmates. "That was her Franciscan spirit. She was feeding the poor even in fourth or fifth grade," said Rev. Maurice Nutt, C.Ss.R., who has written extensively on Sister Thea and has been tasked with helping put together her case for canonization.

At 15, she left home to join the FSPA in La Crosse, Wis. As with most Franciscan Sisters, she began her service as a schoolteacher, just as her mother and grandmother had done before her in the secular world. Her unmistakable talent, and her pursuit of even more education, took her beyond the elementary school level to the university setting. She eventually served as the chair of the English department at Viterbo College in La Crosse and helped found the Institute for Black Catholic Studies at Xavier University of Louisiana in New Orleans. These were done in addition to her emergence as a prominent speaker and singer, using all of her gifts to proclaim the Gospel and help bridge racial divides.

"She knew racial differences occur because of a lack of contact. She used her life to bring various cultures together, to share their joys and sorrows and frustrations and dreams," said Father Nutt, who first encountered Sister Thea when he was a seminarian at Xavier, where she became his "spiritual mother."

One way Sister Thea accomplished this reconciliation of the races was through music. Every culture had a song, she would say, and learning one another's songs was a way of coming together in a non-threatening way.

Nowhere was that power more evident than at the 1989 United States Conference of Catholic Bishops meeting, where she'd been invited to address the Church leaders. During her remarks, she urged the bishops to get to their feet, join hands and sing the civil rights anthem *We Shall Overcome*. As was the case with virtually everyone she met, the bishops felt compelled to comply, her dogged determination running stride for stride with her unshakable faith.

About the event, Tom Roberts wrote in the *National Catholic Reporter*, "The bishops and I were mesmerized and deeply moved. I said to myself then – and have said since to anyone who would listen to the story – that I thought I saw a glimpse of the Church's best future that day."

To Father Nutt, the ability and the willingness to stand and preach or sing or dance before the bishops or schoolchildren or an all-white audience in the Deep South was rooted in her firm understanding of who she was in the eyes of God. "When you're so sure of who you are and that God is really with you, there's no fear to being unapologetically yourself."

In 1984, Sister Thea returned to Canton to care for her ailing parents. She did so while still carrying out her various ministries, which by then included an extensive schedule of traveling the country. Soon after, she herself was diagnosed with the breast cancer that would ultimately claim her life in 1990.

It was back home in Canton where she met Sister Dorothy Ann Kundinger, FSPA, who was serving as a teacher at Holy Child of Jesus, the role she expected to fill for the entirety of her working life. Instead, Sister Thea was looking for someone to move in with her to aid in the care of Theon and Mary Esther and her extensive traveling schedule. Sister Dorothy Ann jumped at the chance. Consequently, she was present for all of the moments in Sister Thea's later life, accompanying her while Sister Thea comforted her dying mother and father in short order in 1984, then filling that same role for Sister Thea when she passed six years later. Her memory lives on, quite vividly, in Sister Dorothy Ann.

"She was so driven to spread the good news that God loves us all and we are brothers and sisters," Sister Dorothy Ann recalled. "That message touched a lot of people, be they bishops or the school kids she worked with or us older people. Sister Dorothy inspired everybody."

Sister Dorothy Ann included. She never did return to teaching, instead moving her ministry into the dual roles of chaplain of Hospice of Central Mississippi and caring for AIDS patients. In the years since sitting at Sister Thea's bedside as she was called home, Sister Dorothy Ann has helped comfort others in their dying days, oftentimes right there in her home outside Jackson. In many ways, her new calling is a direct result of a question she posed to Sister Thea when they first met: "What can I do?"

It's been more than three decades since Sister Thea Bowman died from cancer at the age of 52. But her memory, and her works, live on at Holy Child of Jesus and elsewhere in the Magnolia State.

Myrtle Otto, a choir member at the tiny, but lively, parish, was fortunate to call Sister Thea her music teacher. "She believed God blessed all of us with different talents," she said.

Myrtle organized a community-wide religious music event at Holy Child of Jesus before the pandemic, with plans to renew the event once the deadly virus had passed into a more manageable state. It's a way of recognizing the undeniable. "Her presence is still here in this church," Myrtle Otto said.

Sister Thea's presence is felt throughout Mississippi, both spiritually and visually. She can be found as far away as Starkville, 100 miles to the northeast, at St. Joseph on the campus of Mississippi State, where she's one of eight Catholic people captured in stained glass. Her image graces the envelope for the Catholic Appeal for the Diocese of Jackson. And she's featured prominently on the other side of the county, where a painting of her graces the entry to Sacred Heart in Camden.

Her legacy is not restricted to predominantly Black parishes. At Sacred Heart in Canton, the historically White church in the city, Rev. Michael O'Brien remembered Sister Thea from his first assignment at the parish in the 1980s, and earlier when he was the youth director for the diocese. He said she was instrumental in improving race relations in Mississippi, during her life and after.

In 2020, the state was considering retiring its flag, which had been used since 1894 and bore the battle flag of the Confederacy in the upper left hand corner. Father O'Brien would pray the Rosary nightly, asking for Sister Thea's intercession in helping the state's leaders, most of whom previously expressed support for the old flag, find a change of heart. They did.

"I considered it a miracle," said Father O'Brien of the decision. He subsequently reached out to Father Nutt to inform him of his prayers and Sister Thea's role, as another part of her case for canonization.

"She was a strong woman who would say what was on her mind. She wasn't just a sweet little Southern girl who would say all the right things. She would challenge the bishops. She would challenge me on a number of occasions," said Father O'Brien, who has a photo of Sister Thea sitting in front of the lectern at Sacred Heart.

The same is true just down the road at Holy Child of Jesus. And of all the representations of Sister Thea I saw during my journey through Mississippi, none resonated as profoundly as the one that sat in front of Rev. Guy Wilson, ST, at Holy Child of Jesus. The painting, a rendering I simply could not take my eyes off, was not of Sister Thea in her younger days, the slender, beautiful young nun who would prod even the stodgiest of men and women to rise from their seats and sing and dance in joyful appreciation of the Lord.

Rather, it was the Sister Thea of her final years, after she had returned to Canton and her parents had both passed away. It was the Sister Thea whose own days were dwindling. She's there, her hair shorn to little more than stubble, perched in the chair that was her sole source of ambulation.

But even in her diminished physical state, the image captures the joy, the spirit, the faith that so defined her life and captivated virtually everyone she encountered. It's a remarkable testament that it isn't just the African American Catholic community to whom Sister Thea can remain a personal source of pride and inspiration. She too can show the path to those whose bodies have betrayed them in some way. These men and women can look to Sister Thea Bowman and realize that no manner of physical handicap need be a limitation in our devotion and service to the Lord.

For Sister Thea Bowman, even as cancer ravaged her, remained ever-faithful in her life's work, never succumbing mentally or spiritually to the disease that claimed her body. It was that Sister Thea, who, until her dying breath and beyond, serves as a model for all of us to emulate.

St. Catherine of Siena Newman Center

Salt Lake City, Utah

"I wish you to enlarge your knowledge, to cultivate your reason, to get an insight into the relation of truth, to learn to view things as they are, to understand how faith and reason stand to each other, what are the bases and principles of Catholicism."
Saint John Henry Newman

Rev. Jacek Buda, OP, pastor at St. Catherine of Siena on the campus of the University of Utah, asks his students to envision the ideal campus ministry in three images. One is as a cathedral. Another is as a coffee shop. And the third is of a think tank.

The Dominican priest, a native of Poland, has been serving in campus ministry for more than 20 years and in Salt Lake City since 2016. His perspective on what makes the optimal Catholic university community is founded on decades of seeing what works and what comes up short.

The cathedral setting is obvious; it's where a beautiful, transcendent liturgy is celebrated. And the think tank is consistent with the setting, where the faith complements the intellectual formation taking place there. "Catholicism needs more of that, more encounters with the world," he reasoned.

And the coffee shop is where "modern people sit, read and debate each other."

At St. Catherine of Siena, each of these elements is present, and not just metaphorically. Cate's Café sits not far from the worship space, serving caffeinated beverages and fellowship in equal measure to students and faculty alike.

More important, following the pillars of a meaningful campus ministry has led to a vibrant Catholic community thriving in the shadows of another dominant religious presence.

Catholicism on the flagship university of the Utah system dates to 1920, when Rev. Duane G. Hunt founded the original Newman Club. The Dominicans have had a continuing presence there since the 1980s, and the current chapel was dedicated on Sept. 25, 2004.

Today, the campus ministry is a place where undergrads, grad students, faculty and staff members, and the community at large come together to worship.

"It's a very lively community, always," Father Jacek said of Catholic life in the university setting. "If it's not lively, it means something's happened, a crisis."

There are no such crises at St. Catherine of Siena. In fact, not even the global health calamity has been a deterrent to the community's health. The pandemic was obviously felt at the University of Utah, though perhaps not as dramatically as it was elsewhere. "Our handling of the pandemic was very sober by the governor. There is a strong protection of religious liberties," said Rev. Cody Jorgensen, OP, the director of campus ministry. "As opposed to some other places, where ministries have suffered, here it as very clear that the governor's mandates never applied to houses of worship."

Of course, that doesn't mean the campus ministry was unaffected entirely. Yet, in some ways, the pandemic was revelatory, said grad student Alejandro Jacquez. "I think one of the really cool parts of starting here during the pandemic vs. a more normal time is you see the true stripes, true colors people. That provides an environment of encouragement, people who genuinely want the same thing you do and will push you to that and you can push them as well."

That attitude is precisely what Father Cody wants to see in the ministry. Born an evangelical Christian, Father Cody converted to Catholicism as an undergraduate at the University of Washington and has been involved in campus ministry for most of his life in the priesthood. He has strong beliefs on what campus ministry is and how, too often, the proper model is inverted.

"One of the questions that haunts me is, 'To what are we inviting young people; what do we propose to them?'" he said.

Frequently, the ministry can be based on the attractional model, an idea that can be summed in just two words: free pizza. If you offer food and other freebies to physically hungry college students, they will undoubtedly have their embedded hunger for the Word of God met at the same time, or so the argument goes. Father Cody rejects this model wholeheartedly.

"The free food concept is like cheap tricks. It presupposes that students won't come to the church unless we bribe than somehow, then they'll find something amazing and want to be there."

Instead, he believes faith must be put at the center of the equation. And what you lose in volume is more than made up for in quality. "When you're real with students about who you are and what you invite them to, you get a different caliber of student," he said.

The students there appreciate the focus, whether from the Dominican leaders or FOCUS itself. The Fellowship of Catholic University Students, or FOCUS, has a strong presence at the University of Utah and many other Newman Centers around the United States. The group's missionaries are trained in Church teaching, prayer and evangelization and meet college students where they are as they encourage them to build a relationship with Christ and pursue virtuous lives.

Each of Utah grad student Alejandro Jacquez's roommates was a FOCUS missionary and he appreciates the quiet, positive impact the men have had on him. "They never pushed anything on me, like you should join a Bible Study or we should pray together. But they make me think, 'Maybe I should be going to daily Mass more often,'" he said. "Being with other young people, seeing how far they push themselves, it's provides a nurturing and empowering environment."

In Salt Lake City, there remains one element of the overall environment that's fairly hard to avoid: the presence of The Church of Jesus Christ of Latter-day Saints. Mormons represent a little more than half the population of the state, and the church plays a major role in all aspects of life in Utah.

"The Mormon question is always in the background," said Father Cody. "The Mormons don't tend to proselytize or be in your face. They're just culturally present."

To some students, their presence is actually a blessing to the Catholic community. "I think the Mormons push the Catholics in a positive way. Whether they're fully devout or not, they are very good about doing the right things for their faith," said Alejandro Jacquez, whose Arizona hometown also had a sizable LDS population.

To undergrad student Nellie Webb, the dominance of the Mormon community provides an opportunity to share the beauty of Catholicism, while also pushing her to understand her faith better. "It challenges us a little more to know the why behind stuff, because we're constantly having to explain it to people," she said.

Nellie Webb and fellow sophomore Rolando Quintana have taken their commitment to living the faith beyond the typical college undergrad experience. They are among a handful of students who live at the Newman Center. They both believe that residence there is extremely valuable in avoiding the impediments to a faith life that may be present in the dormitories.

"It helps having a group of people who support you in your pursuit of holiness," she said. "It's so hard to do it by yourself."

"It's very formative, living with a community of men," said Rolando Quintana, who grew up not far from campus. "It's nice to have this network of guys you can live with who share your values."

Though social activities are not at the core of campus ministry, they can't be ignored either. But Father Cody follows the idea that whatever events are created to serve the community, they must come from the students, not him. "At campus ministry, the only people who should be designing social activities are the students," he said, noting he sticks to the faith arena.

That doesn't mean students are discouraged from his side of the equation. When Rolando moved into the Newman Center residence during his sophomore year, he wanted to resume outreach efforts, typically designed for the non-practicing Catholics on campus. Though the student body is heavily tilted toward the Mormon faith, there are still more than 5,000 Catholics enrolled there, a testament to the school's growth as more of a regional university.

He began putting together "tabling" events, setting up a small booth on campus and inviting fellow students to come talk to him about the Newman Center and the Catholic faith. Getting started was a bit scary, but ultimately rewarding. "All I can do, and I do it with great faith, is pray to God that He inspires someone's heart to come up to the table so we can talk to them," he said. "And when you get the one person who does, this is why we're out here."

Though the parish is created to serve the needs of the current student body, its congregation is not limited to those still paying tuition. Michael Mozdy was a grad student at the university in the 1990s, but remains an active member of the parish. For him, it's the Dominican spirituality that forces him to bypass parishes closer to home. "It's really nice to see orthodox Catholicism thrive," he said.

That orthodoxy arrived, he said, with the many Polish Dominicans who have been assigned to the parish through the years, most recently the current pastor.

When Father Jacek was first presented with the idea of working in campus ministry in his native Poland, he didn't think he was qualified to do so. The campus ministers he grew up with were "phenomenal people, a rare breed." But he recognized immediately the absolutely vital role they play in the Church's future.

"I think it's one of the top priorities in the Church," he said. "I don't know how it cannot be. This is the moment when we ask for God. We all search at the same age, and if we don't help that search, what are we planning to do?"

And the results can be transformative. Though Alejandro Jacquez grew up in a devout Catholic household, it was at the Newman Center at Northern Arizona University where his faith truly blossomed. "Growing up I was Catholic, but like most young people, I didn't necessarily know what that meant. It was something I believed in, but not something I centered my life around. Eventually, I became a lot more Catholic."

And Nellie Webb sees that conversion all over the campus of the University of Utah. "I wasn't expecting people to be in love with their faith as they are here. I had never experienced that a lot, especially on a day-to-day level."

St. John of Nepomuk

Yukon, Oklahoma

"The things which you have heard from me from many witnesses you must hand on to trustworthy men who will be able to teach others."
2 Timothy 2:2

In October of 2013, Most Reverend Paul S. Coakley, archbishop of Oklahoma City, exhorted the people of the Sooner State to become disciples for Christ. Coinciding with the tail end of Pope Benedict's Year of Faith, the archbishop released the letter, "Go Make Disciples."

"This is God's word addressed to us as we conclude this Year of Faith. It is our mandate. For all of us and for each of us, it is both an invitation and a challenge; a call and a mission," he wrote.

To drive home his message, in 2019, the fourth archbishop of Oklahoma City released a new letter, "Go Make Disciples! Building a Culture of Conversion and Discipleship for the Archdiocese of Oklahoma City," the blueprint for the next dozen years for the Church in Central and Western Oklahoma.

The people of St. John of Nepomuk in Yukon did not need to be told twice.

Five years earlier, Dr. Carole Brown, the newly hired director of new evangelism for the Archdiocese of Oklahoma City, convened a meeting of some local parish leaders to discuss the path to discipleship creation. She specifically was looking at Catholic Christian Outreach – a program which had been developed by a Canadian campus ministry group – to see how it could be adapted to everyday parish life.

Included in that initial group of church leaders were Ann Cook and Bryan Hooper, the pair who would become the two-headed force behind St. John Nepomuk's unparalleled success at building disciples.

"Ann and Bryan were exceptional in that they went home and made it happen," said Dr. Brown, now the director of the Sioux Spiritual Center, a Catholic retreat lodge in South Dakota. "I had a lot of people who went back and attempted it and it didn't go very well. Some went reasonably well, but not as well as when it was driven by Ann and Bryan."

Bryan Hooper was serving as the director of RCIA when he was invited to the meeting. Ann Cook was just a parishioner at St. John Nepomuk, but she was already fully committed to the cause. "When Archbishop Coakley hired her [Dr. Brown] and I heard what her vision was for the new evangelization in the archdiocese, I called our vicar general, who had been our pastor, and said I need to be a part of this." She went to work for the archdiocese.

When they completed the discussion sessions with Dr. Brown, Ann Cook and Bryan Hooper knew this was something to implement at St. John. They also knew just how to make it happen.

Rather than send out a parish-wide call, they hand-picked 30 or so parishioners they believed would make future discipleship leaders, inviting them to an introductory dinner to explain the process. Of those 30 initial men and women they selected, only two rebuffed their invitations, though a few others drifted away during the course of the program.

That's not surprising. The CCO program, modified by the archdiocese and implemented at St. John, is an arduous one, a nine-month journey that demands commitment. "It's such a slow burn. It takes a long time for anything to happen. You don't just put a note in the parish bulletin about it," Dr. Brown explained.

They broke down the groups by gender, Ann Cook leading two groups of women and Bryan Hooper a single group of men. They walked through the process, which includes a series of five books. The first of those books, Discovery, gets at the heart of the program, the core message of the Gospels and what it means to be a Catholic.

"Pope Francis' 2013 Encyclical had the most beautiful succinct summary of the kerygma I've ever seen. This has to ring out on the lips of catechists over and over: 'Jesus Christ loves you; he gave his life to save you; and now he's with you every day at your side to enlighten, strengthen, and free you,'" Dr. Brown related.

That concept is the root of the CCO program. "With the CCO materials and the process they described, it became so easy to lead people very systematically but also very organically in their own time to Jesus. It really makes it simple to not only lead people to Jesus, but teach them how to do it themselves," Ann Cook said.

Out of that first group of disciples, the subsequent wave of leaders was forged, the men and women who would guide the next cohort of hand-picked candidates for discipleship. This growth is Exhibit A of the mantra that Disciples Make Disciples.

By working in small groups, the program delivers a powerful combination of deep, meaningful study of Christ's teachings and intimate sharing of how these men and women try to navigate the challenges of daily life in a Catholic way. The scripture study is the stepping stone to more robust discussion within the group.

That was the effect it had on Ramona Ritchie, an early participant in the program. "It made me sit down and read scripture and answer questions, but my biggest takeaway was just the different fellowship, and the women who shared things. There wasn't a week that went by when I didn't go home and say, 'Wow, they're carrying a lot of burdens,'" she said.

Over time, more than 100 people had completed the CCO process, resulting in St. John Nepomuk creating more disciples than any parish in the country.

The effect of such development is felt by more than just the individual. "What it's done for the parish, it's a real community builder," said Rev. Rex Arnold, who was the pastor at the parish when the program was initiated but has since moved on to Christ the King. "If you have a program that is small faith groups with scripture and prayer, it's going to build a network of community. It's going to be the rebar in the footings of your foundation."

The basis of the CCO program has not been limited to the discipleship program. It's also used, at a more rudimentary level, in the parish's RCIA program and any other faith formation efforts. Getting the RCIA participants engaged is particularly useful, as too often the enthusiasm that is engendered in that program is squandered when the new Catholic's spiritual journey ends and there is nothing there to fill the void. Or, worse yet, the process was being undertaken as an obligation, rather than a true commitment to the faith.

"I was coordinating RCIA, helping with adult faith formation at the parish, and I kept seeing people going through and never seeing them again. They were going through the motions to please a spouse, but we were not changing lives," Ann Cook related.

And the beauty of discipleship is how it grows in all directions. When Nicole Crumley's discipleship group had finished, she immediately took the lessons she learned and the energized spirit to share with her fellow teachers at St. John Nepomuk Elementary School. She and Ann Cook split the faculty into two groups and began introducing them to the CCO journey. She was heartened by how many of her fellow teachers, some of whom aren't Catholic, embraced the opportunity. "It was amazing to see how the faculty reacted. And I know it made me a better teacher," Nicole Crumley said.

The work has even spread beyond St. John Nepomuk. Emily Pickett was another woman who completed the program, but felt a pull away from the parish during the pandemic. Her family joined Holy Trinity in Okarche, home of Blessed Stanley Rother, the native Oklahoma priest who was the first martyr from the United States. Soon after, she was asked to become the parish's director of religious education, with Rev. Cory Stanley specifically interested in her implementing the discipleship program there. "I told Ann, I really feel like the Holy Spirit has moved us to continue what you started at St. John's," she explained.

For others interested in developing discipleship program at their parishes, Ann Cook has some relevant, first-hand advice. Though it's important to have a pastor who is open to the new evangelization, he shouldn't be seen as the person spearheading the program. A staff member of parish volunteer is better suited, and the program should become that individual's entire focus. Developing a successful discipleship effort requires too much energy and dedication to have someone whose attention is constantly diverted.

Also, never forget that discipleship is not just about absorbing the teachings of Christ and sharing it with one's neighbors. "What makes a disciple is someone who has a definitive experience with Jesus Christ that's evident in their lives," Bryan Hooper said.

Being a disciple is not just spreading the word, but living it. The Pickett family is an example of that idea at work.

One day, during the height of her discipleship journey, Emily Pickett had taken her children to the zoo. She was sitting on a bench, watching her three children playing when she was struck by successive, unexpected thoughts. She wondered how sad it was that some children never got to experience the simple pleasure of a family trip to the zoo. Then she wondered why that idea was planted in her brain at all.

The explanation was soon provided. The following night, while preparing lessons for her family's Bible studies, she read James 1:27: "Religion that is pure and undefiled before God and the Father is this: to care for orphans and widows in their affliction and to keep oneself unstained in the world."

Those zoo thoughts were not a coincidence. No, it was the Holy Spirit calling her to action.

She began praying on the matter with her husband, Matt. Soon, they realized the Holy Spirit was inviting them to become foster parents, to live out that message in James.

Since then, the family has grown dramatically. They began fostering children, which led to the adoption of a daughter. When that happened, they put fostering on hold, but began serving as a respite family, taking on children on weekends to give their foster families a break.

"I thought four kids was a stretch of what I was capable of, but having those kids on the weekend, I was like, 'I could totally do this.'" Her family agreed, with both her husband and son acknowledging how Emily seemed, "so much happier on the weekends when the other kids are here," she related.

So the Picketts began anew, this time taking on sibling sets, a greater challenge but one that allows brothers and sisters to stay together during their most difficult times. The family established a limit of caring for two siblings at once, then almost immediately waived that rule when a trio of sibs were in need of a loving home. As they've learned again and again, when you've been called by Christ, you heed His directives, not yours.

"We had some crazy, complex things going on with our foster child while our own daughter was sick, but we knew 100 percent this is what

Jesus wanted so we kept going," Emily Pickett recalled. "And of course, He took care of us."

Shrine of Our Lady of Guadalupe Copatroness of the Unborn

Bakersfield, California

> *"Your faith spoke for this child. Baptism for this child was only delayed by time. Your faith suffices. The waters of your womb – were they not the waters of life for this child? Look at your tears. Are they not like the waters of baptism? Do not fear this. God's ability to love is greater than our fears. Surrender everything to God."*
> Saint Bernard

SOCIETY HAS NEVER DEALT WELL, OR EVEN ADEQUATELY, WITH MIScarriage. The grief experienced by mothers who have suffered a child lost in the womb goes unrecognized. It is certainly not treated with the same degree of compassion as when a parent loses an infant son or teenage daughter.

Even fathers, lacking that obvious visual biological connection, may not appreciate or understand the depth of suffering a mother endures following a miscarriage.

And those lost children…well, there have been few attempts to recognize them and their existence. They too often slip from our minds entirely, brushed aside in our haste to move on.

At Shrine of Our Lady of Guadalupe in Bakersfield, Copatroness of the Unborn, they are dismissed no longer. They are named. They are celebrated. They are loved. And it is just one example of the parish's profound celebration of the family.

The parish dates to 1921, when it was called Our Lady of Lourdes. Four years later, Bishop John Bernard MacGinley of the Diocese of Monterey-Fresno had the name changed to Our Lady of Guadalupe to reflect the parish's strong Mexican immigrant population, a situation that continues through the present.

That name was modified again in the 21st century. In 2011, following the death of the Most Rev. John Thomas Steinbock, Diocesan Administrator Monsignor Myron Cotta added Copatroness of the Unborn to the parish title. A month later, newly appointed Bishop Armando Ochoa declared it to be a shrine by that name. The changes were a testament to pro-life needs of society and the strong commitment from the parish itself. "Ours is the strongest pro-life parish in Bakersfield," said Rev. Larry Toschi, Oblates of St. Joseph, the current pastor at the church.

The distinction reflects its parishioners' love for the Church, for Mary and for life itself. That love and commitment is demonstrated in the ambitious undertaking a few miles from the church's home.

Since the turn of the century, the parish has been pursuing a new church building at the site. The current worship space was constructed in 1925, and seats only 480. That is not nearly enough to house the 11 Sunday Masses taking place there every weekend – six in Spanish and another five in English.

Many of the services fill up not just the pews, but the aisles and vestibule and, occasionally, out to the curb. "The need for a new church was obvious," said Father Larry.

The need was far greater than the means. Our Lady of Guadalupe is not a wealthy parish, comprised primarily of large, blue-collar Hispanic families. "We haven't had much of a financial base," he acknowledged.

Yet that hasn't stopped the development of the new site. It began with an open-air facility, where five of the weekend Masses are conducted. The pavilion adjacent to the Shrine can seat close to 1,000 parishioners and Bakersfield's location in the San Joaquin Valley makes outdoor services a year-long reality.

More recently, in 2020, the parish finished construction of the Memorial of the Unborn, a wonderful way to honor those children lost before birth. The memorial offers two different ways to properly recognize those who have passed. For children who perished but whose remains have not been kept, a plaque can be added featuring the child's name and date of death. But if the parent has kept the remains, the child can be entombed in the memorial. When I visited, there were nearly 40 names combined, all added in just a little over a year's time.

The opportunity to give these children a proper resting place gives great comfort to the parents.

"The church has helped me acknowledge the loss, face it and heal from it," said Rosa Figueroa, who lost son Francisco in 2014. "I have a plaque any time I feel like I want to honor my baby. That baby is part of our family."

The healing doesn't just work for the mother. Her husband, Arturo Figueroa, said the process of naming and burying Francisco has aided his ability to comfort his wife. "From a male standpoint, it helps me become more aware and connected to the grief she was going through. It's so easy when the pain is not validated to not bring it up or talk about it. This gives me a chance to be part of the experience and know how painful it is," he said.

And that pain doesn't disappear just because the years have elapsed. The healing isn't just for babies lost in the recent past. Mary Alice Lopez lost twins to miscarriage in 1994, a burden she carried with her for a quarter century. The introduction of the various efforts at Our Lady of Guadalupe finally allowed her to find peace. "I didn't have closure until they started talking about this program," she said. "I didn't know if I wanted to come or not, but it was the best thing I ever did. It was a beautiful thing, to give them a name. It's helped me immensely."

The support for the unborn is just one of many ways Shrine of Our Lady of Guadalupe serves the entire family. The parish has successful, life-altering ministries for marriage preparation, sustaining relationships and more.

Teresa Herrera is an active participant at the parish, serving as both a rector and occasionally singing. Though a lifelong Catholic, it was her attendance at a matrimonial retreat that compelled her to do more in service of Christ.

"They talked about the problems in marriage, and when I heard them, I heard my life through theirs," she said. "That changed me. I went in one person and came out a whole new person. I try to be better."

Michelle and Juan Pablo Ayala have had a similar experience with Holy Spouses Society, a spiritual commitment for couples. "Honestly, if we hadn't joined that society, we probably wouldn't be here today," said Michelle Ayala, while her husband nodded his assent.

It's just all part of the pro-family spirit that permeates the parish, which helped it push through the erection of the memorial and beyond. The next phase of construction, which was expected to be completed in 2022, would add a perpetual adoration chapel to the site. It would be the only perpetual adoration available in Bakersfield and will soon become a magnet for the devout community.

Gary Ridgeway, who converted to Catholicism in his twenties, is a relatively new parishioner to Shrine of Our Lady of Guadalupe, drawn initially to the parish when he stopped in for Reconciliation and found parishioners waiting in two lines, 25 deep, to participate in the sacrament. A second visit proved the first was not an aberration. "These people are hearing something different," he thought.

Father Larry invited Gary Ridgeway to join the committee working on the perpetual adoration chapel, as the new parishioner had already been actively involved in adoration at other parishes in the city. He jumped at the chance to give the community a true 24/7 opportunity for prayer, believing the chapel will be packed at all times given the strong faith of the Bakersfield community. "You better have your hip boots on because there are going to be graces all over the place. It's a dream of a lifetime," he said.

Finally, the last stage will be the construction of a new church building at the site, one that will mirror the adoration chapel in design, only larger. That facility will require even more fundraising for a community short on disposable income but incredibly long on the love of Christ.

Before the pandemic, a group of women, many from the now-closed parish Holy Spirit, would sell tacos, tamales and other foods outside Mass every Sunday, attracting both parishioners and neighbors with good taste to the pavilion church. All of the money raised would go straight toward the building fund, helping pave the way for the construction of the memorial, and soon, the adoration chapel. "We're selling food all the time, but 90 percent come from low-economic backgrounds. They make up for it with their faith and their service," said Maria Neri, who serves on the bereavement committee for the parish.

Though Stuart Gordon and his wife worship at another parish in Bakersfield, he has been a member of the building committee since 2020. He marvels at the parish's relentless dedication. "I'm just a minor cog in this. I think it's amazing how much money they have raised over the years for this project, a little bit at a time."

The plans for a new church trace back to 2001, when the devout group of parishioners began to outgrow the facility on California Street. The intention wasn't to replace the existing facility, which sits next door to the elementary school, but merely to supplement it given the tremendous needs of this booming parish.

The land was not an issue. Years earlier, Rev. James Catalano, OSJ, found an empty field where he buried a Holy Family medal, identifying the spot as the ideal location for the new church, school, and hall. When he contacted the property owner about selling the parcel, the landowner instead opted to give nine acres to the church. An additional 11 acres was purchased at a reasonable price in 2002.

But the vision had a hard time keeping pace with the rising costs of everything. Capital campaigns were launched to procure the necessary funds, only to find the price tag had risen by the time the money had been raised.

Ultimately, the parish had to first settle for the 9,000-square-foot pavilion, and developments moved rapidly after that facility become a reality. Today, those involved with the project talk about when the new church will be constructed, not if.

Yet it isn't the progress on the buildings that most impresses about Shrine of Our Lady of Guadalupe. It's the unwavering commitment of Father Larry, the other priests, and the parishioners to honoring the unborn.

Our Lady of Guadalupe's efforts toward healing those who have suffered the pain of miscarriage began shortly after the bishop's designation, when Father Larry and Sandra Garcia attended a workshop sponsored by All Embraced, a ministry that began in the Archdiocese of Atlanta but has grown into an effort that serves all faiths.

When they returned to Bakersfield, Sandra Garcia started her own workshop, addressing the many challenges that families who have experienced a miscarriage face. She spoke from experience, having suffered her first miscarriage in 2015.

Out of those early workshops came the recognition the mothers needed to formally name the children. At the first naming Mass, 129 children lost to miscarriage were given the proper recognition they so richly deserved.

The efforts at healing continued, covering many of the issues faced, from the spiritual to the practical. In California, for instance, the state doesn't recognize the unborn under the age of 21 weeks as human beings, treating them instead as medical waste. That complicated the efforts to collect those remains, though representatives of the local Union Cemetery have volunteered their services to pick up the remains from medical facilities when a mother requests it.

The varying needs led to the creation of still another Our Lady of Guadalupe life-supporting endeavor – the Ministry of the Unforgettables.

"This is wonderful for the pro-life movement," Father Larry said. "It's an indirect way to fight abortion and a direct way to heal miscarriages."

Sandra Garcia and Rosa Figueroa head up the ministry. In addition to the workshops and other programs, they are on call to deal with any parishioner who is in the process of miscarrying, meeting her at her home or the hospital. They come to pray and comfort these vulnerable women, while informing them of their options. The ministers stress the importance of keeping the remains for a respectful goodbye.

Keeping a hold on the remains – either by enduring the pain that accompanies miscarriage to do it at home, or in the face of pressure from healthcare workers to dispose of them in the hospital setting – is not an easy thing to do. "When I see moms who do collect the remains, I know they were very courageous," Rosa Figueroa said.

Sandra Garcia has endured miscarriage on three separate occasions, but she believes those experiences were providential, as it allowed her to find her calling serving other mothers in that most troubling time. "Going through that made me realize there's a big need for this. I feel like God has chosen me to do this. Even at the time when it was painful, I knew it was a blessing," she said.

But of all the people and sacred places I encountered at Shrine of Our Lady of Guadalupe, I doubt anything will stay with me as long as Virginia Santos-Ruiz and her closet.

Virginia Santos-Ruiz is the development director for the parish. Her closet sits unobtrusively in her office in the utilitarian building on the grounds of the memorial. It is filled with blankets, boxes and other materials she's found online or in stores, items she uses in her other role with the church.

When Father Larry and others conceived the idea for the memorial, they considered virtually everything except one detail: Who would prepare the remains for burial?

That singular responsibility has fallen upon her. Each time she receives a miscarried child, remains that range from as small as a few inches to fully developed babies, Virginia Santos-Ruiz is tasked with handling those remains and readying them for their final resting place. She treats this unanticipated obligation with the utmost respect it requires, placing the remains inside small blankets, tenderly wrapping them and choosing the perfect box for ultimate placement inside the tomb. It's an hours-long process that is at once touching and tragic, loving and heartbreaking. Moreover, it is without question excruciatingly painful for the woman charged with the preparation. The accumulation of these burials is evident in her words. "There are times I need to call in sick, if it's just to cry and sleep all day," she admitted.

Yet she keeps returning to this ministry, because these babies, and their grieving parents, demand nothing less than to be treated with kindness and dignity and she has been the one called upon to deliver that. "I never thought I'd go from being a mortgage lender to a volunteer at the church to getting hired to fundraise to running a cemetery. But that's what I do," she said.

But I would make a subtle argument to that description. Virginia Santos-Ruiz doesn't simply run a cemetery. She is, in every conceivable way, a caretaker.

St. Peter

Portland, Oregon

"I am already cut off from human voices, for my ears cannot hear; my gossiping tongue is already silenced, since because of my deafness it cannot speak ... And I would have willingly endured this suffering from birth, so that no words that may have offended or disserved God could ever enter the cloisters of my ears."
Saint Teresa de Cartagena.

About 10 minutes past 10 a.m. on Sunday, March 28, Sandra Kindblade bowed and took her place at the lectern. She delivered the first reading, from the Book of Joshua, to the few hundred gathered at St. Peter.

Just not aloud.

The longtime parishioner did her best to work in tandem with the woman adjacent to her, the other reader at St. Peter that Sunday morning. Sandra was delivering the reading in American Sign Language. But she wasn't translating the spoken words for those in the deaf community. She is a member of that very community, one who was contributing her gifts in service to her Church.

St. Peter is the original American Sign Language Church in Portland, though Our Lady of the Lake in nearby Lake Oswego also offers the Mass for a vibrant deaf community there. The ministry's origins at St. Peter date to the 1980s, under then-Rev. Patrick Francis Walsh, who passed away in 2015 after establishing the Archdiocesan Office for the Deaf Community. In the last five years, the church in a working class neighborhood on Portland's southeast side has become a more permanent home for the city's deaf Catholics.

And Rev. Raúl Márquez hopes it stays that way. Even if he is someday transferred on to another parish, a fate that awaits many diocesan priests, he hopes St. Peter remains a place for Portland's deaf and hard of hearing. "This is their community," he insisted.

Sandra Kindblade was not raised Catholic, instead converting when she met her husband. Most of her life in the faith has taken place at St. Peter in a church that was fluent in her language. The same is not true of fellow parishioner, and fellow lectern, Howard Hammel.

Growing up in Montana, Howard Hammel would sit restlessly in the pews, the beauty of the Mass lost in the silent world he inhabited. At that time, there were no attempts made to speak to him, at least not in his home parish.

Even when he began attending a school for the deaf, he was still unable to fully participate. Though the sisters there made some attempts to communicate, it was not done with translators and ASL. The first time he encountered the Mass in ASL, when he was a college student, the experience was revelatory.

"Now I understand it," he recalled. "It's so clear. I finally got the meaning of what Mass was."

Bringing the full Mass to men and women such as Howard Hammel and Sandra Kindblade is not just a nice perk, but essential for the Church to fulfill its responsibility to its people.

"In an ideal diocese, everything a hearing person would experience in a parish, the deaf would also have available," said Sister Linda Roby, BVM.

Sister Linda had made that objective her life's work. When she was a novice with the Sisters of Charity of the Blessed Virgin Mary in Dubuque, Iowa, her group visited Chicago one summer. There, she had the opportunity to work with deaf children, and she was immediately taken in. She pursued a master's in deaf education, which segued neatly into deaf ministry.

"What I so enjoyed was deaf and hearing parents bringing their deaf kids and watching the kids grow up in a community in a way they could understand," she said.

For more than 30 years she led the deaf ministry in the archdiocese. She saw her role as "helping the deaf community to use their leadership within the Church, both in worship and in ministering to each other and the broader community," she said.

Though Sister Linda retired in 2017, she remains involved with the community at St. Peter. And her work has been picked up by Father Raúl Márquez, pastor at St. Peter.

The Colombia native has tried to build on her legacy, including the invaluable measure of learning and using ASL at Masses when the opportunity allows. During the Mass I attended, Father Cornelius presided over the Mass, while Father Raúl stood beside him and signed parts of the liturgy.

To Howard Hammel, Father Raúl's efforts to become fully fluent in the language is incredibly important. "It's really a blessing to have him. He's improving all the time," Howard said.

The implications are substantial. While each ASL Mass has a fully fluent ASL translator who can deliver the homily and other spoken words to the deaf community, the Church is there for its adherents all year long. A pastor's responsibilities don't end with the recessional on Sunday. Being able to communicate directly with a parishioner when a translator is not available is crucial to fulfilling a priest's pastoral obligations.

Helping the Church meet those needs is the mission of the National Catholic Office for the Deaf. Founded in 1971, the ministry is dedicated to serving as a vital link between the Church and the deaf and hard of hearing.

Rev. Glenn L. Nelson is a board member of the NCOD, having served with the ministry since the early 1990s. Like Sister Linda, he became intrigued by deaf education at an early age, then followed up his work teaching deaf children by entering seminary and helping deliver the faith to those young people.

Monsignor Nelson believes the Church didn't historically exclude the deaf intentionally, but had no understanding of how to accommodate them. Even after some religious orders formed to serve and educate young deaf Catholics, those graduates often returned to home parishes or dioceses that had no programs or efforts to continue that ministry.

That's changed through the years, but work remains to be done. Dioceses or parishes may be limited by financial or personnel resources, such as a lack of qualified translators to go around. The NCOD is available to provide some of those resources, including an online First

Communion preparation program. "We're here to help pastors fulfill their roles. We're bridge builders, I think," he said.

One development that has grown out of this 50-year push has been for the ministry to expand beyond just serving the needs of the deaf to actively inviting them into greater roles in the Church. There are numerous deaf priests and other religious around the country providing much needed perspective and leadership. "It's not necessarily about helping the deaf community, but working alongside of them," Monsignor Nelson said.

Sister Linda echoed that sentiment, while acknowledging the limitations that existed with her decades-long commitment. "As much as my heart is with the deaf, I will never be a member of the deaf community. They will say that I am, but I will never have their life experiences. To have a priest who does is amazing."

She noted the country's roster of deaf priests are very generous with their time, providing retreats and confession, in person and online. "To see so many young deaf priests, some not so young anymore, says to me we have done some things right."

By serving as lectors and other roles at St. Peter, Sandra Kindblade and Howard Hammel are examples of that leadership at the lay level. It's something both parishioners feel quite strongly about, that the deaf and hard of hearing should not be viewed as limited.

"We're not poor deaf people. Some people think deafness is related to our intelligence. But we think, we read, we go to school, all the things everyone else does," Howard said.

Or, as Sandra said more succinctly, "Deaf people can."

Until relatively recently, the deaf community at St. Peter had a separate Mass in the chapel, one catered exclusively to them. Many Catholic parishes that serve the deaf follow that model.

But now at St. Peter, ASL is included in the larger parish setting, an approach Father Raúl prefers. He feels it better reflects the universality of the Church, our inherent Catholicity.

"It's a lot easier that way, but I don't think it's ideal. I think it's worth it to say we're one community."

To Father Raúl, developing that sense of a single Catholic community is important in many ways. He views learning ASL as not just a benefit to the members of the deaf community but to the hearing parishioners as well. He believes the priest needs to be a model to the entire St. Peter family and he would be failing in his duties if he took no steps to learn how to converse with a subset of his parishioners. "If I am not signing but we have a deaf community, I wonder what the hearing parishioner sitting in the pew would think. 'If this is not important to him, why is it important to me?'" he asked.

But it's clear that embracing the language of the community is important to many congregants at St. Peter.

That point was beautifully delivered during the singing, and signing, of *Holy* during the Mass I attended. As the St. Peter choir performed, Father Raúl signed the words in companionship. And his signs were mirrored by others in the church, not just by the deaf community but many hearing members from the parish as well. They did so with unadulterated exuberance, and at that moment I truly wished I was conversant in the language to sign along with them.

It was a wonderfully moving sight. It also served as a stark reminder that sign language is not just a substitute for spoken English, but a varied, expressive method of communication and that its application at Mass only complements the spoken parts of the liturgy.

At St. Peter, and elsewhere around the country and world where ASL is offered, the Mass is delivered in two languages simultaneously. The people of those parishes are all the richer for it.

Church of the Visitation

Topping, Virginia

Church of Francis de Sales

Mathews, Virginia

"The aspect under which our neighbor is to be loved, is God, since what we ought to love in our neighbor is that he may be in God. Hence it is clear that it is specifically the same act whereby we love God, and whereby we love our neighbor. Consequently the habit of charity extends not only to the love of God, but also to the love of our neighbor."
Saint Thomas Aquinas

Embarking on a building project is rather common for Catholic churches. Whether constructing a new sanctuary, a new parish hall or a renovation to existing space, parishes across the country are often called to build.

But the parishioners of Church of the Visitation, the small parish in Topping, not far from the Chesapeake Bay in Virginia's Middle Peninsula, undertook a more unique challenge. The people of COV took on a building project in the middle of a building project.

For years, the parish had been looking to replace its original, low-ceilinged worship space, a place that simply never called out, "Catholic Church." That sense wasn't aided by the fact the worship space doubled as the main social gathering area, with the individual chairs reconfigured for various events, such as its popular Italian Feast in the summer. There was no doubt a new worship space was needed, and the parish began fundraising toward that effort around 2010.

The push was moving along nicely, the parish families notable for their generosity. However, the project was put on hold in the later part of the decade, shortly after Rev. Gerald Kaggwa was assigned to pastor at Church of the Visitation and Church of Francis de Sales, another small parish located "across the bridge" in Mathews, Va.

As he settled into life on the Middle Peninsula, Father Gerry relayed tales of his hometown in Uganda and the hardships faced by the young families who simply wanted a Catholic education for their children. Soon, the parishioners of Church of the Visitation and Francis de Sales had another, more pressing, matter at hand: building a suitable school building for the students of Kitangira Village.

Father Gerry was born in a family of nine boys and four girls. His father, the late Leonard Magembe Ssalongo, was the catechist of the location. He had started the original outdoor school so the boys and girls of this Ugandan village didn't have to walk 4 to 5 miles one way, through dangerous areas, to receive an education. They met at the old church building, which his father had constructed.

Shortly after his assignment to the churches, the priest was discussing his upbringing with parishioners. At Church of the Visitation, several members of the congregation were teachers, and thus asked about his schooling. He told them he had been among the first students at the church decades earlier and how the children there were now dodging water from the leaky roof and in danger from crumbling walls.

Though the old building still housed classes, the church, St. Noa, had been replaced. The effort was aided by a campaign driven by Father Gerry's brother, Father Josephat, a fellow priest in New Jersey, and overseen by another brother, Tony Lukwata.

The needs for the school and the community in general were and remain plentiful. Clean water is a rarity, with the only sources provided by a nearby stream and improvised wells dug by local residents. Other necessities, such as first aid and ready availability of food, are also concerns. Some of those issues have been addressed through Father Josephat's efforts, but the instructional limitations remained in place.

The parishioners of Church of the Visitation and Church of Francis de Sales realized they could complete that next step, constructing a school building for the children of Kitangira.

Father Gerry reached out to his brother back home to inquire how much it would cost to build a school. Not surprisingly, the figure was quite a bit lower than a project in the States.

"Our church is really good when it comes to helping out when we're presented with a need," said Kathy Kauffman, one of the COV parishioners who helped organized fundraising for the effort. "And this was an accessible need. It was something we could do."

That the project also delivered a tangible result made the giving easier. The parishioners weren't just sending money away with no knowledge of how it would be used. They could see the results themselves. "I'm a firm believer that you want to make people feel good about helping," Kathy Kauffman said. "We're in a rural Virginia county. Nobody has a whole lot, but we want to share what we have and feel good about it. When we have an opportunity to do it, we take it seriously."

Church of the Visitation, led by Kathy Kauffman, Mary Ellen Sherwood and Eileen O'Brien went to work, creating fundraisers to raise the $45,000 necessary for the initial phase of school construction. "I sold Magic Cloth for cleaning windows," Eileen O'Brien said. "They went like hotcakes."

So, too, did the hotcakes. Regular fundraising breakfasts were established, with one attracting a $1,000 on-the-spot gift from a parishioner.

The breakfasts also gave the parishioners the opportunity to track the progress of the project. Regular updates and photos were presented at the breakfasts, making the endeavor very real for the members of Church of the Visitation. "It was very direct aid," Kathy Kauffman said. "Everybody felt really good about that."

Similar efforts were launched at Church of Francis de Sales. One anonymous parishioner from Francis de Sales put up a $30,000 matching grant, designed to spur giving from both of the two parishes.

The first phase of the project resulted in the construction of four classroom buildings, a kitchen and a toilet. A second phase was also launched, adding more classrooms, fencing and a playground for the children. The school can now serve more than 300 children, ages 3 to 10.

The payoff for the project was not just felt halfway around the world. The dividends are also shared by the people of Church of the Visitation and Church of St. Francis de Sales.

"We recognized very well that this type of activity is not only good for the beneficiaries, but it's very good for the people who are organizing and giving of themselves. And the more people we could involve, the better it is for the health of our community here," Mary Ellen Sherwood described.

The contributions of the parishioners of the Middle Peninsula didn't end when the first school bell rang. Since then, they've taken up other efforts to aid the education efforts of the young people of Kitangira. The parishes have helped collect shoes of all sizes. They also purchased reams of fabric to be sent over to Uganda to be turned into clothing. The cycle was also completed when Ugandan-made jewelry was sold back in Virginia, with proceeds going toward the fundraising efforts.

Moreover, the parishioners continue to look at ways to help the Kitangira community's educational system thrive, now and in the future. Eileen O'Brien noted they would like to send the teachers to university, to help them improve their educational levels to deliver higher quality instruction to the students.

The lack of good schooling is a significant issue in Uganda, and propels a cycle of an underdeveloped population. "The schools are only in the big cities. If you live in a rural area, you have to walk a long distance," Father Gerry explained. "Most of the rural people, they have very low education. Because of the distances, most of them drop out when they're still very young. They don't even finish elementary school."

Father Gerry has been back home twice. First, for the groundbreaking for construction. Then again when the school opened for good. He's hoping on his next visit, some of the parishioners from the two churches will join him on the journey, to get a first-hand look at what their generosity has meant to his family and friends in Kitangira. As for him, his appreciation for his parishes' efforts is indescribable. "I have no way of expressing it, because I didn't expect it."

Upon completion of the school building, Church of the Visitation also resumed its efforts at home. On the weekend I attended Mass, the second Sunday of Advent in 2021, the new worship space was nearly complete. Only a few details remained, the completion of the marble top altar, installation of the sound system and construction of the platform for the choir among them.

Appropriately, the space was being used to house some of silent auction items, another event in the parish's near-perpetual state of fundraising. Even more appropriate, a parishioner walked in and informed Donald Delagrange, the church building committee chairman, that he was in possession of some valuable prints he'd be willing to add to the collection if the committee thought it would help. "Of course," was the reply. That kind of impromptu generosity is a way of life there, Donald Delagrange observed.

When talk of the project in Africa emerged in the middle part of the last decade, some parishioners suggested taking the money already on hand for the new church and using it there. That idea was quickly squelched, realizing the cash raised, some in the form of money willed to the project, had already been earmarked for the new building and it would be inappropriate to reappropriate it. If they wanted to help there, they had to start fresh.

And so they did, while putting their plans to have a space fitting their commitment to the faith on temporary hold, to be resumed after their work 8,000 miles away was done.

That day arrived a few months later, though it wasn't the completion of the altar, the sound system or the choir platform that signified its suitability for worship.

"Father won't let us worship here until the bishop comes in," Donald Delagrange said to me in December.

Most Rev. Barry C. Knestout, 13th bishop of the Diocese of Richmond, dedicated the new Church of the Visitation on Feb. 26, 2022.

St. Joseph University Parish

Buffalo, New York

"The Spirit of the Lord is upon me because he has anointed me to bring glad tidings to the poor. He has sent me to proclaim liberty to captives and recovery of sight to the blind, to let the oppressed go free, and to proclaim a year acceptable to the Lord."
Luke 4:18–19

At the imposing oxidized copper-crowned church on Main Street in Buffalo, you can get your mission statement in official and unofficial formats. The official version would not look out of place at most U.S. parishes, save for a single word that would raise the occasional eyebrow: St. Joseph University Parish is a diverse, progressive, spirit-filled Catholic Christian community where all are welcome to deepen their experience of faith, join in vibrant worship, share their talents and gifts and live justly.

But the unofficial version, what the people of St. Joseph's mean when they say everybody is welcome, offers the truest picture of the community that's been built not far from the shores of Lake Erie.

"Single, twice divorced, under 30, gay, filthy rich, black and proud, poor as dirt, can't sing, no hablo Ingles, married with pets, older than God, more Catholic than the Pope, workaholic, bad speller, screaming babies, three-times divorced, passive-aggressive, obsessive-compulsive, tourists, seekers, doubters, bleeding hearts… Oh and You!" It is an invitation the parish found printed in a newsletter from the National Federation of Priests' Councils and made its own.

To the parishioners at St. Joseph, it isn't just a perfunctory message, a statement crafted by a long-forgotten committee and then left to languish. Living this message is at the heart of parish life, pursued through commitment and effort.

"We tell people at our new parishioner welcome there are no hoops you have to jump through to come to this parish to become a member," said Rev. Jacob Ledwon, who has served as pastor at the parish for more than 30 years. But St. Joseph doesn't merely open the doors and expect the parishioners will come.

Years earlier, the parish participated in a study by Parish Catalyst that examined all aspects of ministry, focused on connecting with millennials. The results were eye-opening. "I operated under the old model, when they graduate from college, they'll drift for a while and then they'll get married and have kids baptized in the Church. It doesn't work that way any longer," said Father Jack, as he's known.

The parish needed to adjust its thinking, not just in serving the millennial cohort, but all demographics. What emerged was a new approach to becoming intentional about hospitality. In California, where the idea was born, it's called "radical hospitality." In inherently less radical Buffalo, they refer to it as "extraordinary hospitality."

Making it work is a parish-wide effort, not just the mission of a few put-upon volunteers. It involves things big, such as encouraging the entire parish community to embrace newcomers, and small, like improving traffic flow in the parking lot.

Creating an environment of hospitality is one of the three pillars of the stool discovered in a Notre Dame longitudinal study on why families choose a specific church. The quality of the music and the quality of the preaching, the study argues, are the others.

The parish has taken steps to strengthen all of those areas. The parish invests heavily in the music, offering a diversity of styles from Gregorian chants at Advent to contemporary Christian music at its 11:30 a.m. service. Both of its music directors are professional composers. For the weekend Masses I attended, held during the 20th anniversary of the September 11th tragedy, a bagpiper led the procession in and recession out, delivering poignant versions of *Amazing Grace* and *Highland Cathedral*. Offering music both inspiring and reverent is the rule at every Mass.

On the preaching side, it has a stable of priests who assist with services, including a seminary professor of philosophy, a retired Jesuit, and a trained architect. The diversity of voices keeps the preaching fresh.

But at St. Joseph, the parish choice stool is actually a chair, with the fourth leg being social justice. "Without that commitment to social justice, there are people in our congregation who wouldn't be here," Father Jack said frankly. "That's their passion. That's where the rubber meets the road for them."

The parish operates an overall Social Justice Concerns committee, which is the umbrella group over up to a dozen subcommittees, including environmental awareness, human trafficking, anti-gun violence or, really, any area of life where a need and the desire to address it co-exist.

Sister Jeremy Midura, CSSF, had been intimately involved with the church's social justice efforts since her arrival at St. Joseph a quarter century earlier. At the time, there weren't a lot of activities ongoing, though there "were a few people interested in bringing about the Kingdom of God by advocacy and change," she said.

Sister Jeremy left the parish in 2021 to undertake a new role with the Felician Sisters in Chicago. But she left quite a mark at St. Joseph. A science teacher for 24 years, she was active in local efforts to clean up Love Canal, the toxic disaster in nearby Niagara Falls that caused significant health and environmental damage. "My areas were science related, but I was always a person who strived for that sense of justice," Sister Jeremy said.

That's a fundamental part of life at St. Joseph University Parish. Most parishioners are involved in one or more committees. Other people from outside the congregation also come aboard, drawn by a particular social ill that moves them.

Perhaps more important than their commitment is their ability to produce tangible results. Sister Jeremy points to the announcement of plans to close a local psychiatric center in the community. The parish's mental health committee, created to reduce the stigma associated with mental illness, went quickly to work. Over the course of one weekend, they got 400 signatures protesting the proposal, contributing to the reversal of the decision.

The community mental health committee, which is currently overseen by Kathy Aman, is the perfect encapsulation of the way the parish operates. In the late 1990s, the parish surveyed its members to see what areas of society were not being served. Three women answered mental health and the committee was soon formed to address the challenges.

There was initially some reluctance to create such a committee, wondering just how it fit into social justice. But the skeptics were soon won over, learning how mental health touches on criminal justice and equality and poverty and so many of the areas of life the parish was already addressing.

Their solutions range from larger societal efforts, such as the one dealing with the psychiatric center, to more church-related concerns. Kathy Aman recalled a committee meeting where an otherwise quiet parishioner noted that the typical Mass, with large crowds and booming music in the imposing worship space, may be intimidating for those dealing with mental health issues. He asked if a smaller Eucharistic service could be created to cater to those parishioners' needs.

The man then went home that evening and died in his sleep.

"We took that as a mandate. We'd better get that going. And we've been doing it ever since," said Kathy Aman, noting that even with COVID regulations limiting options on gathering, the Eucharistic service never paused during the pandemic.

Individuals throughout the community will join the committee that matches their interests. But it's also important to recognize what the parishioners want out of the experience and allow them to pursue that. Father Jack points to a hypothetical accountant who joined the parish, and the immediate thinking was to put that person on the finance committee. "That may be the last thing they want to do. They look at numbers eight hours a day, 40 hours a week. They want to get out and do something for Habitat for Humanity, where they can use their hands."

Sister Eileen O'Connor, who now chairs the social justice committee, advises volunteers to find the cause that most resonates, rather than try to tackle every issue the parish is involved in. "We cannot be passionate about every single social justice issue. We don't have the emotional energy for that. Find your passion and where you want to spend your energy going forward," said Sister Eileen, a member of the Sisters of Mercy.

On the other hand, it can help to have experienced talent on hand. The parish is able to call on lawyers who worked in immigration work to mental health practitioners. Joining Sister Eileen in overseeing the broader social justice effort is Dennis Walczyk, who previously served as CEO of Catholic Charities in Buffalo and thus brings a wealth of knowledge of the resources available and key decision makers in Western New York. Among his numerous responsibilities is to stay on top of issues facing the community and then meet with committee chairs to see if and how they fit into the parish's existing groups.

He marvels at the dedication of all of the parishioners involved. "What amazed me, but it speaks to the passion and commitment these people have, is how all through the pandemic we have been able to keep the groups going, 99 percent through Zoom meetings. People have really hung in there and stayed involved and committed their time."

The parish uses these social justice ministries to expand on its pursuit of intentional hospitality. Efforts are undertaken intergenerationally, such as a Christmas project for prisoners that brings in small children and senior citizens working together. "It's not excluding certain demographics or age," Father Jack said.

And that's just one way in which the progressive in the mission statement fits in. The church has been pushing the proverbial envelope for years, such as making a place for female altar servers in advance of formal Vatican approval. "Liberal has some bad feelings for some people. We say progressive," Father Jack acknowledged.

Employing a softer term doesn't always deter its detractors. Some have simply written off St. Joseph as the diocese's lunatic fringe. Other objectors will try to point out the error of the parish's ways. The staff gets calls and letters from residents and others who aren't comfortable with its approach to the faith. Father Jack engages with those willing to do so. Anonymous screeds are ignored. Occasionally, the chancery gets involved when a complaint is lodged there, though the church remains in the diocese's good graces.

And its wide-ranging approach is getting through. The parish has grown substantially in the last two decades, today numbering more than 2,000 parishioners from 37 different zip codes.

"I refer to this parish as the last car on the train, often for people who are thinking about leaving or people thinking about coming back. We tell people, you come as you are. That's how people went to see Jesus. You never saw Jesus turn anyone away," Father Jack said.

"That's our model."

Sacred Heart

Colorado Springs, Colorado

"He was pierced for our transgressions, he was crushed for our iniquities; the punishment that brought us peace was on him, and by his wounds we are healed."
Isaiah 53:5

A dozen or so years ago, Cathy Kusman's life "fell apart." A lifelong Catholic who served as director of one of the largest youth programs in the Diocese of Colorado Springs, she was suddenly living through the unexpected pain of divorce.

It was a devastating experience, made more so by an absence of support within the church to serve people like her. Instead, she was directed to the divorce group at the local Presbyterian church. That didn't help. In her estimation, the group was more faith-based singles club than a place for healing.

She realized there had to be something better, something helpful for a Catholic man or woman whose entire existence was being rewritten, often against their wishes. She knew they were out there, spotting them as they entered Mass late, sat alone in the back pews, then departed early. They were as lost as she was, with seemingly nowhere to turn.

She became that place to turn.

After reading an article about an individual working to support the newly split, Cathy Kusman realized that was the role for her. She went to school to get licensed as a divorce coach to help walk people through the process, but from a Catholic perspective.

Initially, when she approached the diocese about starting a ministry for divorced Catholics, now-retired Bishop Michael Sheridan was reluctant. He feared, and not without some historical precedent supporting that concern, the ministry would become like the dating group Cathy Kusman found at the Presbyterian Church.

Cathy Kusman pleaded her case, suggesting the men and women of the diocese she wished to serve weren't looking for phone numbers to stockpile or romantic dinners to plan. "These people are broken. They don't need to date; they need to heal," she insisted.

Fortunately, she had an ally she had never met. In 2015, Pope Francis began to alter the Church's message toward the growing number of divorced Catholics that populated our rolls. Though the catechism of the Catholic Church is unambiguous on the indissolubility of marriage, the pope has instructed priests to change their approach toward the divorced among their congregations. His Amoris Laetitia, Latin for "The Joy of Love," exhorted the faithful to treat divorced Catholics with greater mercy.

Soon, the retired bishop reversed course, opening the door for Cathy Kusman to begin her ministry. She now serves as the diocese's director of divorce survival and recovery.

She hosts programs throughout the diocese for those men and women who are now in that awful place she was more than a decade ago. Twice a year, she conducts three-month-long programs for the newly divorced, guiding them through the many phases of the process and the challenges their new lives create. The program is similar to the one advanced by author Rose Sweet, though Cathy Kusman said, "we use it as a base and build on it."

The first month resembles a support group for those who have lost a loved one, which in many ways it is. "Your old life dies and suddenly you're left with no idea" she said. "You don't know what pieces to pick up to recreate a life."

That description fit Larry Kotik, another program graduate. "It seemed like my whole identity, everyone I thought I was – a husband, a father, a protector, a co-provider, the person who provides an example and molds my children into the people I want them to be – that was all destroyed," said Larry Kotik.

Like many recently divorced Catholics, he had no idea where to turn when his marriage dissolved.

"People who belong to the parish and the diocese, it's almost like they shun you, instead of reaching out to help. If it wasn't for Cathy starting the group and doing the research and putting together the videos that were approved by the church, there's really nothing out there," said Larry Kotik.

Lorraine Stickle, married 28 years before her split, needed to go through the program twice to rebuild her life. "I had always considered myself a strong person, but I had to find that again. A lot of those people helped me become strong again," she said, noting she remains in contact with many of the participants in her second group.

The presence in the group of divorced Catholics from both genders was a blessing to Kathryn Whitfield. Having felt betrayed by her former spouse, she found herself becoming distrustful of all men. "I felt it helpful to hear what men in the group had to say about their experiences and their thoughts and feelings."

And the value of the program wasn't just speaking with and commiserating with men and women who were enduring the same things, "it was that I wasn't alone because Christ was with me. I depend on that," she said.

Over the course of the two-hour, once-a-week sessions, each group works through the anger, sadness, and denial that comes with the end of a relationship that was supposed to remain undivided until death. "For every person it looks different," Cathy Kusman said.

The second stage is more practical, involving finances and other tasks that will be handled as a single person rather than a couple. She brings in realtors, financial planners, divorce advocates – a range of professionals to help walk the participants through their areas of expertise. These experts are all divorced themselves, allowing them to be more than Rev. sympathetic voice, but an empathetic ear.

Mark Bauer completed the program, then was asked by Cathy Kusman to come back and speak to a later session about his divorce and how things changed over time. "My divorce took me down to almost ground zero. I had almost nothing left. Now I'm back on top, better than I was before," he said.

"The most valuable thing about the program was just finding my ability to acknowledge what had happened and how to move on," he added.

If the divorced individual is seeking an annulment, the group leaders will help them identify whether the participant would be eligible and how to pursue it. Traditionally, this is the area of vulnerability. Catholics who discover they are not candidates for an annulment may use that as an excuse to walk away from the Church. "The group helps them stay in the faith by making them understand it better," said Cathy Kusman, who is now serving as the faith formation director at Sacred Heart in Colorado Springs, an assignment that signifies her own recovery is continuing to progress.

Before enrolling in the program, Cathy Dixon attended a similar effort offered by a local Protestant church. "I didn't feel the connection with the other group because, in other religions, I don't want to say divorce is not frowned upon, but it's not as life-changing as it is in the Catholic faith. It was very difficult to be Catholic and still attend Mass and reconcile that with the fact you were divorced from your spouse."

In the program, Cathy Kusman uses the final sessions to help the recovering Catholics begin building new lives. Again, not by seeking new romantic relationships, but understanding how they can develop new interests, new goals and a healthy outlook on the rest of their lives.

Though her recommendations aren't binding, she asks each of the recovery program's participants to eschew dating during the 12 weeks they're meeting. A lot of the participants feel the need to date, though she routinely sees that attitude dissipate over the course of the three months. "You need to heal," she explained. "Otherwise you're just taking your broken self into a new relationship."

No aspect of the sessions are more difficult than when there are children involved. That's even true when the offspring are no longer children, as was the case for Cathy Kusman and her daughter. Co-parenting is rife with challenges, whether it's dealing with joint custody of young children or merely navigating the holidays with offspring who have kids of their own. "We teach how to co-parent well, no matter how old your child is."

The program is also valuable for the children, who are not immune from the pain of their parents' split. "It doesn't matter what age they are. Everybody goes through it, not just the two people who were married," said Lorraine Stickle.

As all of the participants understand, the process of recovery doesn't necessarily end when the 12 weeks are over. "I continue to work on healing and recognizing deeper and deeper layers of what needs healing, focusing most on trying to rely on Christ rather than whether there's a partner in my future," Kathryn Whitfield said.

About six weeks after the sessions end, the groups reunite to gauge where each person is in the ongoing process of recovery. For some groups, the reunion is merely one of many events, as some of the cohorts continue to get together after the 12 weeks are over.

While Cathy Kusman's classes accept both men and women, there is one ironclad rule she follows: if both former partners are interested, they will not be assigned to the same group. The first one will be invited in; the other partner must wait for the next session to start. But she also recognizes the needs are immediate and will make allowances to address them. When a man tried to sign up for a class his wife was already registered for, Cathy Kusman met with him privately once a month until the next group began.

As with so many other things, the pandemic thoroughly disrupted the ministry. While the technology exists to run classes, it's simply not conducive to the kind of intimate sharing that goes on in a typical session. If a recovery group had been ongoing at the time the coronavirus shut down life, she said, they might have been able to continue through Zoom or other web-based programs. But starting a new one simply wasn't an option. The potential candidates for the sessions – men and women who are at their rawest when a group starts – were not going to share their pain with strangers looking at them from the small box in the corner of a monitor.

Of course, the cruel irony of that situation is the pandemic was even more devastating for the newly divorced. When they most needed the mutual understanding and companionship the recovery group provides, they were shut out from the experience and confined to their suddenly empty homes.

To Cathy Kusman and others, It only further highlighted the importance of this ministry, and the need for similar efforts around the country.

"Catholics are going through divorces. Even though you're a Catholic does not mean you're not going to face this. Cathy's program is wonderful. I feel more churches need to offer that to Catholics who want to remain Catholics and feel welcome," said Cathy Dixon.

Cathy Kusman agrees, noting the absence of divorced Catholics in the pews is not always a positive sign. "People don't think they need one. They look around and say, 'We don't have any divorced people here,'" she said, then explained why. "Yes, because they left."

St. Peter Claver

Lexington, Kentucky

"This means that you are strangers and aliens no longer. No, you are fellow citizens of the saints and members of the household of God."
Ephesians 2:19

For more than 10 years, Joto Mbirizi was confined to an area smaller than the worship space at Saint Peter's Basilica. Day after day, night after night, the Congolese man's world was limited to a patch of earth no larger than 100 square yards, his penance for doing nothing more than trying to protect his family.

Several years earlier, Joto Mbirizi joined many of his countrymen in fleeing the war-torn Democratic Republic of the Congo. He had already lost family members to the fighting and its bloody aftermath, and was determined to steer his wife and children away from the violence and war-related illness and disease that have claimed more than 5 million Congolese people in the past two decades.

He left his home in 1999, first settling into a Tanzanian refugee camp for two years. Then after trying and failing to resettle in South Africa, he spent the next 10 years in a Malawian camp, a prison by any other name.

But in 2014, the devout Catholic man and his family realized their long-sought dream, relocation to the United States of America.

Specifically, Lexington, Kentucky, where many other Congolese refugees have resettled to escape the fighting that resumed in the late 1990s. Since the refugee resettlement efforts began, approximately 4,000 Congolese men and women have found sanctuary in the Kentucky city of 320,000. And their numbers continue to grow. Though the war officially "ended" in 2003, many parts of the DRC remain mired in lethal conflict, with more Congolese men and women awaiting their chance to find stability in the Western Hemisphere.

Kiko Lusiwe's story is eerily similar to Joto Mbirizi's. He and his family escaped the Congo for Namibia, spending almost a dozen years there. Initially, he hoped to spend only a short time in the camp, with plans to return to his home country shortly after peace did. In time, he recognized that wasn't going to be possible and he started examining a more permanent solution for his family. He saw the U.S. as the place where he could find that elusive peace.

"I wanted to go somewhere better, where my kids could go to school," Kiko Lusiwe recalled. "In a refugee camp, there's no hope for education."

Joto Mbirizi's description of his time in guiltless captivity is even more blunt. "In a refugee camp, you're not a human being."

His arrival in the United States changed that outlook immediately. "Here, we feel very much like we're human beings. We can help each other, even if we don't have much. I have some, and I can help others," he said.

Those two men have been doing just that. The two Christian refugees – Joto a Catholic, Kiko a Protestant – have not just adjusted to life in their new home, but have dedicated themselves to easing the transition for those who follow. They do so through the organization the Kentucky Congolese Catholic Association. The KCCA is headquartered at St. Peter Claver, which has become the unofficial home for the Congolese diaspora in the bluegrass.

Initially, the Catholics from the Congo worshipped at several sites around the city, depending on where they lived. But over time, there arose a desire to let the community celebrate the liturgy it had grown up with, one that used the language and played the music and followed the traditions of Central Africa. Aided by Bishop John Stowe and others in the diocese, they ultimately settled at St. Peter Claver, a downtown church. Over time, services grew from once a month to twice-monthly to the current schedule, when the community can praise God in a Mass that recalls the Catholic Church of their homeland every weekend.

Each Sunday at 2 p.m., the Congolese community conducts its worship service at St. Peter Claver. Most weeks, the entire Mass is handled in Swahili, one of the many languages of the Congolese people.

Joto served as deacon at the Mass I attended, one presided over by Rev. Anthony Muthu. Father Muthu often serves at the 2 p.m. Mass, having learned Swahili during time spent in Africa. When St. Peter Claver's pastor, Rev. Norman Fischer, says Mass, he will do it in English but the songs and Mass parts will still be in Swahili, which he's slowly absorbing over time.

St. Peter Claver seems, in retrospect, an ideal landing spot for the Congolese community. Founded in 1948 as the Catholic Church for Lexington's African Americans, today St. Peter Claver is among the most diverse parishes you're likely to find. While still a favorite place to worship by Black Catholics, it's congregation is equally split among Whites, Asians, and Hispanics, a diversity that developed not by fiat, but organically, said parishioner Brian Fox.

And Swahili isn't the only foreign tongue that's been spoken at the parish. St. Peter Claver has offered Korean Masses when a pastor is available, and even the occasional Filipino Mass from time to time. The parish is clearly a place where there are no strangers.

Finding a church where the community could develop and grow on its own was imperative, Father Norman said. "I think there's a sense of ethnocentrism, of 'Listen to us and we'll give you what you need.' With this, there's a level of empowerment rather than enablement."

Given the opportunity, the community has indeed been unshackled. They have created their own choir, their own ministries, and other programs. Ushers and lectors and altar servers have been identified and developed.

All the while, they haven't ignored the homeland. When flooding devastated an area of the DRC where many of them were from, the parishioners were able to raise several thousand dollars to support loved ones 8,000 miles away.

But it's not a closed community, either. They also found opportunities to interact with the English speakers at St. Peter Claver. The teenagers from the two sides had a combined Confirmation service and the entire parish joins for the Taste of Heritage, where the foods from all of the parishioners' ancestral homes are shared.

Moreover, they all will benefit in 2023 when the new worship space is completed adjacent to the current church. The new sanctuary will replace the existing low-ceiling space, which will be converted into a multi-purpose hall. Seating will nearly double to 400 in the process, realizing a long-time dream for the more seasoned members of the parish.

The immersion of the Congolese Catholic community into St. Peter Claver has been beneficial not just for the entire parish, but Father Norman as well. That's particularly true when he presides over the 2 p.m. Mass, his language shortcomings notwithstanding. "My experience is you get transported to the Congo. They know their prayers. They know their music. They know their liturgy. They may not have a lot, but they have their faith," he said.

For people like Joto Mbirizi, his commitment to the faith inside St. Peter Claver is just half of his ongoing responsibility. His investment in the KCCA is equally important.

Settling in a new country, particularly one so far removed culturally from the homeland, is an extraordinarily challenging proposition. It's made even more so if the newcomer is not conversant in the native language, as is the case with many of the refugees who come to Kentucky.

"The first problem people face is the language. It's a problem for getting a job," he said. The KCCA's maiden objective is to help the refugees overcome that obstacle.

And a job is an absolute necessity. Contrary to myth, refugees are expected to quickly become contributing members of society. Refugees get three months of assistance when they arrive, after which they're on their own.

That's where the KCCA comes in. The association can provide additional assistance where necessary. More important, the association provides the responses to questions that three months in the States aren't enough time to answer.

Though Kiko Lusiwe has been in the U.S. for longer than most, even he is occasionally confronted by issues that perplex. A problem with shoddy work at his home left him needing the services of a lawyer, a concern that hadn't previously arisen during his first 10 years in the States.

"In life, no one knows everything," he said, explaining the KCCA's mission. "What are the issues the Congolese community is raising and facing and how can we help each other? And if we don't have a solution, at least we can get a reference."

The arrival in the U.S. can be humbling in many ways. In the Congo, Kiko Lusiwe was a doctor, an educated man. But diplomas from many foreign schools are not valid in the U.S., so they must adapt by finding jobs that are seemingly beneath their skills and experience. Yet, none of the refugees I met had any complaints about life in the U.S. To the contrary, they were truly delighted to be here.

"The Congo, for me, is now just a place to visit," Joto Mbirizi said proudly. "Here in America, this is my home."

Each new year brings in a small new group of Congolese refugees to Central Kentucky, all facing the same issues as those who came before them. A more recent arrival is Mwenebatu Apolo, who I met after Mass. A student at the nearby University of Kentucky, Mwenebatu has quickly improved his fortunes and comfort in his new home by mastering his second language, English. His aim is to pay that forward, aiding the next wave of refugees in their efforts to acclimate themselves to their new homes.

Mwenebatu Apolo has been here slightly longer than Godefroid Nyembo, who serves as the choir director at St. Peter Claver. The music is crucial at the 2 p.m. Mass, as it is one of the elements that unifies the parish community. Though Swahili is the chosen language used at the Mass, it's actually one of 242 different languages spoken in the DRC, with official language French, English, and Lingala among the more commonly used tongues. The music, however, is relatively universal, drawing from many Congolese traditions.

Like most refugees, Godefroid Nyembo arrived in Kentucky with little to his name. But, he insisted, he didn't come entirely empty-handed, a fact that made this otherwise daunting transition much easier than it had any right to be.

"I'm comfortable," he said. "I have my God."

Little Sisters of the Poor Sacred Heart Cathedral

Gallup, New Mexico

"Be kind, especially with the infirm. Love them well…Oh yes! Be kind. It is a great grace God is giving you. In serving the aged, it is he himself whom you are serving."
Saint Jeanne Jugan

In 1839 in France, Sister Jeanne Jugan found an elderly blind woman left on her own on the streets of Saint-Servan. The sister took the woman home to her apartment, launching the legacy of care that would build a global congregation and lead to her canonization in 2009.

The extraordinary work of Saint Jeanne Jugan, and the Little Sisters of the Poor congregation she founded, continues here in the U.S. and around the world. Those sites include Villa Guadalupe, a nursing home located in Gallup, New Mexico.

The home, one of 22 in the U.S., is designed to provide care for the elderly poor. A mix of sisters from the congregation and lay staff serve the needs in two separate facilities, for assisted and apartment living. Most other homes operated by the Little Sisters in the U.S. offer skilled nursing as well.

Here in the States, there is no place more in need of the Sisters' remarkable commitment. The Diocese of Gallup, which encompasses four counties in Northwest New Mexico and another two in Northeast Arizona, is at the heart of Navajo Nation. It is, by most measures, the most economically disadvantaged diocese in the country.

Villa Guadalupe can house up to 23 residents in the assisted living section, plus another 12 in the apartments. The home is usually filled, with a list of potential residents waiting for placement. When the mission was established in 1982, the plan was to always have at least 50 percent of the residents come from the Navajo reservation.

"We've always considered it a 'mission house' here in the United States," said Sister Constance, who serves as U.S. communication director for the congregation. "Gallup has always been special."

A decade ago, the Little Sisters of the Poor operated more than 30 homes in the United States, though that number had fallen through consolidation of homes and a declining number of sisters. Moreover, new homes will now be located elsewhere in the world, where poverty is more endemic and the existing social services are often lacking.

The congregation's ability to draw in newer sisters has also become more difficult in recent years. Many of the existing order were introduced to the community in high school through volunteer programs. Sister Constance admits she began volunteering at age 15 to bolster her college résumé, not out of any great desire to serve the elderly. However, the sex abuse scandal that plagued the Church has curbed those programs, as the homes can now only allow younger women to volunteer if they're accompanied by a parent. "As you can imagine that kind of puts a damper on young people volunteering," Sister Constance said.

Those who follow the path now, like Sister Rose, must be more self-motivated, called by "the simplicity of life and the sisters' joy in serving the residents and their faith," she explained.

Formation typically begins in a sister's country of birth, or at least on the same continent if no such formation houses exists there. The second year of formation takes place at the motherhouse in France.

Temporary vows are made on multiple occasions prior to taking permanent vows, done when a sister "has to choose if this is what you believe is God's will," Sister Constance said. Once perpetual vows are made, a sister can be assigned to any house in the world, depending on the needs of the homes and the gifts each woman possesses.

That plays out at homes such as Villa Guadalupe. Sister Rose serves in the office, while others perform such roles as directing resident care, collecting for the home's operation or pastoral duties.

The residents can come from all faiths, or none at all, as long as they're "old and poor." That's the only requirement, said Sister Rose, administrator for the facility. However, the quiet faith exuded throughout the home often has an effect on the residents, with many coming to Catholicism after arriving.

A typical day begins with coffee and breakfast, followed by Mass at 11 a.m. Group activities and other social events are supplemented by praying the Rosary in the chapel and evening prayer services. The opportunity to express the faith is a fundamental aspect of Villa Guadalupe.

Alas, as with everything else, the typical day has changed dramatically since March 2020.

Like many nursing homes, both secular and religious, Villa Guadalupe was devastated by the pandemic. In fact, the home was one of the hardest hit, a product of the unfortunate timing that saw Navajo Nation become an early hotspot in COVID-19's spread, before much was known about it and treatment efforts were in their infancy stages. Conditions were so bad locally in early 2020 that highways into Gallup were blocked, with only residents permitted entry into the town of 21,000 people.

The leadership of Villa Guadalupe reacted immediately to the virus's emergence in the U.S., limiting admittance to the facility to staff in mid-March 2020 and imposing other preventive measures. However, the insidiousness of the virus, coupled with the unique vulnerabilities of elderly care homes, were simply too great to overcome.

"Even before we had any cases, life was already changing," said Sister Rose. "When the public health guidelines came out, there was no visitation. Residents couldn't have family come in and we couldn't have residents go out."

In fact, during the height of the outbreak, residents were restricted to their rooms, forced to dine there as well. It was an enormous change, particularly for the home's more social residents, but the effects of the pandemic demanded those measures.

Over the course of 2020 and into 2021, the home's Mother Superior, a position held initially by Sister Sarah and then assumed by Sister Theresa Louisa, alerted the outside world to the pandemic's progression through the home. In a string of near-weekly updates on the Villa Guadalupe website, Mother Superior related how the first positive case led to the virus sweeping through the facility. It's a heartbreaking chronicle, one that ultimately described how 12 residents of the facility succumbed to COVID-19.

Not surprisingly for women of such deep faith, the terrible toll the pandemic took on the home did not come without blessings. "We always appreciated our residents, but I think it helped us appreciate them even more. And we value even more the things we took for granted before the pandemic," Sister Rose said.

Over time, as the surges waned, some allowances were made, first through non-contact visits and then opening the house to visits in specific locations. Masses remained off limits to family members throughout the first two years as the chapel simply isn't large enough to accommodate visitors and still maintain adequate distancing. Even with 100 percent vaccination rates among the residents, the pandemic still had a hold on the home two years in.

My hope was to celebrate Mass in the chapel at Villa Guadalupe, sharing the Eucharist with the sisters, residents and other guests of the home. But that was neither feasible nor responsible. Instead, I found myself a half-mile away, joining a few other early risers for daily Mass at Sacred Heart Cathedral, seat of the Diocese of Gallup. Sadly, it seemed fitting.

While all of us may bemoan the disruption the pandemic caused, a dry and reasoned analysis suggests the day-to-day inconveniences had become rather mild two years in. Mask-wearing requirements still existed in some locations well into 2022, and the occasional new spike might have affected our dining-out options for a spell. But, for the most part, our daily lives largely resumed as before.

That's not so for the men and women in homes such as Villa Guadalupe. For two years and counting, their lives were upended, limited by the extreme precautions necessary to keep them safe.

Thus, it was only proper I was in the same position as so many others over these last two-plus years: worshipping by myself. And for me, it's a one-time disappointment instead of the weekly suffering so many have endured, a painful circumstance I prefer not to contemplate.

Across the world, there are thousands, if not millions, of family members who have been routinely attending religious services in their own quiet isolation. They are unable to join their loved ones, perhaps close in distance, but still out of reach. Worse, these people may be cut off from relatives or friends who don't quite understand why a beloved son or daughter, granddaughter or grandson, lifelong friend or recent acquaintance, no longer comes around to visit them or join them at Mass.

So, like them, I sat here in this lovely worship space and I prayed.

I prayed for the sisters and lay staff members at Villa Guadalupe, individuals who have answered one of the most important calls on earth – to serve the elderly poor. I asked God to protect them, to support them, and to give them the strength to continue to do His work.

I prayed for the family members outside, men and women who have been shut off from loved ones in most need of their presence. I asked that they someday soon are able to reunite fully and without restrictions with their loved ones.

And I prayed for the residents, whose vulnerabilities to the insidious virus make every day a source of worry and fear. I asked the saints for their intercession so they stay may safe and healthy, both in mind and spirit.

I prayed for all of them, the healthy victims of COVID-19.

St. Elizabeth Ann Seton

Bear, Delaware

"For where there are two or three gathered in my name, there I am in the midst of them."
Matthew 18:20

52 Masses has joined the conversation

For devout Catholics, Sunday Mass is not an option, a task to be fulfilled if your schedule allows. It's a requirement, one that millions of Catholics in the U.S. and elsewhere around the world treat with the utmost fidelity.

But in March of 2020, bishops and archbishops around the world found themselves in the previously uncharted territory of issuing widespread, diocesan-wide dispensations. The unknowns of the rapidly developing coronavirus demanded putting the health and well-being of the parishes, and the communities that surrounded them, ahead of the weekly foundation of Catholic life. It was not easy for any bishop, any priest, to accept, but the clergy across the world largely fell in line.

The inability to conduct Mass in-person, or for the parishioners to share in the Eucharist, didn't mean the liturgy needed to be denied entirely. Getting the Mass into the homes of its congregations simply required the Church embracing the technologies that were already available to them.

In the Diocese of Wilmington, that was the expectation. Immediately upon issuing the dispensation, then-Bishop William Malooly announced to the 57 parishes in the diocese they were expected to use the Internet to deliver the Word to where those parishioners were – in their homes.

And very few parishes embraced that call as fully as St. Elizabeth Ann Seton in Bear, Delaware.

Rev. Roger DiBuo has joined the conversation

52 Masses: Father, how was Seton parish set up to handle this sudden transformation?

Father Roger: We had nothing before COVID hit. That's when Tom Arena volunteered his services.

Tom Arena has joined the conversation

Tom: I've been with the parish for the past 16 years. At the beginning of COVID, I touched base with Father Roger and mentioned, 'If you want to livestream so everyone can see, we can start a Facebook page.' It all went from there.

Father Roger: All that technology you see, that's all Tom creating this and guiding me and asking me what it is I wanted.

Initially, Tom Arena created a Facebook page and a You Tube channel, and he and fellow parishioner Kevin Meinhaldt would use their cell phones to film and livestream it to both locations. Eventually, they shifted the entire operation to the You Tube channel.

Kevin Meinhaldt has joined the conversation.

Tom: When we heard the bishop was going to have a more formal presence online, we decided to look at more permanent options.

They did so enthusiastically. Father Roger authorized the removal of two pews at the back of the church, where a new studio booth and sound board were set up. One camera was fixed at the back of the church, then a second added near the altar, both of them capable of moving to capture the entire worship space. A large television screen was added near where the choir sits. There, the responses, readings, and other information is readily visible to virtually everyone in the pews, as well as those parishioners watching Mass from home. After the initial construction, some generous parishioners donated the money to create an electronic carillon bell system, also housed in the tech booth.

The second camera was designed to eliminate all of the blind spots in the church, and allow the viewers at home the closest replication of the Mass as possible, at least from a visual perspective.

Kevin: During Communion, when the deacon goes to the Tabernacle, the people can see the reverence of it.

Within a few months, as the initial wave of COVID-19 started to relent and socially distanced and mask-wearing attendance became the norm, Father Roger realized the value this new method of Mass delivery offered, particularly for those parishioners who can't make it to the church, regardless of the reason.

52 Masses: Were we doing enough for our home-bound before the pandemic?

Father Roger: It has opened our eyes and our vision to see we weren't doing enough, other than bringing them Communion or the Anointing of the Sick. The Church was present through the priest or a minister, in a very deep but small way. We went into their homes to do that. What this gives them is the opportunity to be a part of us. It's not just going to them; they can come to us.

The parishioners of Seton parish appreciated that opportunity.

Joan Ansalvish and daughter-in-law Lisa Kennedy-Ansalvish have joined the conversation

Joan Ansalvish is a founding parishioner of Seton parish, and has been fixture there for decades, serving on virtually every committee imaginable. Even through the pandemic, into her 90s, she was still an active presence at the parish, but COVID stopped her in-person participation immediately.

52 Masses: How much did the ability to experience Mass mean to you?

Joan: It meant a lot. It worked out really well, having the church on TV. I think Seton does a good job of reaching out to shut-ins. Father would go out and give Communion. He's good, but he can't be everywhere at every moment.

Lisa: Mom comes from a generation that isn't technically savvy. It was a challenge for our house to find a way to stay connected with the Church. We're still on a learning curve, but we're getting there. It helps us stay connected. Not as connected as we'd like, but still connected.

And it's not just through Mass they can stay connected. Joan's son Joe, a Los Angeles resident, passed away from COVID while he was back home visiting the family. When the family was finally able to conduct a proper funeral, Tom and Kevin filmed and livestreamed the funeral Mass to Zoom, allowing his friends and colleagues from all over the country to participate in the Mass in a way previously unavailable.

Lisa: We have to find a way to take the best of a terrible situation and apply it for good.

Diana Moyet-Trerotola has joined the conversation

Diana Moyet-Trerotola also spent many hours in the early days of the pandemic at home with her mother, a regular Mass goer the family relocated from New York to Delaware.

Diana: She lives in New York. Other than going to church, she doesn't go out very much. It was good to be able to sit on the couch and watch the Mass with her.

But Diana wasn't just a passive participant in Seton parish's efforts. A hospital chaplain with a master's degree in theology, she developed 30 spiritual devotions that Seton would post on its social media sites. It was one other way, in addition to Sunday Mass livestreams, a Wednesday Holy Hour and a virtual bible study program, that Father Roger and others at Seton were serving the spiritual needs of the parishioners sheltering in place.

Diana: The live Mass led to those other online spiritual programs. We were already doing some things for my ministry and for the front-line staff, but once they got connected, I said I could do this for you. It really took off.

When I attended Mass in late summer, most of the COVID precautions had been lifted, at least temporarily until the delta wave took over. The 8 a.m. Mass was still being livestreamed, though after a year of serving the parish virtually but dutifully every week, Tom and Kevin finally had some support in their digital ministry efforts.

Tom: We've just started getting the younger people involved. It's something they're interested in.

For this Sunday morning Mass, the booth was manned not by the two adult parishioners, but a quartet of young people mastering the skills. College students Jacob Clark and Francis Chacko served as the director and livestream operator, respectively, while high schooler Deron Tchuente ran the slide presentation and his younger brother Declan Takam operated the cameras.

It is by no means a simple operation, though I'm sure it's much easier for teenagers and twentysomethings to get up to speed than it would be for someone my age. The boys can't lose focus at any point in the Mass, and must adjust to any hiccups that happen in the course of a typical Sunday service. Still, the boys handled their duties with nary a glitch, though they later acknowledged some buffering issues with the stream.

Francis Chacko has joined the conversation

For most of the boys, working in the booth is an opportunity to serve the Church in a way that also taps into their interests. But Francis Chacko has an additional incentive. Francis's family is part of a growing Syro-Malabar population at St. Elizabeth Ann Seton. The Indian-American parishioners have hopes of establishing their own parish, possibly purchasing available land right on Seton's campus, a move that has Father Roger's complete blessing. If it happens, Francis would like to be at the forefront of delivering a similar livestream to the Syro-Malabar community.

Francis: I think it's something we've had in our minds for the future. Father Roger has been very instrumental in helping us build out our community. Livestreaming it is food for thought.

The embrace of technology has not been limited to livestreaming. From the outset, the parish turned to Zoom to keep parish committees in constant contact and the parish's operations running smoothly.

Father Roger: Our finance committee hasn't missed a monthly meeting since COVID started. The Knights of Columbus have Zoomed meetings. I think they're fantastic. It saves travel and gas pollution and accidents. Obviously, a church is a community that gathers in a physical space. But for some of those meetings, we don't all need to be sitting in the same room.

One of the great assets of these technologies is how they expand the presence of the parish well past the church walls. A family vacationing elsewhere can watch a live or rebroadcast of Sunday Mass being held at their home parish. An out-of-town grandmother with a Zoom invitation can see her granddaughter receive First Holy Communion. A hospitalized parishioner, perhaps alone in a sterile, impersonal room, can digitally join friends and family at Mass. And the bishop's annual

Mass for the state corrections facilities can be safely filmed at Seton, then shown to the prisoners with no fear of spreading the virus to that vulnerable population.

Father Roger knows nothing can replace the experience of in-person attendance at the Mass, which must be the objective unless circumstances legitimately prevent it.

Father Roger: It's not full and active participation. You cannot be present to the Eucharist just staying at home.

Still, those circumstances do arise, and the suboptimal solution need not be ignored in our quest for the ideal.

Father Roger: It's an evangelizing tool. We're reaching people who otherwise wouldn't have tuned in to a religious setting. It's exciting to have Seton parish a part of these things, to be part of a bigger audience, a bigger congregation, as we go forward.

52 Masses: Thank you, Father.

52 Masses has left the conversation
Christ is still in the conversation

Holy Family Syro-Malabar

Phoenix, Arizona

"Disorder in society is the result of disorder in the family."
Saint Angela Merici

It is a name most appropriate. Holy Family, the Syro-Malabar parish in Phoenix, is an exquisite example of the role the entire family plays in a healthy faith community.

It is also the key to the church's continued ability to flourish in the United States.

On the last Sunday in January when I participated in my first Holy Qurbana, the pews at Holy Family were not just filled, but done so in a most orderly fashion. The kindergarten children took the first row, followed by first graders on up. Children are, literally, front and center at Holy Qurbana, a practice that traces back to the Eastern church's home in India, where many of the worship spaces don't have pews.

"We want the attention from the little ones," explained Rev. Justin Puthussery, who was appointed to serve the parish in 2020 during the early days of the pandemic. "Little ones should not see the gimmicks of the adults. We want them seeing Jesus and the priest."

That child-centered approach wasn't restricted to the seating. The readings for the liturgy and the music were all led by young people, which is the parish's practice when Qurbana is conducted in English. Each week, the service rotates between English, the native tongue of most of the young people, and Malayalam, the language of the church's home in Kerala, India. It's a nod to the push-pull the Syro-Malabar Church faces here, with Indian-born adults preferring Qurbana in the language they were raised in while their children naturally lean toward the language they hear every day.

"The language fight is there in every community," said Father Justin. "Practically, we need to use English to communicate with them."

When Qurbana ends, all of the young people move from the worship space directly on to catechism classes, which take place in various rooms around the small campus. Their parents, who may have traveled up to 90 minutes to get there, enjoy fellowship outdoors as they wait for their children's lessons to be completed.

To parents such as Vinesh Peter, a father of three, catechism classes are every bit as vital to his children's development as their formal K-12 education. "It has the same importance, to keep the children grounded, so they know what to do, respect others, respect their parents," he said. "It's not about being Indian-Indian. It's about doing the right thing."

Principal John Rinson heads up the catechism program. "This is how we bring kids to the faith. We let them know this is the most important thing to do on a Sunday, to be in the presence of God."

Beautifully, the education process doesn't start with kindergarten or even preschool, but in the womb. Pregnant mothers are invited to sit in on catechism classes, educators Gracy Mathew and Ainie Tom explained.

And this attitude of growing the faith in the young is not just held by devout parents or religious educators, but reaches to the highest level of the Church in the United States. "I have to concentrate on the formation of the second generation," said Mar Jacob Angadiath, the first and only man to serve as bishop of the St. Thomas Syro-Malabar Catholic Diocese of Chicago. "That's a primary concern, how to keep them within the Church."

The Syro-Malabar Church, was founded during the first century by Saint Thomas the Apostle in Kerala in South India, where it remains based. But the 20th century has seen it take root in the United States, in any city where a healthy population of immigrants from India call home.

In 1984, then Father Jacob Angadiath came here as the first Syro-Malabar priest assigned to the United States. He was sent to Texas, serving under a Roman Catholic priest in the Diocese of Dallas at the behest of the growing Indian population there.

The young priest began offering Holy Qurbana once a month, then bumped it up to twice a month so the Catholics could experience the liturgy they had grown up with. In time, the community grew large enough, and raised enough money, to establish its own parish. They purchased a former Baptist church and the first parish outside India was born.

And that structure remains the template in the Indian diaspora of the United States. A community develops within a Roman Catholic parish, Qurbana is added to the liturgy schedule, then if the growth is strong enough, the community strikes out on its own.

Mar Jacob Angadiath has overseen it all. As the Syro-Malabar presence in the United States grew, to Chicago, New York, New Jersey and beyond, Saint Pope John Paul II instructed Cardinal Mar Anthony Padiyara to study the needs of this unique community. As a result of that study, the pope established the diocese of Chicago in 2001, the first eparchy outside India. Jacob Angadiath was appointed the diocese's first bishop, a position he retains.

When I sat down with Mar Jacob Angadiath at his home near Mar Thoma Sleeha Cathedral in Bellwood, Illinois, there were 48 parishes and another 36 missions spread out across the United States. Though the growth has taken place almost entirely under his leadership, he's quick to refuse any credit for the Syro-Malabar's development in his adopted country.

"This was God's work. I had nothing to do with it," he said humbly.

And for him, the work God does to build His kingdom does not necessarily begin on Sunday morning at Qurbana, but in the homes of all of its adherents.

"The family is of great importance in our values and tradition," he said. "For us, everything begins at home." It's where faith formation begins, where prayers are spoken nightly.

Their family invocations include the Holy Rosary, prayers for the dearly departed, prayers to particular saints and simple praise to Christ. "It brings unity to the family," Mar Jacob said of these family prayers. "Even when there has been some discord, during that time everything is gone. We are all reconciled."

Mar Jacob Angadiath, like Father Justin Puthussery, know the special challenges Eastern churches face in the U.S. Most of the adults and parents at Holy Family are Indian immigrants, men and women who grew up in the traditions of the Syro-Malabar Church, with Malayalam their first language.

Their children, however, are most often U.S. born, or at least have spent most of their formative years growing up in the States. English is their first language, American traditions the ones they encounter every day at school and through consumption of media and entertainment.

It a challenge for Indian-Americans to preserve those values and traditions they hold dear and one the Church plays a key role in supporting.

"Mass helps reinforce what we teach at home. When they go to school, they see other things," said Tessy James, a parishioner. "Here, they know what they belong to and what they need to practice."

Buoying the hopes of inculcating the faith in the second generation of families is the emergence of vocations of U.S.-born Syro-Malabar men and women. In 2018, two priests born in the United States were ordained, "the first fruits of the Syro-Malabar Church in America," Mar Jacob Angadiath calls them. More have followed their footsteps, while a group of young U.S. women have similarly answered the call and joined U.S. religious congregations. Attracting young people into vocations is imperative to the Church's vibrancy, since it faces the obstacles of not having schools or other facilities that are common to the Roman Catholic Church here. The parish church, one that typically serves congregations spread out over large distances, is the entirety of the Syro-Malabar infrastructure here.

Holy Family was founded in 2013, five years after the community first formed in the Valley. Its first families originally worshipped at Our Lady of Fatima Mission before setting off on their own.

Their location is centrally located in Phoenix, which was no accident. Given the distances many of the families must travel to attend Qurbana and any other events, they wanted a site that was most accessible to the largest number of families. They found one on 24th Street, just a few blocks north of the Roman Catholic parish St. Agnes, a fact that became meaningful in early 2021.

Already struggling to deal with the effects of the pandemic on church life, the parish was dealt a second blow when a small fire broke out in the church. The sacristy suffered significant harm, and smoke damage existed elsewhere in the worship space. The parishioners of Holy Family were displaced.

They found welcoming neighbors in St. Agnes. Holy Family transferred Holy Qurbana services to the church down the road. Just as important, the parish opened up its school to use for Holy Family's catechism classes. "Everything that happened here was done over there," Father Justin said. "They were so cooperative."

Daily Qurbana was the only activity taking place at the Holy Family location, as the small number of attendees allowed the parish to use a church in a separate hall on site. By late October 2021, the community was back worshipping at its home parish.

Though Holy Family is their Sunday home, many of the parishioners feel equally welcome continuing to worship in Roman or other Catholic parishes. That's true of Matthew Jose and his family. Though they have been part of the community since its founding, their home 30 miles away means daily Mass attendance takes place at a Roman Catholic Church in closer proximity.

The man charged with leading the Syro-Malabar Church here in the U.S. is thoroughly supportive of that nod to practicality. "Whether Syro-Malabar or Ukrainian or Byzantine or Latin, Catholic is Catholic," Bishop Mar Jacob Angadiath said.

St. Vincent de Paul

Tallassee, Alabama

"In simplicity of heart I gladly offer everything, O Lord."
Blessed Maria Gabriella Sagheddu, model of Christian unity.

THE RELATIONSHIP BETWEEN CATHOLICS AND OTHER CHRISTIANS in the United States has a spotty history. Our arrival in the U.S. in large numbers in the 19th century was viewed suspiciously by the dominant majority Protestant population, an unfortunate condition that has largely been erased by time.

Yet in areas where the Catholic presence was not so substantial, it has often taken longer to eliminate that inherent distrust of us, and, in some extreme cases, even our claim to the Christian faith. Places such as Alabama, a state where 85 percent of the population is Christian, but only 7 percent of those Christians belong to the Catholic Church, have been slower to truly welcome the Church and its people. As noted by Saint Anselm College's Andrew S. Moore in the Archdiocese of Mobile's Encyclopedia of Alabama, despite a presence in the area that long predated Alabama statehood, "persistent anti-Catholicism meant that Alabama's Catholics rarely felt entirely comfortable."

That anxiety has waned considerably in the more recent past, and organizations such as ACTS have gone a long way to eliminating those decades of uneasy co-existence. ACTS stands for Association of Christians in Tallassee for Service, an interdenominational effort to meet the needs of the impoverished in Elmore and Tallapoosa counties in East Central Alabama.

From the beginning, Tallassee's St. Vincent de Paul has been an important contributor to the group, providing the three Ts to the organization. Moreover, the parish's contributions have helped play a role in reshaping the view of Catholicism in this rural southern community.

"It has probably broken down some of the negative attitudes," said retired Rev. Charles Troncale. "The attitude has changed for the better."

Monsignor Troncale served for several years at St. Vincent de Paul. He came to ACTS through his participation in the community's ministerial association, another significant tool in chipping away at anti-Catholic sentiment. At each monthly meeting, the ministers would sign up to volunteer to be at the ACTS physical location in the city in the event on the clients wanted spiritual assistance along with their material needs. "Every now and then, they would want me to pray with them or pray for them. Many people had never met a Catholic priest," said Monsignor Troncale, himself an Alabama native.

His successor at St. Vincent de Paul, Rev. Mateusz Rudzik has a background that couldn't get much more different. Father Mateusz is a native of Poland. He came to the States decades ago but found his original destination in the Upper Midwest too cold, precipitating a relocation to sunnier Alabama. He finds the ACTS experience a welcome, and wonderful, change.

"It's something I haven't encountered in the South before, with different churches working so close together and putting any differences aside to focus on how they can help the people of the community," he said. "For me, it's a phenomenon."

Of course, ACTS primary goal is not ecumenism, but fulfilling the obligation of all Christians to care for the least among us.

The organization was founded in the 1980s when a number of local pastors were looking for a central location to handle each church's commitment to the needy of the community, a way to improve the services to the impoverished in Eastern Alabama. Currently, 17 churches in Tallassee participate, contributing financially and with gifts of material goods. The city allows the organization to use the former city hall building at no charge.

Barry Adair serves as director of ACTS, running both the physical location and directing the community volunteers, both religious and lay people, who aid the operation. ACTS typically offers help in three primary ways: with food assistance, clothing help, and to aid with utility payments. When available, it can provide furniture or appliances or other gifts that come its way.

"Even though we're small, I can't think of another organization in our immediate area that does all the things we do," Barry Adair said.

Better yet, everything the organization provides is free of charge. "If John and Jane walk out of here with something, they walk out with no expense. Other agencies might charge a little," he said.

And, being a Christian organization, the aim is not just to arm the clients with those corporal items, but aiding them spiritually as well. Each client is invited to pray or speak with a local pastor. ACTS also provides instructional videos on a host of topics, including smoking and drinking cessation and budgeting, to better prepare the clients for the days and years ahead.

Though clients are not required to participate in ACTS' spiritual services, Adair believes faith is an inherent part of the work the association does. "For me, personally, it should be that way. It's in our name."

Jan Brienza had recently joined St. Vincent de Paul when she began volunteering at ACTS. The experience was transformative, both in the true ecumenism of the operation and the work being done.

"I was raised a Methodist, I have five uncles who were Baptist preachers, a very Protestant upbringing. But I walked in as a Catholic and it didn't matter. We were there to be the hands of Christ or the Face of Christ. It was amazing. I've never been part of an organization like that," she said.

Over the course of the past decade, she graduated from volunteer to St. Vincent de Paul's representative to the board and eventually to chairman of the board of the nonprofit organization, each step and each experience a revelation in the value of Christian service to both the recipient of our charity and to the giver.

"Seeing the people that we were serving crying because we were giving them 40 pounds of food for their family and I'm griping because I have to buy Hunt's ketchup instead of Heinz ketchup, it was so humbling. It made me grateful for what I do have, instead of wanting more," Jan Brienza recalled.

For the parish, ACTS is not the only way the church integrates with the larger Protestant community in the area. On Saturdays in the summer, the parish steps away from the clapboard church in downtown Tallassee and holds services in Church of the Pines, a beautiful open-air facility located just a few feet from Lake Martin a half-hour north of the city.

The A-framed structure was built in the 1970s – replacing a pine-straw covered arbor where services began being held in the 1950s – to serve the Protestants at the lake. Sunday mornings are still given over to a nondenominational Christian service at the location. But on Saturdays between Memorial Day and Labor Day, the building's owners yield the facility to St. Vincent de Paul, which replaces its vigil service in Tallassee with the outdoor Mass. The weekly service appeals to travelers, lake residents, and some SVdP parishioners, who enjoy celebrating the liturgy with God's beauty as an impressive visual backdrop, while the gentle lapping of the waves against the shore also serve to soothe.

Joining Father Mateusz at the front of the church most Saturdays is Glenn Person, the entirety of the music ministry for the vigil service. It's clear no other persons are needed, as Glenn's rich tenor voice seemed to emanate from somewhere in the pines themselves.

Glenn Person is another example of the Christian fellowship running throughout the community in Elmore and surrounding counties. He is a member of an AME church in his native Tuskegee, but does the music for both the outdoor service and for the Sunday 1 p.m. service at St. Joseph in Tuskegee, where Father Mateusz also serves as pastor.

The multifaceted musician enjoys the experience at the Catholic setting, which provides a much different set of songs and requirements than he gets at his home church.

"I'm getting back to my roots when it comes to classical voicings," he said. "I have done a lot of foreign language material, a lot of Latin, some Spanish. I'm Gospel born and raised, but I also have this classical background, and for two hours out of the weekend, I'm back to my roots when it comes to music school."

On the Saturday I attended, Father Mateusz was confronted with all the challenges the outdoor Mass provides. The evening began in the typical sweltering heat of an Alabama summer, but gave way to ominous clouds, distant thunderclaps, and an eventual downpour that pinched many parishioners to the inside pews, trying to escape the blowing rain. But by the end of Mass, when parishioners were filing out to return to beach homes and boats, by God's providence the storm had passed. By the following day, the Church of the Pines would again be claimed by Eastern Alabama's other Christians.

Building stronger relationships with our Christian brothers and sisters has been an objective of the Church for decades. The restoration of unity among all Christians was one of the principal concerns of the Second Vatican Council, it was written in Unitatis Redintegratio. And then-Pope John Paul II built on that idea in his 1995 encyclical, Ut Unum Sint: "This unity, which the Lord has bestowed on his Church and in which he wishes to embrace all people, is not something added on, but stands at the very heart of Christ's mission."

In Tallassee, and elsewhere, that heart is beating vigorously.

St. Peter the Apostle

Schulte, Kansas

"You are called like the apostles to make God known to others."
- Saint Jean-Baptiste de La Salle.

Most Rev. Michael Jackels, then bishop of the Diocese of Wichita, sat over a late-night coffee in a dimly lit kitchen with Rev. Bernard X. Gorges and posed a simple question to the priest: "Do you believe Totus Tuus is of the Holy Spirit?"

It was a question Father Bernie had not previously considered. Totus Tuus, Latin for Totally Yours, the motto of Saint John Paul II, was founded by Father Bernie years earlier, shortly after he was ordained.

From its humble beginnings serving small parishes in the farm country around Wichita where Father Bernie was raised, Totus Tuus had already grown into a massive undertaking, extending not just past the borders of the Diocese of Wichita, but outside Kansas as well.

Father Bernie's program was on the verge of another round of growth. The priest was getting set to aid the program's arrival in Iowa into three of the four dioceses in the state. As was customary, such an expansion would begin with him offering training for those who would implement the program within a diocese.

Father Bernie answered in the affirmative but was curious where the now-retired bishop was going. The priest talked a little of his aspirations for the program and what his future role could realistically be while still maintaining his growing pastoral duties. Bishop Jackels followed up with another question, asking whether Father Bernie would like to "test that spirit?"

Again, Father Bernie pondered the question, still confused at the bishop's intent.

"Get out of it completely," Bishop Jackels advised, surprising the priest. "If it's built on your personality, it will stagnate and fail. If it's not, it will grow."

"I did get out," said Father Bernie, now the pastor at St. Peter the Apostle in Schulte. "And it exploded." Today, Totus Tuus is in place in more than 40 dioceses around the country. Each summer, new dioceses get on board with the program, with its time-tested formula of true-to-faith Catholic instruction delivered by inspired young people.

Liz Clark serves as the director of Totus Tuus, coordinating not just the program in the diocese, but across the country. She oversees the growth of the operation into new areas, while pushing to see more uniformity in the program from one diocese to the next, both in what's being offered and how.

"We're trying, with national, to get everyone on the same page. It's such a Catholic program, so strong in the sacraments, we don't want to see it get watered down."

The program's origins date to 1987, before Father Bernie had even entered the seminary. He had been teaching religious education at his farm town parish when he was asked to travel with two nuns to help with Sister School, a rural tradition in Southern Kansas. "It was what the Protestants would call Vacation Bible School," he explained. Soon, however, they started running short of available sisters, so his monsignor asked him to set out on his own.

It began in the small parishes – he would teach kids in grades 5-8 and a young volunteer from the parish would handle younger children in a two-room schoolhouse kind of arrangement. The following year, he invited a seminarian to join him. That exponential type of growth continued throughout the 1990s, recruiting spirited young Catholic men and women to provide the teaching that serves as the lifeblood of the Totus Tuus experience, all the while serving more children in larger and larger parishes.

That first volunteer teacher was Lisa Munn, a lifelong parishioner at St. Peter the Apostle. She was serving as a teacher at the school in 2000 when Totus Tuus was implemented at the parish and she's helped out every year since.

"I personally feel very attached to it," she said. "Totus Tuus taught me how to discern my vocation. I feel the life I have right now has its roots in Totus Tuus."

Lisa Munn had grown up learning the Baltimore catechesis, memorizing its message that "God Made Me to Know Love and Serve. Father Bernie took that further, explaining, "you cannot love what you do not know, and you cannot serve what you do not love," she recalled. "To me, that's Totus Tuus. It's teaching these kids about their faith and inviting them to come and love Jesus. If you love something, you want to serve it."

She said there are two elements that drive the success of the program, what makes so many other dioceses around the country want to implement it at home. The first is it's "authentically Catholic," deriving its program from the basics of the faith – Mass, Confession, the Rosary, and the Eucharist.

The program is operated on two separate yearly rotations. In one, a six-year rotation, the program covers the Ten Commandments, Virtues and Beatitudes, Prayer and the Our Father, Salvation History, the Apostles Creed, and the Sacraments. Another four-year timetable deals with the four Mysteries.

Additionally, Father Bernie developed the program with four pillars: Eucharistic adoration and worship; catechetical instruction; Marian devotion; and vocational discernment. A few years later, he was advised to add a fifth pillar, one he claims was a little outside his purview: fun. "I'm not a fun guy," he concedes, a statement few, myself included, would agree with.

Yet, Father Bernie and others believe the program's effectiveness hinges on the missionaries who drive these lessons home in a way that simply wouldn't be possible for parents and grandparents. From parish to parish, all summer long, the college-aged kids who serve as missionaries relentlessly and joyfully bring the faith alive.

"I think the other secret ingredient is the example and witness of these college kids who come in. Your mom and dad and teachers tell you this stuff, but when you have a young person who's energetic and fun and they're saying the same thing, you think 'Maybe it's the real deal.'" Lisa Munn said. The college students are undoubtedly the real deal. From the moment the Totus Tuus kids walk in on Monday morning until they're released to mom and dad on Friday afternoon, the missionaries lay bare their love for Christ, their enthusiasm matched only by their endurance.

They cheer and cajole every kid in camp, displaying an excitement and positivity that would come across as forced if attempted by someone my age. In the hands of Dominic Jirak or Nicholas Samsel, it's completely natural. As it should be. Like most missionaries, the young men were Totus Tuus campers long before they returned to teach. The experiences the young men had in camp were instrumental in their discernments to pursue the priesthood.

"Totus Tuus showed me that faith isn't just for old men and women," said Dominic Jirak, entering third-year seminary at the House of Formation in Wichita. "There's something more. My faith is worth living for."

Likewise, Liz Clark's path to the position she holds is a well-trod one in the Diocese of Wichita. She attended the program as a child, served as a missionary during her college years, then assumed her post after first working as a teacher. She joins the dozens of priests and other men and women in religious life who recognize the program as a catalyst to their own callings. It's also served as a place where many young Catholic men and women first met, individuals whose discernment took them to married life and the delivery of the next generation of Totus Tuus participants.

"It's a beautiful thing to see how many vocations have come through this program, to priesthood, to religious life and to married life. It's been a blessing for sure to the diocese," Liz Clark said.

Even with the faith-centered life that comes with the seminary, both young men say the experience of working with the children at Totus Tuus offers an entirely different kind of encounter with Christ. "As a college-aged kid, I think I've got my prayer life figured out. But there's so much more joy I can bring to the world. And you can see that by interacting with all the kids," Dominic Jirak said.

Nicholas Samsel, too, gets a much-needed pick-me-up, whether he's teaching the students about the mysteries of the Rosary in the classroom or leading a slapstick-style skit to keep them entertained in the cafeteria. "God is calling me to be a priest to serve the people of God.

It's something I sometimes lose in seminary because it's so much structure and so much classwork. That's one of the beautiful things about Totus Tuus," he said.

In the Diocese of Wichita, the program's beauty runs even deeper. In addition to the parish-based sessions, the diocese also offers weeklong overnight camps, broken down by age and gender, girls attend one week, boys another. It's for those young people who are even more energized by the faith and with an even greater desire to strengthen their relationship with Christ. Expanding the camp program into the other dioceses served by Totus Tuus is one of Liz Clark's not-so-secret ambitions.

Yet the heart of the program will always sit at the parish level, where the pre-teen and high school-age parishioners may get their first meaningful encounter with Christ. And almost 40 years on, the engaging priest who started it all claims to have turned over most duties to the younger Catholics, though his success at fully detaching himself from the program is questionable. He still opens the rectory to all of the young men serving as missionaries at St. Peter the Apostle, engaging them in spirited discussions of faith long into the evening. And he presides over the Mass that serves as the anchor for each day's activities. Still, the pastor admits, "I've slowed down a lot in the last five years."

True though that may be, Father Bernie can take considerable comfort in the knowledge that his legacy of programs will continue to educate and energize young Catholic men and women for decades to come. For Totus Tuus is his creation, but it remains forever of the Holy Spirit.

Blessed Sacrament

Stowe, Vermont

"Art is able to manifest and make visible the human need to surpass the visible, it expresses the thirst and the quest for the infinite. Indeed it resembles a door open on to the infinite, on to a beauty and a truth that go beyond the daily routine. And a work of art can open the eyes of the mind and of the heart, impelling us upward. However some artistic expressions are real highways to God, the supreme Beauty; indeed, they help us to grow in our relationship with him, in prayer. These are works that were born from faith and express faith."
Pope Emeritus Benedict XVI

THE STORY OF BLESSED SACRAMENT INVOLVES A WORLD-FAMOUS Austrian matriarch, the righthand man to a Belgian saint, a French resistance fighter and a retired art professor. But Blessed Sacrament is not an 800-year-old parish in some postcard-worthy Alpine village. Rather, it's a barely 70-year-old church in the similarly picturesque Stowe, Vermont.

The church was founded in 1949, though not without some delay. When the local priest's request to create a parish where a mission church existed, the initial attempt was rebuffed by the bishop. In went a future parishioner in his place, who successfully pitched the Diocese of Burlington on granting a parish. That parishioner was Maria von Trapp. Yes, the Austrian-born, Vermont-relocated Maria von Trapp, the matriarch of the Trapp Family Singers, the inspiration for The Sound of Music, was integral in the foundation of Blessed Sacrament.

But that's only part of the fascinating history of this resort town parish.

Though lacking a building, the budding Catholic congregation already had the land, and it couldn't have been more appropriate. The site was on the grounds where Joseph Dutton was born and raised.

Dutton was a Protestant-born native of Stowe who converted to Catholicism after serving in the Civil War. In 1886, he left the continental U.S. for the island of Molokai, to aid the work of the resident priest, then known as Father Damien. By then, the tireless priest had already contracted the same Hansen's disease suffered by the island's residents, an ailment that would eventually claim his life.

Brother Joseph spent the remainder of his days in Hawaii, carrying on the work of Saint Damien and alerting the world to his efforts. The drive to similarly canonize Brother Joseph is ongoing in Hawaii, with support from the people of Blessed Sacrament, the parish dedicated to him. In May of 2022, the Diocese of Honolulu held a ceremony to open the Diocesan Inquiry Phase for Joseph Dutton.

And that's not all. Next to enter the picture, literally, was André Girard, a famed French painter and World War II resistance leader, who, like the Trapps before him, fled Europe for the United States in the 1940s.

After the war, the Catholic magazine *Liturgical Arts* put together an enticing proposition for smaller Catholic churches of the United States. A wealthy family had commissioned Girard to paint the Stations of the Cross for a parish with limited resources.

Blessed Sacrament was just such a parish. While the diocese had agreed to the construction of a new church, funds were scarce, and thus a small, dark, boxy structure was all the fledgling parish could afford. The finished product was completely naked in terms of adornments, existing merely as a worship space. That proved to be quite beneficial.

Father Francis McDonough, Blessed Sacrament's first pastor, was friendly with Maurice Lavanoux, an editor at *Liturgical Arts*, earning a visit to Vermont by Girard, the editor and benefactors.

The utilitarian edifice somehow caught the eye of Girard. While others stood aside, the French artist broke from the group to study the church from all angles, inside and out, mumbling variants of "c'est magnifique."

He returned with a simple proposal. He would choose Stowe to do his work, but on a single condition – that he be allowed to do the entire building. The Stations, the walls, the windows, and the ceilings all would be touched by his artistry. Blessed Sacrament would become his ultimate artistic creation, done at no cost to the parish.

There are few Catholic churches anywhere in the world where all of the adornments were done by a single artist. It was the perfect enticement to the deeply devout craftsman.

His paintings have transformed the small wooden church structure into a showpiece, now recognized as one of the Green Mountain State's most important historic buildings.

Upon my arrival, it was easy to see how André Girard was so inspired to do his work here. Though simple, the structure fits perfectly in its setting; one could easily imagine it being the best-built barn on a 1950s Vermont dairy farm.

Girard's work is wholly unconventional compared with what's found in most Catholic churches in America. In some ways, it can be an acquired taste, and one not every visitor comes to obtain. "My first take on it was how strange this was. It was like nothing I grew up with in the traditional Catholic church, with marble and beautiful stained glass windows," said Beverly Bishop, a parish historian.

But the work won her over, in part because of how clearly Girard was in tune with the faith. "I didn't understand how deeply André Girard understood the scriptures. Even now, I'm amazed at how deeply felt these paintings are."

I concur wholeheartedly with her assessment. The passion for the faith the artist possessed is undeniable, something you recognize before you even enter the space.

On the exterior, the story of Brother Dutton's work with Saint Damien is told, with black paint against the gold-colored walls. More artistry is evident above the single entrance to the church.

It only gets more enticing inside. Behind the altar is a mural, depicting the Holy Trinity in light strokes, the followers of Jesus below painted with darker strokes, and Christ's likeness done with a touch of dark lines, representing how he came down from Heaven to become man.

Near the ceiling are 36 colored windows, not the stained glass as you'd find in most parishes, but one of Girard's signature styles of painting on glass. The windows depict an array of scenes from Christ's life: The Wedding Feast at Cana, The Agony in the Garden, The Sermon on the Mount. Each painting uses colorful strokes offset against dark spaces to tell the specific story captured on the single pane. It also gives the impression of ample movement, something much more difficult to capture through stained glass.

Like Michelangelo before him, André Girard's work was not limited to the walls. The ceiling has 60 panels, each featuring lightly drawn faces of Christ, angels and more. They provide a heavenly covering to the worship space.

But to me, it was Girard's original assignment, the Stations of the Cross, that was the most absorbing. His paintings detailing Christ's Passion were like none I'd ever seen. The paintings ranged from brightly colored to blackness, offering vivid details and blurred backdrops, but all telling the story in full detail and showcasing the pain and suffering in a way that only a true master is capable of. I don't know if André Girard considered Blessed Sacrament to be his artistic masterpiece, his opus. But I doubt there are many works that more perfectly marry artistic brilliance and profound faith as this one does.

The artwork has been attracting visitors to the church for decades. Stowe is a popular tourist site, with out-of-towners coming to ski in the winter, relax in the summer, and take in Vermont's spectacular foliage in autumn. "Between the activities in the community, whether it's different sports tournaments for the kids or the leaf peepers in the fall, probably half the congregation every Sunday is people who are visiting," said Rev. Jon Schnobrich, the current pastor of Blessed Sacrament.

Girard's art may draw them to Blessed Sacrament, but the parish keeps them coming back. "One of the hallmarks of the community is hospitality. We really try to extend the hospitality we think Christ would show to the stranger, welcoming them to worship with us, to celebrate with us, have coffee hour and make this place part of their home away from home when they're on vacation," Father Schnobrich said.

They find that home in Blessed Sacrament, which André Girard turned from a common country church into a work of brilliance. Alas, there was a near-fatal flaw to Girard's plan. A masterpiece is only as good as its canvas and Blessed Sacrament wasn't built to support world-class art. Within two decades, the wood planks and windows were showing their age, and Girard's creations were on the verge of becoming a casualty of that deterioration.

By this time, Girard has passed on, so his widow, Andrée Jouan Girard – herself a heroic figure in the fight against the Nazis, serving time in an Axis prison for her role in the resistance – suggested the next best thing. She called on Josephine Belloso to carry on his work.

At the time, Josephine Belloso was an art teacher at St. Joseph's College in Brooklyn. She met the French artist when she invited him to deliver a lecture at the school, then accepted his invitation to study under him. It began a long friendship with the artist and his family, which culminated in restoration work on both his remarkable series of painting on film, plus the church in Stowe.

Josephine Belloso arrived in Stowe believing she would simply be restoring the windows, which would be consistent with the work she had done on his films. Instead, she was called upon for the full restoration, a task made more challenging by the constant interruptions of well-meaning parishioners.

On her final day, she was determined to not let anything distract her. Standing on a platform, absorbed in her work, she heard a twittering "Ahem, ahem," down below. She tried to ignore the tiny pleas, but eventually turned to find the visitor was Maria von Trapp, who had come to thank Girard's protégé for her skillful rehabilitation. "I would like to shake your hand, but you're up too high," she told Josephine Belloso, who practically tripped in her haste to come down from her perch.

When I spoke to her, the now-retired teacher still cherished the opportunity given to her to restore one of her mentor's greatest artistic endeavors. "In this simple, rustic church, with walls that were peeling, this distinguished artist put his hand," she said. "Using rudimentary materials and simple strokes, he managed to create something at once very humble but also one that shows extraordinary visions of not just the artist, but a believer."

Another two decades passed and the same problem arose, the building materials still not holding up its end of the bargain. "If it even touched anything, if the wind blew, it would just peel away," recalled Josephine Belloso, who chronicled the history of the church's artwork in the book, *Painting on Light.*

This time, the caretakers of Blessed Sacrament were looking for a more permanent solution. Using digital printing and other modern techniques, the latest restoration recreated Girard's vision in a way that is better prepared against any battering from Vermont's four equally assertive seasons. The breathtaking final result, now permanently a part of the Blessed Sacrament story, was the byproduct of "art, science, and good old-fashioned Yankee carpentry," said Lynn Altadonna, a parishioner and retired aerospace engineer who helped oversee the second restoration, skillfully executed by local artist Matthew H. Strong.

Today, Blessed Sacrament is a thriving parish, gifted with a healthy balance of young and old families, which isn't always the case in Vermont, one of the nation's oldest states. "That is a great sign of hope. We have a lot of young people, young families," said Father Schnobrich, who was appointed pastor in 2019.

He points to a larger than average recent Confirmation class as evidence, which he hopes will turn into more active participants in the church community. "When you receive Confirmation, it's not graduation from catechism class. It's the launching pad to get more actively involved in your parish."

The objective, of course, is to ensure the present of Blessed Sacrament is as rich and rewarding as its hard-to-fathom past, where the extraordinary was carved out of the commonplace, and where the vision of a parish for a small community to call home has grown into one the world comes to see.

"They just needed a place to worship," Beverly Bishop tells of the first parishioners of Blessed Sacrament. "They hadn't gotten around to adorning it when this gift fell out of the sky. To imagine all of the work this artist did is pretty mind-blowing."

Holy Cross & St. Katharine Drexel-St. Mary

Kaukauna, Wisconsin

St. Katharine Drexel-St. Francis

Hollandtown, Wisconsin

> *Jesus said to his disciples: "Beware that your hearts do not become drowsy from carousing and drunkenness and the anxieties of daily life, and that day catch you by surprise like a trap. For that day will assault everyone who lives on the face of the earth. Be vigilant at all times and pray that you have the strength to escape the tribulations that are imminent and to stand before the Son of Man."*
> Luke 21:34-36

DEACON JIM TRZINSKI IS LIKE A LOT OF OTHER MEN FROM THE Diocese of Green Bay. He fishes in the spring, camps out in the summer, and hunts in the fall. And when the many lakes freeze over in the brutal winters of the Upper Midwest, he fishes again. It is not a law that men of the near Northwoods of Wisconsin live for the outdoors, more of a general rule of thumb.

But Deacon Jim turns his love for the outdoors into something more. Something holy. Since taking his vows years ago, he has been bringing the Word of God to the men who share his passions in a place where they feel at home.

His ministry was inspired by a similar effort from Jim VandeHey, a local Catholic man who is involved in Colorado Leadership Retreat, an effort to bring people to Christ in the Rocky Mountains. Deacon Jim, then serving at St. Paul in Plainfield, volunteered his property for a local meeting, which in turn sparked his own effort.

"He planted the seeds with me. He thought I should take the reins and run, because so many guys are hungry for this," Deacon Jim recalled. "My goal is to plant the seeds and see how they blossom."

He carried, and expanded on, the program when he moved on to his second assignment, serving as the pastoral director at All Saints Parish in Denmark, a responsibility that included overseeing three churches and a school.

In addition to the Bow Hunting for God outdoor retreats, he developed a Campfires with Christ Bible Study program in the summers. Both are founded on the same basic principle: "It's the theme of taking Christ outside the walls of the church," he said.

In his Bible Study sessions, it's less about memorizing passages from the Good Book and more about discussing how Christ's message can be applied to our daily lives. "It's relationship building. What does this passage say to you?" he asked.

The programs were quite popular, which can be its own problem. The goal of any evangelization effort is to multiply disciples, to appeal to as many people as possible. On the other hand, these particular programs often work best when the group is more intimate, where sharing is more comfortable and trust can be forged.

But all, including the Learn Christ, Live Christ ministry for children he built in Denmark, have the same goal in mind – pushing the faith outside Sunday Mass and into our everyday lives.

"Ministry is not a whole lot different than the pandemic. If you stay at home, the illness isn't growing. And if you keep the ministry at home, it's not going to grow either," Deacon Jim said. "It's kind of like the coronavirus in reverse."

And like so many other aspects of Church life, those ministries were derailed by the pandemic, as well as his decision to step away from the diaconate to pursue another line of work. Fortunately for the people of

Northeastern Wisconsin, his sabbatical didn't last long, with Deacon Jim recognizing his proper place was in the Church.

It was something his good friend Jeff Van Rens knew all along. When he learned Deacon Jim was moving on, he thought it was a mistake. "This is what he should be doing. He's really good at it," said Jeff Van Rens, a parishioner at All Saints.

Jim Trzinski's return to the diaconate was not in the all-encompassing pastoral director's role he held previously, but as the pastoral associate and evangelization coordinator at Kaukauna's Catholic parishes, which consist of St. Katharine Drexel-St. Mary's, Holy Cross, and St. Katharine Drexel-St. Francis. It seems the perfect fit for a man born to evangelize.

Even in the period when he was not serving the Church, his passion for marrying the outdoors and his faith never wavered. Thus, he forged a relationship with Ironman Outdoor Ministries, a nondenominational Christian ministry that was pursuing the same ends he had.

Founded by a group of Bible study participants at Patrick Tyndall's Baptist church in his Columbia, South Carolina, hometown, Ironman Outdoors Ministry is now a year-round endeavor, hosting hunting, fishing, shrimping, and other expeditions. "Pretty much anything in the outdoors men want to do, we want to do it with them," Patrick Tyndall explained.

In November of 2021, a group of Ironmen made its first foray to the Upper Midwest, with Deacon Jim serving as the retreat leader. A dozen men, most from outside the state, joined Deacon Jim for hunting during the day and meaningful discussions of faith in the evening.

Also accompanying him there was longtime friend and local farmer Duane Pionke. The two met when Deacon Jim served at St. Paul in Plainfield, Duane's parish. They shared a love of God and the outdoors.

For the hunt, Duane relinquished use of his land to the Ironman group, an act that has given him great joy over the years. He revels in the time an out-of-state visitor, who had longed to hunt whitetail deer with his father before the dad suffered a fatal stroke, bagged a doe on his land and buried a Rosary at the spot in his father's memory. Or the time a boy barely in his teens got his first deer on Duane's land, and rushed up to the farmer, not to boast or describe the event, but rather to thank Duane for the opportunity.

Yet it's when the sun goes down that the retreats gain their true meaning. The men, a group that extended to include me, gathered in a circle to share nightly "manhood talks," opening up about all matters of importance. "After the second day, it's less about the deer and more about God and what's going on with people's lives," Patrick Tyndall explained.

Indeed it is. In the comfort of a supportive group of fellow outdoorsmen, and guided by Deacon Jim's and Patrick's talents, the men opened up in a way that isn't common for them. Duane Pionke cautioned the gathering that he doesn't express himself well in front of a group, then shattered those expectations with powerful accounts from his own life. "I didn't say it for attention or sympathy. I just wanted to express how important deacon has been to me and my family," he explained to me.

Again and again, the gathered men of all ages did the same, exposing themselves and their weaknesses for God and all to see. With each revelation, Deacon Jim skillfully noted how faith and prayer can be employed to comfort or heal or understand.

And it isn't just outdoorsmen who can benefit from the process. I'm neither a hunter nor a fisherman, and found the experience challenging, fulfilling, and enlightening. So too did Jeff Van Rens. He doesn't go on the hunts, but rather serves as the group's gofer, chauffeuring the men to their various hunting spots during the day but fully partaking in the nightly talks.

"It opens your mind when you realize you're not the only one, that we're all in the same boat. We have so many similar struggles. And you always learn a lot of things that you really knew, but never practiced or took seriously," he said. "I don't know why we need to get old before we figure out what life is really about."

I couldn't agree more.

For some, the word "manhood" may conjure certain ideas and traits, not all of them positive. But Patrick and Deacon Jim didn't operate under some archaic definitions of manhood, where power or dominance were mistaken for strength. Rather these were more Biblical ideals of manhood. Victory over sin. Caring for those we love. Being there for our families. And being there for other men to guide them, to help them become better Christians, better husbands, better fathers.

There were bold admissions about frailties, where we were lacking in our relationships with our families, with our wives. The conversation also turned to lust and how some had wrestled with that particular demon and what had been done to conquer it.

Just as important as our own admissions were hearing the confessions of others, seeing ourselves in those same sins. When one or another man lamented his tendency to become impatient, his unwillingness to compromise, or his propensity toward inattentiveness, others could be seen murmuring assent or nodding in agreement, myself most definitely included. There is immense value in knowing that our sins, our weaknesses, our simple failings are not ours alone, both for the sake of recognition and for the shared wisdom in how we may overcome them.

These were good men trying to be better, which is what all of us should aspire to. Yes, the hunt undoubtedly drew them in, these outdoors lovers. But it is the talks, the engagement with fellow Christians, they will long remember. It is these moments they will take back to their wives and children, friends and girlfriends. The hope, as always, is the lessons imparted and the wisdom shared are not fleeting, that they withstand the next time there's a dispute at home or life's challenges intercede.

That's the idea. And that's what Deacon Jim and Patrick Tyndall have dedicated themselves to – making these practices part of a permanent change. That's where faith comes in. Where prayer comes in. Where Christ and our Church must fill in.

Because when Deacon Jim or Patrick or others like them are not by our side, challenging us to do the right thing, Christ always will be. These manhood discussions create an excellent blueprint for Christian men to follow. But we all need God's ever-present hand to guide us day to day.

St. Ignatius Mission

St. Ignatius, Montana

"The Holy Land is everywhere."
Black Elk, Servant of God

BEFORE THERE WAS A ST. IGNATIUS, MONTANA, THE SMALL RESERVAtion town in Southern Lake County, there was St. Ignatius Mission, the Jesuit-founded church that gave the municipality its name.

Logic and a rudimentary knowledge of earth science tells us the spectacular nearby Mission Mountains got to Big Sky Country long before the Society of Jesus, though the range also earned its name from the spectacular church that sits near its base.

In the mid-1800s, Jesuit missioners arrived in the area, establishing the first Catholic parish in the Jesuit tradition in the Western United States in the process. But they didn't come, set up shop, and hope to convert the Natives living there. Instead, they came at the persistent invitations by the tribes.

In 1829, 1832, and 1839, the local tribes sent delegations to St. Louis, trying "to get the black robes to come here," explained Rev. C. Hightower, SJ, pastor at St. Ignatius Mission. The Jesuits finally responded in the 1840s, initially settling in Stevensville, Montana, before coming to the current property in 1854 when the Natives there were forced from the land 70 miles south.

The parish was once 100 percent Native, though that changed in 1908 when the Homestead Act opened reservations up to white settlers. Today, the parish is a relatively even mix of Natives, men and women from the Salish and Kootenai tribes, and non-Natives.

That the Jesuits were sought out by the Salish, known as the Flathead in the non-Native world, has been crucial to the longstanding warm relations between the Native people and their guests from the West.

The Society of Jesus was welcomed to the reservation land and they've responded by being loyal to the Native people and its culture.

"If you think about California, the padres came with the soldiers. It was conversion by sword. Here, it was conversion by desire," Father Hightower explained.

That loyalty was best illustrated in 1891. The U.S. government, as it was wont to do through much of its history in relations with indigenous people, was pushing to shrink the reservation to open up more land to claim. The Jesuits responded by building the incredible church that exists today, a gorgeous cathedral-like structure on the prairie. "They said, 'No, this is Salish land. This is the reservation,'" Father Hightower said. The church building, long listed on the National Register of Historic Places, is a marvel, a shocking brick structure that stands well above everything else in the town it gave its name to.

The grounds around the church are also dripping with history. On the north side of the parish sit two log cabins, one built in 1854 to house the first set of missionaries, the other constructed a decade later for the Providence Sisters. Both have been impeccably preserved.

The older structure is used now for the St. Ignatius Museum. Audrey Ehlert has volunteered at the museum for several years, and is still surprised when visitors from all over the U.S. and the world descend on her adopted parish. "We've had people from New Zealand, Australia, Africa, The Netherlands. You name it," she said. "It amazes me they find it."

But it's the inside of the worship space that is the most eye-catching, the aspect of St. Ignatius Mission that keeps these tourists descending on this small town in Western Montana. Lining the walls of St. Ignatius are 58 frescoes painted by Brother Joseph Carignano. The lush paintings include numerous portraits of the saints, scenes from Christ's reign on earth, and other visions that only a true person of God could create.

This is a community that proudly preserves its past, a fact that was illustrated in 2021 when a multi-year restoration project was completed at the church. It was a long overdue endeavor, designed not just to repair the gorgeous church after 130 years of wear and tear, but to correct some of the mistakes made during previous cost-conscious fixes.

Before the construction project, the plaster on the walls was delaminating, among other headaches large and small. The project this time was undertaken using historically correct materials in the renovation to more closely return the church to its original state.

The work required sacrifice. Most of it was done in the summer months, which is the prime tourist season in Montana and when much of the church's funding is supplied. "It's funny. Being a priest you study a lot of theology and philosophy and all you do is construction and finance," Father Hightower joked.

If the road was rocky, the end result was worth it, he acknowledged. "People are overjoyed. For the elders, it looks like it did when they were little kids."

But it isn't just elders who are taking to the church. Upon relocation to the area, the Balderas family sampled another church before choosing St. Ignatius. Its suitability for the young, but large, family was why it immediately felt like home. "Everyone has been so welcoming and gracious," Natasha Balderas told me after Mass.

The parish's comfort with children extends to the Mass itself. On the Sunday I was there, regular musician Anne Stewart was accompanied by a pair of vocalists, sisters Amelia and Anna Cronk, just 15 and 12 years old at the time. The following week, when Anne Stewart was going to be elsewhere for the 5 p.m. Mass, the sisters were scheduled to handle the musical duties alone.

The Cronk sisters are merely following in the music director's footsteps, who also began playing at Mass as a teenager. She's been performing at St. Ignatius for decades. She came to her first Mass in the 1970s and approached a woman playing the pump organ afterwards, asking the woman to let her know if she ever needed a someone to fill in. "She lifted up her hands and said, 'Thank God, I haven't seen these notes for years,'" Anne Stewart recalled the 89-year-old organist telling her. She's been in charge of the music ever since.

She cherishes the opportunity presented to her at St. Ignatius, particularly the chance to balance the traditional Western songs she's always played with the Salish songs she's been introduced to at the parish.

Incorporating Native culture and traditions are part of the mission at the mission. While there were some early issues of "cultural insensitivities," when the Jesuits arrived, the Society of Jesus missionaries have largely been allies of the Salish people. They still are.

Carole Lankford is an elected official with the Confederated Salish and Kootenai Tribes council, the government entity that oversees the 1.2-million acre reservation. She's also a churchgoer at St. Ignatius. She said the parish continues to work hand in hand with the local tribes, which also include the Pend d'Oreille.

"We try to work with each other, like on COVID situation. The parish worked really well us and followed the rules the tribe had set down, even though there was a county government on the reservation that also put down rules," she said. "Father Hightower felt like, 'we were invited to this reservation and we will follow the rules of the First People.'"

That also means understanding the distinctions between tribes on the reservation. The Salish, Kootenai, and Pend d'Oreille have their own customs and dialect. There is no monolithic 'Indian,' as some outsiders might assume.

But a commitment to faith and spirituality is one area the First People share and extol. One of the cultural highlights of the year for the local tribes is the Arlee Espapqeyni Celebration, an annual gathering to celebrate Native culture though dance, music, art, games, and more. The first attempts to organize a powwow began in the late 1800s, though Bureau of Indian Affairs rules at the time prevented Indian dancing. The tribes attempted to get around this embarrassing bit of history by planning an event for the Fourth of July, reasoning the government couldn't possibly be upset by a celebration on the nation's birthday. The powwow continues to be celebrated around the Independence Day holiday.

The Year 2022 marked the first full return of the Arlee Celebration in three years, with COVID calling off the 2020 event completely while only a limited one-day schedule was held in 2021. But in a testament to the strong connection between the local tribes and the Catholic faith, one of the few events on the 2021 calendar was the annual Mass.

The Mass is immediately followed by the Memorial, a march for all of the people lost during the past year. The 2022 event had a new inclusion to the Memorial – recognition for the indigenous women who have gone missing over the years. It's an enormous problem that's faced Native women on and off the reservation, an issue just now being understood outside Native communities.

"There is widespread anger and sadness in First Nations communities. Sisters, wives, mothers, and daughters are gone from their families without clear answers," reports the organization Native Hope through its Missing and Murdered Indigenous Women campaign.

Responding to and aiding the Native parishioners' grief prompted by this and other hardships facing indigenous people is just one of the many responsibilities of the Dominican Sisters who serve at St. Ignatius.

Sister Margaret Hillary has been at St. Ignatius for 13 years, a natural relocation spot after she earned a degree in cross cultural ministry. "I work with all of the people here and it's difficult to know who is tribal and who is not," she said, which is further complicated by the number of intermarriages in the community.

Of course, she's not trying to isolate one group or another. Her religious ed classes, populated by both reservation and non-reservation children, are taught traditional Catholic catechism and Native spirituality, where she sees a considerable amount of overlap. "Their basic experience of God revealing Himself to them is very similar to what Christians have experienced," she said.

The religious education program she runs is exceptionally well-attended by all of the students living on the reservation, Native or not. "Our parents are holding their youngsters to the values and history of their Catholic faith," she said.

Sister Margaret is also engaged in another major endeavor, the Kateri Ministry, a monthly gathering of women. Formerly conducted in person, the ministry has kept going through the pandemic via Zoom. Through the Kateri ministry, women of St. Ignatius and other tribal parishes gather to discuss and learn about the Native Catholic experience, such as the study of important local Catholic figure, Black Elk.

Over time, the program has transformed into more of an ongoing faith sharing exercise, with one of the women guiding the group through the upcoming Scripture readings. "The people interact exceptionally well," Sister Margaret said. "It's kind of nice."

Any of the efforts undertaken at St. Ignatius follow a simple formula inherent to the Jesuit tradition, Father Hightower said. "Whenever we do something, we evaluate it. If it worked, good. If it didn't work, we try to do it better. It's always moving forward for the greater glory of God."

Sts. Peter and Paul

St. Louis, Missouri

"Love the poor tenderly, regarding them as your masters and yourselves as their servants."
Saint John of God

On Sunday June 12, Deacon Tom Gorski returned to Sts. Peter and Paul after an extended stay in Florida. Tasked with delivering the homily, the deacon spoke on the inscrutability of the Trinity, the natural topic given this was The Solemnity of the Most Holy Trinity.

Deacon noted that the mystery of the Trinity – that God, Christ, and the Holy Spirit were one – was beyond full comprehension for meager human minds. But still, we could see the fruits of the existence of the three persons in one true God in our lives.

God's love is paternal, caring for us the way a father would. Moreover, as deacon said, we are called to "parenthood over the earth and all within it." Jesus is the Word that reveals truth in life. And the Holy Spirit can be seen in the graces in the everyday. "I watch two elderly people on a park bench patiently listen to each other, completely attentive to the other, and I see grace and experience Spirit," he said in his homily.

Those elements were present on Sunday, and every day, at Sts. Peter and Paul and parishes everywhere. Christ's Word, of course, is at the heart of the liturgy, and June 12 was no exception. "Everything that the Father has is mine; for this reason I told you that He will take from what is mine and declare it to you," He said in John 16:12-15.

God's paternal love? Well, that's where Sts. Peter and Paul truly distinguishes itself and has for more than 40 years.

In the frigid winter of 1979, the tragic death of a man in the Soulard neighborhood of St. Louis launched an effort that didn't just result in a home for the homeless. It started a movement that would become a model for the rest of the country to emulate.

The pre-Civil War neighborhood that Sts. Peter and Paul has resided in since 1849 was once among the city's most vibrant, though that had changed dramatically a century later. The residents of the neighborhood began fleeing for the suburbs shortly after World War II. Plans by the city to raze the entire area to create an industrial and distribution center never materialized. Malignant neglect was the overriding principle for the community.

By the late 1970s, all that remained were some lightly attended churches and an increasing transient population. The parishioners of those churches became intimately familiar with many of those down-on-their luck neighbors. When a familiar face froze to death one brutally cold Midwestern night, the people of Sts. Peters and Paul, as well as St. Vincent de Paul and Trinity Lutheran Church, felt the call of God to act.

"In those years, homelessness had not raised its profile nationally. It was not something that was routinely discussed on the news," said Tom Burnham, who has been active in serving the homeless community since those early days. "This was just a group of folks from a handful of churches in the neighborhood responding to a neighborhood issue."

The initial solution to the growing concern was to create a winter shelter to serve the city's homeless population. That shelter was opened in the parish hall at Sts. Peter and Paul, with congregants from the other two houses of worship aiding in serving the church's nightly guests.

The following year, the shelter was relocated to the basement of Sts. Peter and Paul, where it remains in operation to this day. Every day of the year, 60 or so men who might otherwise go without shelter can rest comfortably in the basement of the historic church.

The early days were more of a seat-of-the-pants operation, with volunteers filling jobs as needed with little in the way of direction. Burnham recalled one of his first responsibilities was filling the reservoirs on the kerosene heaters nightly. The church basement had no forced air and no running water, renting out Johnny on the Spot portable toilets in lieu of traditional bathroom accommodations. "We didn't worry about the fumes from the heater because the place was so drafty," Burnham said.

Initially, the church would host upwards of 85-90 people nightly, men, women, and children. On the worst nights, they would jam 120 people into the undivided room. "Today, we have 60 beds in there and it feels crowded," he said, acknowledging how much has changed in the past 40 years. "When I think back to when we had twice as many people, I just shake my head and wonder."

Over time, the church basement was reconfigured, leaving space for 60 bunks in one location, and another three beds segregated for those residents who may not function well in crowded conditions. A kitchen area, laundry room, shower facilities, meeting rooms, and offices were also created to better serve all of the needs of the residents.

One floor above the shelter, the church has also undergone a transformation since the 1980s. Rather than continue to serve people in the historic configuration, which would leave dozens of empty pews, the worship space was transformed. All of the pews were removed. The back ones were not replaced, turning the space into a gathering area for fellowship around a gorgeous baptismal font. The altar was pulled to the floor, with terraced, in-the-round seating creating a more intimate space to celebrate Mass.

That's the space where the parish community exists now, many traveling from other locations in the city and county to worship. Though not a large community, the parish, led by Rev. Bruce Forman, still works to serve the people housed below and elsewhere in the neighborhood.

For three weeks per month, Sts. Peter and Paul relinquishes use of the parish hall for daily meals for the area's impoverished. Each meal is supplied and served by a local group, more than half of them other Catholic parishes in the area. Other local houses of worship, including Baptist, Methodist, and Jewish, plus college students from nearby Webster University and professional staff from Mercy Hospital contribute.

Such growth in the services offered mandated a more organized operation. By 1986, the group overseeing the shelter registered as a 5013C, setting the stage for the transition into Peter & Paul Community Services, the non-profit organization that oversees 4,000 annual volunteers and runs dozens of programs for the city's most vulnerable citizens.

While still managing the shelter at Sts. Peter and Paul, now a men's-only facility, the organization operates two transitional housing programs, one focused on individuals with major mental illness diagnoses and the other for people with HIV or full-blown AIDS. Each of those facilities has a clinical staffs comprising of social workers, nurses, occupational therapists, and substance-abuse counselors. A permanent-supportive housing program also has 25 beds.

"Every year, we see about 200 people move from the streets to some type of permanent housing. Some of them live independently, some move over into group homes or into some sort of supportive living situation. We're assessing and trying to develop their living skills and search for housing appropriate for their skill set," said Burnham, who transitioned from enthusiastic volunteer to a full-time staff member of Peter & Paul, now serving as its community relations officer.

The organization also works with the other agencies in the area, such as the Salvation Army, to ensure all of the needs of the homeless and impoverished community are being met. Rather than merely looking at the basic necessities of food and shelter, Peter & Paul and its partners have expanded the offerings to include legal and healthcare services, the best way to ensure the optimal outcomes for their clients. It's known as the continuum of care, a phrase that originated right there in St. Louis.

"We wanted to know who else was out there, who's doing what and where we're coming up short," Burnham said, explaining the genesis of the program. "From that, we started to bring other services into the mix."

Others took notice of the agency's initiative. The U.S. Department of Housing and Urban Development, or HUD, declared the Peter & Paul method of continuum of care a best practice, a blueprint for other agencies to follow.

It's not the only way Peter & Paul has been at the forefront of the field. In 1990, the organization developed a Homeless Management Information System, a database where all types of information is uploaded, from demographics to services being provided. The database is used to measure the agency's effectiveness. That too became a standard practice for agencies across the country.

The system continues to be refined and improved, with other city and state agencies pushing forward. There is no competition between cities on the topic, with each agency looking to others for both support and to share knowledge. "We have been approached by and served as consultants for other cities. And other cities have developed programs and systems that we have learned from," Burnham said. "We're all in this together, and there are wonderful ideas and strategies and approaches that have been developed around the country that we pay attention to."

But ideas don't just come from volunteers and paid personnel. Peter & Paul also leans on the people it serves. Several of its former clients are part of the staff of 15 individuals. Some are even on the board of directors.

Having that input is critical to successfully serve the community. "We can come up with an idea and it seems perfectly reasonable to us, and we put it in front of our clients and former clients and they'll give us 10 reasons why it's not going to work," Burnham said. "We've got to pay attention to that. They know better than we do."

Even with a professional staff devoted full time to the various programs and services, the agency couldn't operate without its thousands of volunteers. These people are particularly valuable when it comes to dealing with the clients, many of whom have grown to become skeptical about people in power. Burnham has experienced that firsthand. He began as a volunteer, moved into a part-time staffer and eventually became director of the shelter. "Each step of the way was like closing the door in the way folks relate to me. As my power and authority increased, folks simply became more circumspect around me," he offers.

This is particularly true with a large segment of the people the agency serves, those who deal with mental health issues. "The people we serve are instinctively more at ease with a volunteer," he said.

Or, just someone they know well. Teri Dunn has been the director of the shelter for the past three years, which means she's been there throughout the pandemic, a particularly taxing time for shelters. When it came time to promote vaccinations for this high-risk population, she helped the physicians and other medical personnel communicate with the residents.

Teri Dunn had the option of shutting down the shelter or closing off the daily meals it provides during the worst of the coronavirus, but she simply couldn't.

"In my heart of hearts, I see the need. I can't turn a blind eye," she explained.

And she found herself particularly reliant on God during this most trying time. "I said, 'You have to give me the manpower. You have to give me the help so I can take care of these people and be able to go home and take care of my children.'"

That element of parental love, God's Love, is pervasive at Sts. Peter and Paul, above and below. Yet, there is one final aspect of the Trinity the Deacon cited in his homily and that too was present at Sts. Peter and Paul. It was a moment made visible by the church's unique design.

After The Lord's Prayer was said and signs of peace exchanged, a small moment from across the worship space caught my attention. Long after other grips had been relinquished and gazes returned to Father Bruce, Fluffy and Bob Juergens kept their hands entwined. That touching moment said so much.

It was the grip of a love that had carried them for decades, the couple just a few weeks shy of their 54th anniversary at the time.

It was deacon's homily brought to life, the Holy Spirit at work revealing His wondrous presence in their connection.

It was, in a word, grace.

Tri-Parish Catholic Church
Assumption

Ferdinand, Idaho

St. Mary's

Cottonwood, Idaho

St. Anthony

Greencreek, Idaho

"He alone loves the Creator perfectly who manifests a pure love for his neighbor."
Saint Bede the Venerable

IDAHO, LIKE MUCH OF THE WEST, IS NOT OVERWHELMINGLY CATHOLIC. According to the most recent data, only 10 percent of Idahoans identify as Catholic, about half the total of Evangelical Protestants or Mormons.

But in the parishes that comprise the Tri-Parish Catholic Church in Northwest Idaho County, the odds are being defied. The area is a Catholic oasis on the Camas Prairie.

The rich Catholic heritage is evident everywhere you turn. Idaho is home to just two Catholic schools for high school students – Bishop

Kelly in Boise, the state's largest city, and St. John Bosco Academy in Cottonwood, its 93rd biggest.

St. John Bosco opened in 1997 as Summit Academy, a tiny operation in a residential basement, determined to bring Catholic primary education back to the area. The academy has grown steadily, building a traditional school building in Year 5. It had 102 students enrolled in 2021-22, with 114 on the books for the following academic year.

Veteran Catholic school administrator Jim Hickel serves as the principal at SJB. He said it's the finest Catholic school he's worked at, high praise given he once started his own. Among its attributes is a hard-working student population. Many of them are the sons and daughters of ranchers and farmers, which breeds a more responsible student body.

The external demands on his students and their families are why St. John Bosco operates on a four-day school week, extending the hours of instruction over the remaining days to make up for that lost time. The move was made because many of the school's families, students included, were working extensively on the weekend, sacrificing the day of rest commanded of us in the process. "We didn't do it to save money. We did it to provide a better family life for everybody," Jim Hickel said of the decision, which the community unanimously supported after the initial trial run.

A few miles west of Cottonwood and a few hundred feet up is the Monastery of St. Gertrude, a home for Benedictine Sisters. It is the only community of women religious with a motherhouse in the Gem State.

Built in 1907, the monastery is still home to 30 nuns. Most are in their 60s, a fact of life in America for women religious. A museum, inn, farmhouse and spiritual center are located on site, bringing travelers to the community all year long. I was one such visitor.

During my afternoon at St. Gertrude's, I opted to take the uphill path lined with the Stations of the Cross to the monastery cemetery. It was a beautiful, if taxing, experience, my sea-level lungs not suitable for the nearly mile-high altitude. The views are gorgeous, whether of the area's many nearby mountains – Buffalo Hump, Round Tops, and fittingly, Gospel Peak – or the miles of green farmland below. The monastery is also spectacular, a twin-domed building constructed using porphyry stone mined from the quarry behind it.

Yet the community's Catholicity is most evident on Saturdays and Sundays in the worship spaces at Assumption in Ferdinand, St. Mary's in Cottonwood, and St. Anthony in Greencreek, a triangle of towns no more than 10 miles in any direction. And in the summer months, a fourth church, Holy Cross, resumes Masses in the nearby town of Keuterville.

"The people here are very devout," said Rev. Paul Wander, who arrived in the community about 10 years earlier. "They care a great deal about their faith, and it shows." It does, in so many wonderful ways.

At the start of the pandemic, Father Wander added a second Mass at St. Mary's to allow for greater social distancing between the parishioners. What happened, instead, was more people showed up for Mass.

In fact, the Tri-Parishes have the distinction of having more people attending weekend Masses now than there were before the outbreak. Father Wander speculates the surge may be due to the possibility the short time away drove a greater yearning for the sacraments. Still, he's somewhat perplexed at this welcome turn of events, which is surely a disappointment to others wondering just what the secret recipe is in Idaho County.

As at all of the Masses I attended, Father Wander invited parishioners to stay after the final prayer to offer their thoughts on the possibility of a change in Mass times. Even at Assumption, where the 5 p.m. vigil Mass was not being considered for a shift, opinions were sought. Welcoming that input reflects the desire to treat this as a single parish.

That same attitude is reflected in the Tri-Parish prayer, recited at each of the churches.

We are many parts...
We are all one body.
May we find...
Christ in our hearts...
Christ in our thoughts...
Christ in each person we meet...
Christ in all that we do. Amen.

It can be a challenge, operating three parishes as one, a trinity of a different sort. Parishioners can get protective of their own turf, resisting calls for any change to the way things have always been done.

That may have been an issue in the past when the churches were first consolidated in a nod to the still-going shortage of priests. But over time the people have accepted the new reality. "They're more comfortable now moving around depending on what Mass times they can hit, whereas once it was they would only go to 'this church.'" Father Wander said.

The three churches are consolidated in many ways. There's a single Knights of Columbus, though one church maintains a separate men's group. There are single parish councils for finance, liturgy, and religious education. Creating single entities did not happen overnight, but developed over the years. The single religious ed program offers still more evidence of just how strong the faith is in these communities. A half-century earlier, local nuns borrowed a program popular with the Mormon Church and implemented it in Idaho County, whereby once a week students are released from school to attend religious ed. The parish owns one building next to the public high school and another next to the elementary school to ease the commute from school and back.

It isn't just the public school students who attend, but also home schooled and St. John Bosco pupils. "Our diocese wants religious ed to come from the parish level, not the school level," said Heather Uhlenkott, the parish's religious ed director. Perhaps more extraordinary than the Catholic participation is the number of non-Catholic kids whose parents also sign them up for the classes, just ordinary Christians who want their sons and daughters exposed to some kind of religious education.

"A lot of kids enjoy coming, and they go back to the public school and talk to their friends. Little kids become evangelists," she said.

The evangelization efforts are paying dividends. Approximately 10 years ago, there were 80 kids in the program. By 2021, it numbered close to 200.

While each parish retains its own character and charm, there were obviously similarities that run through all three churches.

The sign welcoming you to Ferdinand announces the population of 135, and it isn't missing any numbers. It was most gratifying to see Assumption had a capacity much larger than that. It was even more encouraging when most of those seats were filled for the vigil Mass. And it was more inspiring still to notice just how many of those parishioners had not yet reached voting age.

That's the norm in all three churches in the Tri-Parishes, sisters Danielle Spencer and Tara Stubbers say. "There are so many big families, here. We always laugh, because if you have eight kids around here, you're just normal," said Tara Stubbers, a pre-school teacher at SJB.

The women come from just such a family, and one whose Catholic roots in the community are strong. Their grandfather, John J.H. Uhlenkott, helped build the monastery.

The story was the same in Greencreek, where the sign welcoming you to town doesn't list the population numbers; it merely identifies the residents by name and how far it is to their homes. These are, safe to say, welcoming communities.

Once again, the Mass was teeming with families. This was most noticeable when the parade of kids flocked to the front for the children's offertory.

Generosity is a way of life at the parishes, and not just financially. When St. Mary's completed some facility upgrades, the parish outlay was a fraction of the total cost, with three-quarters of the labor and materials being contributed by the parishioners.

But if there was any single event that encapsulated the beautiful Catholic spirit that envelopes the Tri-Parishes, it was the story shared to me of the Prigge and Rehder families and young child, Leo.

In 2021, Leo was the fourth child born to Dylan and Emily Prigge. Leo was born with almost no natural immunity, a condition which forced the family to retreat to their home, the only surefire way to protect their child from the natural world's dangers the rest of us fend off without a thought. Mom and dad worked from home. Their oldest daughter, Gianna, a student at St. John Bosco Academy, could no longer attend in-person classes.

The community outside their walls never forgot them. Gianna's teachers prepared daily lesson packets for her. The meal train, which rolls every time a mother in one of the parishes delivers a new baby, put on extra rail cars, providing meals to the family far longer than normal. Parishioners supplied games and crafts for the home-bound kids to keep them busy in their new reality. Facetime calls were set up by other moms to keep the kids connected with friends and relatives. Kids even wrote letters, harkening back to the days of pen pals. One day, the family packed tightly in the car and drove to the parking lot at St. Mary's, where parishioners gathered around them in prayer. Most were getting their first look at baby Leo.

"I know the secretary at St. John Bosco, and she told me 'Every single day we pray for Leo.' That means the world to the family," said Leah Prigge, Leo's grandmother.

And there were financial contributions, too. When the family had to travel to Seattle for Leo's battery of doctor's appointments, the community supplied enough funds to secure an Airbnb for a month, which allowed the entire family, plus Leo's grandmother and aunt from the Rehder side of the family, to accompany mom and dad. That generosity permitted Emily and Dylan to handle Leo's appointments while the kids stayed back at the rental.

The generosity even extends to the next generation of parishioners. As part of a Confirmation class project, Jane Schwartz crocheted a stuffed animal lion and raffled it off, with the proceeds going to the family.

Fittingly, a 3-year-old girl won the raffle. And Jane raised $2,200 for the Prigge family.

Danielle Spencer, who experienced the same kind of outpouring of community support when she unexpectedly lost her husband in 2021, marvels at the Catholic spirit that permeates the area.

"It's very holy ground. There is a larger number of religious who have come from here," she said. "Even the people who don't have a vocation, they just live the faith so deeply and they incorporate it into everything."

University of Iowa Health Care System Newman Catholic Student Center

Iowa City, Iowa

"Sick people are Jesus Christ's creatures. Many wicked people, criminals, swearers, find themselves in a hospital by God's mercy, He wants them to be saved! Nuns, doctors and nurses that work in a hospital have a mission: cooperating with this endless mercy, helping, forgiving and sacrificing themselves."
Saint Joseph Moscati.

Rev. Timothy J. Regan is not, as some fear on their initial encounter with him, a harbinger of doom. His presence in the hospital room of a God-fearing Catholic man or woman is not a sign that death is imminent.

Nor is he merely a sacramental dispensary, the Catholic equivalent of a door-to-door salesman, quickly and dispassionately making the rounds with the Eucharist or to anoint the sick.

A hospital chaplain with the University of Iowa Health Care system, Father Regan is one of hundreds of Catholic men and women around the country involved in this specialized ministry, offering the full range of pastoral care to any and all who populate the healthcare ecosystem where he serves.

Father Regan's involvement in healing began before he entered seminary. The priesthood was a second career for him, having worked previously as an occupational therapist. He doesn't know whether that pre-seminary background was a factor the first time he was given a hospital chaplaincy position – immediately after ordination – but he's sure subsequent assignments have been made with his extensive history in mind.

He served first as a temporary chaplain at the university, then, after standard parish assignments, was named to the permanent position at Genesis Hospital in Davenport. His current appointment is his third time in the role and the one he expects will be his last. "I could ask for a different assignment, but I choose not to. I do love the ministry I'm in, and at my age picking up and moving again is not high on my want-to-do list."

It is not for everyone. But it's most definitely for him.

"One of the things I like about it is the fact that, in some ways, I can be more of the priest I was ordained to be. As a pastor, you have to do a lot of administration. As a chaplain, there's always some administrative and bureaucratic stuff that needs to be taken care of, but the real focus in not on management, it's on providing ministry. That I appreciate," he said.

Hospital chaplaincy places specific demands on the priest or others filling the role, most obviously the ability to deal with the emotional and visceral difficulties that are endemic to a healthcare setting. It's certainly not for the squeamish.

Primarily, chaplaincy is about presence, being there for the patient, the family members and the doctors and nurses as well, said Erica Cohen Moore, executive director of the National Association of Catholic Chaplains. The NACC is an organization dedicated to forming and certifying chaplains, primarily in the medical field though it's beginning to stretch into other forms of chaplaincy. Membership is open to all who feel called, not just men and women in religious life.

"The hope is they're considered part of the medical team that surrounds a patient and a family in whatever kind of care that is, whether it's acute, palliative, hospice, mental health, behavior health," she said. "Some of our chaplains have specialties in different areas, but they're part of the team that assesses the spiritual needs of the patient and goes beyond the patient into their supporting structure."

To Father Regan, one trait stands out above the others in the ability to successfully serve as chaplain, whether that's in a hospital or a correctional facility or even an educational setting: non-critical listening. The effective chaplain must be able to hear not just what is being said on the surface, but to unravel the real need behind those words. And it must be done in a way that harbors no judgments, no condemnations.

"You must have a compassionate heart, and the willingness and openness to accept the other person for who and what and where they are in their life journey without being critical, without trying to pass judgment on things," he said. "Basically, trying to bring that compassionate heart of Christ to the situation so that it's His response that is being made, not just human to human."

Yet there are times that test even the most merciful of priests. When a child is admitted with burns or broken bones from abuse, Father Regan is confronted with comforting the man or woman who is likely responsible for those injuries. That's when the ability to be the compassionate heart of Jesus is most difficult for a flesh and bones man, even one in a collar. "It can be very challenging to try to minister to that person in front of you who in all likelihood is the abuser," he admitted.

"You have to be able to set aside your emotions?" I asked.

Father breathed deeply. "Yes."

Experience also teaches him some things. When he enters a room and a patient defiantly blurts out, "I don't need a chaplain," that's usually the time to pull up a chair. It's going to be awhile. The floodgates open, and the pain and everything else that's been bottled up will soon come rushing out. And Father Regan, like all hospital chaplains, will be there as the perfect sounding board.

Doing it well is imperative, and it can't be done by just anyone with a desire to serve. "Our chaplains have worked very hard for their certification. They are professionals just like a doctor, like a nurse. They have to get credentials, they have to go through continuing education. It's a huge responsibility and they all do it so well," Erica Cohen Moore said. They must, because the alternative is frightening. "We don't want to create more trauma; we want to create support."

As with so many other areas of priestly life, there is a dire shortage of chaplains. On any given day, there will be approximately 800 active patient beds in the University of Iowa system, with around one-seventh of those beds filled by known Catholics. And there are just two priests to serve them all.

It's simply not possible for Father Regan to see all of them on a given day, or even most. On a good day, he might see 10. Some days, it might just be one, as that is the need presented to him. If that description sounds like tending to the one lost sheep and leaving the 99 behind, it should.

As one can imagine, the COVID-19 pandemic only amplified the challenges faced by Father Regan and his ability to serve the needs of everyone who came and went at University Hospital – patients and their families and staff members alike.

The people admitted to University Hospital during the height of the pandemic were extremely sick, the coronavirus at its worst. Many were on ventilators, literally gasping for breath. Their physical pain was only exacerbated by the protocols in place to prevent the spread of the virus, which meant they were cut off from friends and family members. Father Regan fought to at least give chaplains access to the patients, to provide the afflicted a source of support in those most difficult times. He was fully willing to put on the full arsenal of personal protection equipment if it gave him access to these patients in the most dire need, absorbing the risks to his own health along the way. "Just being able to have a physical presence with them was the first barrier," he recalled.

Equally meaningful was the effect the measures were having on loved ones, who were denied access to the facilities altogether. Those times demanded an increase of phone chaplaincy and even some Face Timing, not the easiest adjustment to make for a technically unsavvy priest.

Yet his pastoral duties didn't end there. The pandemic's ramifications on the hospital staff were profound, which were only compounded by the shortage of workers. The nurses and doctors, therapists and counselors, housekeepers and orderlies were working day after day in an environment where a deadly, invisible virus lurked in every room. And they, unlike Father, would go home at nights to husbands, wives, children, and grandparents, not knowing whether the coronavirus was making the commute with them. The stress through all of it was unimaginable and remained a meaningful presence in the healthcare space two years after the first cases came to the United States.

Similar to my experience with the Little Sisters of the Poor Nursing Home in Gallup, N.M., I was kept from attending Mass at the University Hospital Chapel due to the ongoing protocols governing hospital visitation. Instead, I opted for the nearby Newman Center where Father Regan and I had earlier spoken about his ministry. He longs for the day the final barrier is lifted and the last mask is removed, but having experienced a few false starts already, he and all the others who populate the staff at hospitals here and elsewhere will continue to proceed with utmost caution in their vocations.

But, to Erica Cohen Moore, the coronavirus also highlighted the tremendous value these servants of God deliver. "In the COVID environment, it's really lifted chaplaincy up in a beautiful and kind of ironic way," she said.

There are times of highs and lows, with God's blessings evident in both. Hospital chaplaincy provides an opportunity for beauty in all of life's mysteries. Obviously, when a patient's condition is seemingly hopeless, only to have her pulled back and leave the hospital healthy just a few days later, those times are going to resonate deeply. The chaplain doesn't manufacture miracles, Father Regan said. He just gets to witness them.

However, there is also grace when the result is not what the family was praying for. Offering a man the blessing of the sick, then being there as he takes his last breath is a powerful experience. He sat beside a woman on a ventilator, resisting death because of her fears that mistakes in her past were going to damn her to hell. Father Regan eventually understood what was troubling her and made the woman understand she was forgiven and could let go, allowing her to experience a happy death with family surrounding her.

"To be able to be present at those times and, by the Grace of God, to be able to speak words of healing, of forgiveness – His words – those are the things that stand out," he said.

But it's in the middle ground between lives saved and lives lost where the bulk of his work is done, where the hospital chaplain is at his most pastoral. It's when he's simply being there, to bring the Eucharist or hear a confession or welcome someone back to the Church who has been lost for a while. It is at those times when he must simply be present for the patient, praying for them at whatever level is necessary at that moment. There have been countless instances where he will anoint someone or offer a blessing, while placing his hands on their heads or in their hands. And then the tears flow. "Theirs. Occasionally mine," he said.

"And that release comes. Then the trick is, I sit there and I hold their hand and I shut up. They don't need me to say anything at that time. Whatever their burden is they're letting go of," he continued. "When that burden is released, you walk out of there and say, 'That's why I'm here.'"

Shrine of St. Anthony

Boston, Massachusetts

"During the time immediately before and quite some time after my conversion I ... thought that leading a religious life meant giving up all earthly things and having one's mind fixed on divine things only. Gradually, however, I learnt that other things are expected of us in this world... I even believe that the deeper someone is drawn to God, the more he has to `get beyond himself' in this sense, that is, go into the world and carry divine life into it."
Saint Teresa Benedicta of the Cross

IN THE HUB OF THE HUB, THE FRANCISCAN FRIARS OF HOLY NAME Province have been meeting the physical, emotional and, most important, spiritual needs of the people of Boston for seven decades. All from the "Church on Arch Street."

Located about as close to downtown as you can get without being inside Faneuil Hall, the Shrine of St. Anthony provides a place for prayerful respite in a raucous urban environment. Founded on Ash Wednesday in 1947 and named after St. Anthony of Padua, the original Shrine was a tiny facility that required a commute for the friars to reach.

By 1954, it was welcoming thousands of Mass goers daily, which prompted the construction of the current multistory facility. "I gave the Franciscans permission to build a chapel and a friary, and they've constructed a basilica and a hotel," said Archbishop Richard J. Cushing at the dedication of the new Shrine just seven years after its opening. "No other order but the Franciscan Order would ever undertake a work of such magnitude. The difficulties were enormous, with whole litanies of trials, troubles, and worries, and its completion is a perfect tribute to the Wonder Worker of Padua."

The days of 5,000 Catholics attending Saint Anthony Novena Devotions each Tuesday have passed, but the Franciscans' commitment to serve the people of Boston has never wavered.

I came to the Shrine of St. Anthony on a Thursday, a visit providentially timed so I could be there to participate in the once-a-month food pantry, where hundreds of Bostonians are provided an array of healthy foods from the Greater Boston Food Bank and distributed by the Shrine's cheerful volunteers. Always open to an additional set of hands, pantry organizers found me a slot in line and put me to work, distributing soup and milk.

The food pantry is just one of more than 20 ongoing ministries taking place at the Shrine, services and programs staffed by a mix of religious men and women and, on occasion, ordinary lay people. The food pantry day was kicked off by Father Harry, who led us in prayer and kept track of how many guests were served. Stationed just before me in the distribution line was Brother John Gill, a 28-year Franciscan friar whose duties often involve outreach.

In addition to serving here and with another food pantry, Brother John has begun work with a new ministry – Identification Services. Lost or stolen IDs, such as birth certificates or driver's licenses, are a huge issue for the homeless and a major impediment to getting a life turned back around. The ministry helps in that regard, whether that's assistance navigating the tangled bureaucratic webs that can sabotage any effort or simply paying the $25 fee for a client.

But lay people represented the largest share of the men and women who worked the food pantry on the day I visited. Most are veterans of the once-a-month service at the Shrine, and they patiently walked a neophyte like me through the process. It's a challenging role, the desire to engage with the men and women being served crashing hard against the obvious need to keep things moving, no easy feat when the line of people stretched all the way around the block and back to the main entrance to the Shrine.

Still, most of the volunteers managed to engage in true Christian fellowship while still meeting the demands of the process. Two experienced hands learned how to say "eggs" and "potatoes" in Cantonese, the better to ease communication between the women and many of the individuals they were helping. Their commitment to that strategy was particularly impressive to me, as the frenetic pace of the food pantry had me struggling to remember the English words for "broccoli" and "cheese."

Other ministries include such varied programs as counseling services, Emmaus Ministry for Grieving Parents, the Haitian Ministry, the Arch Street Band, and the Women's Medical Clinic. The clinic, operated in partnership with the Boston Healthcare for the Homeless Program, is a location where the city's most vulnerable women can receive necessary health services in a safe and confidential setting.

Moreover, the Shrine doesn't just wait for the most disadvantaged people of Boston to come there. Mary Ann Ponti, St. Anthony's outreach coordinator and a licensed drug and alcohol counselor, will engage in street outreach in conjunction with a nurse practitioner.

And the Shrine's ministering to the homeless extends beyond the lives of the men and women. St. Anthony's Lazarus Ministry provides burial to the homeless and abandoned without next of kin. With assistance from local funeral homes, the ministry provides the Mass of Christian Burial and grave space at New Calvary Cemetery in Mattapan at no charge.

Despite this, the outreach efforts are complementary to the primary focus of the Shrine, its chief objective for all 70 years – providing a convenient and prayerful setting for people to praise and worship God. It offers plenty of opportunities to do so, with seven weekend and 15 weekday Masses on the schedule, plus daily Confession.

Among the most interesting ways it fulfills this mission is through spiritual direction, the Ignatian practice delivered here with a bit of a Franciscan twist. The Shrine of St. Anthony provides opportunities for spiritual direction, while also training lay and religious people alike who would like to become spiritual directors.

A spiritual director is someone who accompanies someone else on a spiritual journey, helping them notice how "God is moving in their lives," said Carol Mitchell, who heads up the Shrine's training program for spiritual directors. While spiritual direction has been a feature of the Shrine for decades, the program to turn willing men and women into directors has only been around since 2015, when it was founded by the now-retired Nancy Nichols Kearns.

The training program, open to religious men and women as well as lay people, is a two-year process that begins by inviting the participants to explore their own spirituality while learning the nuts and bolts of spiritual direction. The second year is a practical session where the new directors are given practice directees to perform individual direction.

All of the instructors are trained in the tradition of Ignatius. "We want people to know Ignatius's Rules for Discernment because they're really important. The Franciscans are a little more free-flowing. The blending of the two is what has juice for me," Carol Mitchell said. Before becoming the director of the training program, she spent years as a clinical psychologist. While the two disciplines share many features, chief among them the critical importance of listening, she ultimately chose to focus her work on spiritual direction. "What I found over the years is that psychotherapy helps people a lot, but true healing comes from God," Carol Mitchell said.

The Shrine had five people serving as spiritual directors when I visited, including two lay women and three friars. Among them is Brother John Maganzini, OFM, who has been leading spiritual direction for more than 20 years.

After leaving his work as a teacher in various archdiocesan schools, Brother John studied both pastoral counseling and spiritual direction, but ultimately chose to focus on the latter. "I did both for a year and found my role was more to walk with people on their spiritual journey than to fix people's lives."

Over the course of a typical month, he has approximately 40 people from around the Boston area come to him for supervision. They meet for a variety of reasons – some are in recovery from addiction and need the spiritual component that greatly aids the physical process. Others want to improve their spiritual lives. And while it's mostly Catholics he's served, there are any number of other religious who have found the value in spiritual direction – other Christians, Hindus and Jews among them.

Brother John believes the process is captured in a few Gospel stories, including the Road to Emmaus when the disciples don't recognize Jesus until He has broken bread with them. "This is to help people get in touch with Jesus, to notice Him in their everyday lives."

He also sees it as example of Jesus instructing the disciples to push the boat out deeper when fishing. "Spiritual direction is about a willingness to go deeper from our head to our heart, which we call the meeting place of God."

One key element of the process is the ongoing need for a director to switch roles, even someone who has been leading the process for decades such as Brother John. "I know myself when I go to my own spiritual direction, I always come out with new insights, something to think about and ponder from one month to the next."

It's part of the code of ethics that directors should still be seeing supervisors. "Otherwise, you can think you're some kind of expert," Carol Mitchell said. "But the notion is, we're all seekers. I'm not any better than the person I'm sitting with. I'm accompanying them."

The journey isn't always easy, even for people who have been through the process. Brother John recalled an encounter with a spiritual director he supervised who came to him one afternoon and stated flatly that "God is gone."

Rather than challenge her directly on that black vision, he listened patiently to her conversation and merely asked of her one thing. "If you wish to come back, look at the end of the day and ask what was a blessing in your life."

She did return, though almost as forlorn as she was on that first visit. He continued to advocate that same line of thought. By the third time, she came with a gift in tow, a plaque with an inscription taken from Psalm 23. "The Lord is my Shepherd. He restores my soul."

That plaque still sits in his office, the same place where this once-lost woman visits monthly to re-engage with Brother John as they both look for God in the everyday.

St. Mark

El Paso, Texas

"Do not oppress a foreigner; you yourselves know how it feels to be foreigners, because you were foreigners in Egypt."
Exodus: 23:9

THE HOME OF ST. MARK PARISH IS A CITY SO INTRINSICALLY TIED to its border status that this link can be found in its very name. El Paso. The Pass.

Located as far west in Texas as state lines and the Rio Grande allow, El Paso is the quintessential border city. It doesn't just sit alongside the famed river, but across from it lies an even-larger metropolis, Mexico's Ciudad Juárez. The Borderplex, as its also known, features the Western Hemisphere's largest bilingual and binational work force. The past, present and, in all likelihood, future of El Paso is connected with immigration in a way no other U.S. city is.

The people of St. Mark understand this completely, and the relatively young but bustling parish has devoted much of its energies to serving the needs of El Paso's immigrant population as well as the migrants who are trying to find a home here in the United States.

St. Mark is much like El Paso itself – bilingual, vibrant, and growing. The parish was founded in 1992 under the humblest of origins. Mass was first said in the living room of the rectory, then transferred to the cafeteria at nearby Benito Martinez Elementary School. The original parishioners went door to door in the community, inviting their east side neighbors to join them in celebration of the Lord.

Deacon Jesus Cardenas has been there for most of the parish's growth, joining St. Mark in 1994. He recalled the early struggles, even getting turned away from homes that bore signs proclaiming the residents were "proud Catholics." But the founding parishioners were not deterred and their persistence at evangelization ultimately reaped rewards.

A multipurpose building was erected in 1996, followed by the construction of the spectacular existing church building in 2003. Urged on by then-Bishop Armando Ochoa not to "think small," the parish opted to build a 1,200-capacity facility in anticipation of continued swelling of the congregation.

The expansion Bishop Ochoa anticipated has taken place. Today, St. Mark hosts five Masses on Sundays – three in Spanish and two more in English. The St. Mark's campus features not just the gorgeous worship space, but an office building with bookstore and the 30-foot tall Virgen de Guadalupe statue between the two structures.

Deacon Jesus believes St. Mark's healthy growth is primarily attributable to one person. "Seven years ago, our bishop sent Senor Arturo [Bañuelas] to the parish, and that was an explosion. Father Arturo has brought so many people in because of his theology and the way he perceives life," he said. "His homilies are so fulfilling for all of us."

Under Rev. Arturo Bañuelas' leadership, St. Mark has indeed grown, and not just inside the church walls. For the pastor subscribes to Pope Francis's notion that we're all missionary disciples. "It's not about coming to church. It's about being the Church in the world and helping the world transform into a better humanity," he said.

Though the parish has long been an ally of the immigrant community, its efforts picked up steam a few years back when the first surge of people from Mexico and Central America began to reach the border. The parish council voted to turn the parish hall into a shelter, where St. Mark would provide the basic necessities to men, women, and children who may have not enjoyed those bare minimums for days or weeks on end.

The parish offers those sheltered a warm meal, a place to shower, and clean clothes. For many it is their first time sleeping inside a non-detention center setting. "They would have beds. They would sleep, and we would pray with them," Father Arturo said.

If the migrant has family members in the States they are visiting, the parish assists with the travel arrangements, supplying bus tickets or taking them to the train station or airport. Gift bags or Target cards to assist their journeys are also provided, when available.

Father Arturo said the experience of dealing with immigration on such a human level, rather than as a source of conflict between shouting television pundits, has had a dramatic effect. "This was profoundly life-changing for our parish because you put a human face to the suffering. People got to hear first-hand stories of why people come, and they realize they're the same as our families. They are mothers and fathers with children. They want to feed their kids, to offer them a better life."

During the times of the most crushing surges, St. Mark's was housing as many as 80 people at a time. They also serve the spiritual needs of the people, many of whom are Catholic. "Every Sunday, we invite the migrants from the different shelters to come to Mass at our parish. And after Mass we take them to some of our classrooms where we have food for them and they can talk and have some catechesis," Deacon Jesus said. "We are so proud to receive these migrants every week."

In addition to serving the immediate needs of the migrants in the community, the parish also has numerous ministries devoted to serving those who want to make the United States their permanent home. St. Mark offers English language classes for those Spanish speakers who wish to become proficient in the predominant language here. There are also citizenship classes for those in the immigration system.

"Our last class had 72 persons. Most of them were able to become U.S. citizens, though two didn't because they couldn't afford it, so they're still in the process," Father Arturo said.

Occasionally, their work also calls them to the other side of the border. During one surge, a team of parishioners visited Mexico and Guatemala, to talk with leaders in those communities to understand why so many were taking such risks to come to the border.

Father Arturo and others in the parish hope they could help change some of the more incendiary rhetoric that surrounds the topic. "When we get people involved in meeting with them, talking with them., that's the most transformative way to change the narrative."

Alas, there is still a long way to go, as Father Arturo and others in the community know all too well. In 2019, the St. Mark community got an excruciating reminder of what happens when anti-immigration sentiment becomes radicalized, watching in horror as 23 people from the city were gunned down in a local Wal-Mart. Father Arturo joined several other members of the El Paso Catholic community, including Bishop Mark Seitz, in responding to the tragedy. Father went to the site of the shooting, comforting frantic men and women who had family members inside who couldn't be reached, some of whom would never walk out alive.

Father Arturo was inspired by the broader community's response to the shooting. There were food drives and other city-wide efforts to support the victims and make sure the tragedy "didn't define us."

He was also tasked with conducting several of the funerals, and recalled how the parish and beyond came together as one. "There was one man who had nobody other than his wife, so the whole town showed up for the funeral. It was very moving, very beautiful," he said.

Father Arturo urges this kind of participation from the entire congregation, prodding parishioners to find their calling. "The focus has been to move the community to an adult understanding of our Catholic faith, to get them involved in mission work, so they see their job is to serve the community."

Not all, or even most, of St. Mark's 62 ministries are focused on efforts involving immigration and related matters, though many of them overlap from time to time. Yolanda Estrada's Women of the Well is designed to uplift women and teach them their role in the Church and how to execute that in the greater El Paso community. As is customary with St. Mark, her ministry was created by the perception of a need and Father Arturo's encouragement to pursue it.

She had already been involved in several liturgical ministries, serving as a lector and a Eucharistic minister. But one day, sitting in Mass, she was struck with a new thought: "Where are all the women?"

"I felt there was a need and space that needed to be filled where women could find their place in the Church. Not to sound cliché, but to help better this world," she said. "I want to empower women to say, 'I want to do this.'"

Their work involves any number of activities, simply going where a need is seen. The Women of the Well have helped prepare meals for those at the shelter, worked side by side with the parish's Misión Chapas ministry, and joined with other groups, Catholic, other religious and civic, on various projects. "Anybody who needs help, they approach us and we're there."

Other ministries are centered on a more spiritual side of the faith. Ricardo Vargas is coordinator for the Guadalupanos, the parish's ministry that celebrates all things Mary. The Guadalupanos are responsible for maintaining the parish's shrine, praying the Rosary throughout the month of May and planning the activities for St. Mark's nine-day Guadalupe festivities in December.

Ricardo Vargas's commitment to the Guadalupanos is driven by his love for the Virgin Mary. "My mom passed away a long time ago. She's like my mother, giving me comfort in my life. I feel a connection to the Virgin Mary," he said.

Just as this devotion to Mary buoys the lives of Ricardo and other Guadalupanos, the parish does the same for the El Paso community and beyond. Or, as Yolanda Estrada sums St. Mark's mission: "Anywhere our Church calls us to be present, that's where we're at."

Holy Rosary

Dillingham, Alaska

"I have made you a light for the Gentiles, that you may bring salvation to the ends of the earth."
Acts 13:47

If there's a Catholic man or woman living somewhere, anywhere, in his region of Alaska, Rev. Scott Garrett is determined to find that individual and serve his or her needs. It's just a product of his most unique priesthood.

Father Scott is the pastor at Holy Rosary Catholic Church, the largest parish by area in the United States. His territory, which consists primarily of small villages, covers hundreds of miles across the southwest corner of the state, places only accessible by air and, sometimes, by water. No sea captain he, Father Scott is a licensed pilot who routinely rolls up the wheels of the Archdiocese of Anchorage-owned Piper Cherokee airplane and sets off for the remote villages to bring Christ to the people of the appropriately named Last Frontier.

For the last six years, and 12 years total, Father Scott has been assigned to Holy Rosary, the small church in Dillingham that serves as his hub of operation. Its remote setting is a perfect fit for the self-described introvert, who prefers the quiet isolation of the area and the small parish communities that make up his congregation.

Dillingham, like much of the area, is a combination of native Alaskans, the Yupik people, plus non-native year-round residents. In the warm weather months, the population of 2,000 quadruples with the arrival of thousands of fishermen, professional and hobbyist anglers alike. Mass attendance is often much higher in the summer, though only if the timing is right. "We get a lot of fishermen at Mass, unless the tide is high," Father Scott acknowledged.

But the size of the flock is never a concern for the pastor. There is no community too small for him to serve. If a single Catholic lives in one of the villages, Father Scott will make the effort to meet with that parishioner whenever possible.

When I first began reaching out to parishes to determine where to go in each state, Father Scott invited me to join him in Dillingham and beyond in his air-aided ministry. Despite my natural disinclination toward heights of any kind, it was an opportunity I couldn't possibly turn down. But if I was going to join him in the sky, I was determined to do so with as much distance as possible between me and Alaska's notorious winter weather. I traveled to Alaska in late June of 2022, one of the final stops on my year-long trip.

A native of Oregon, Father Scott Garrett was ordained in the Archdiocese of Anchorage at the start of the 21st century. Though he had years earlier gotten his pilot's license, college, grad school, and his original career in finance kept him grounded through most of his twenties and thirties. When he was called to the priesthood, he chose Anchorage as a site where he could combine his interest in flying with his passion to serve the Lord.

His first permanent assignment as a priest was to Holy Rosary, serving there from 2005-2011. He was then called back to serve in the Anchorage area, but his heart remained out west, and thus he jumped at the chance to resume his work in Dillingham.

Make no mistake though, flying will always be a secondary consideration.

"I fly because it helps my mission, but I'm not passionate about it," he said.

That's evident in his approach to the skill. To my eternal appreciation, Father Scott is an exceptionally cautious flyer. He won't take off if visibility is limited, either by the fog rolling in or smoke from the infrequent, but potent, fires that may rage through Alaska's ample wilderness. If the cloud ceiling is too low he will keep the plane grounded. And if the wind is above 25 knots, Father Scott will not risk conditions getting worse. He's landed the single-engine aircraft in 35-knot winds before, but he has no desire to attempt it again.

These policies are thoroughly practical. Small craft flying is fraught with peril, as the people of Holy Rosary know all too well.

Rev. James F. Kelley was a retired Naval chaplain when he came to Holy Rosary in 1991. He founded the St. Paul Mission – the model of serving those far-flung communities that Father Scott has maintained – flying across Western Alaska to bring Christ to the residents of communities such as Port Alsworth, Sand Point, and the Aleutian Islands town of Unalaska. Such was his zeal for the ministry that on Christmas Day in 2001 he braved Alaska's typically frigid winter weather to celebrate Mass in seven different villages.

Less than six months later, on his way to celebrate Palm Sunday services, Father Kelley's plane crashed on Tuklung Mountain near Manokotak. He died at the age of 73, another tragic reminder of the potential danger the pilot of small crafts hauls with him on every flight.

We walked from the rectory to the open aircraft lot where Father's Piper Cherokee was parked, taking advantage of Holy Rosary's convenient location less than a quarter mile from the airport. He gave me one foolproof job, untying the ropes that tether the craft to the ground. The lines securing the craft were unmistakably his, with three knots on each for the Father, Son, and Holy Spirit.

We boarded the single-engine plane and were soon on the runway, my excitement at the prospect of this first small plane experience engaged in a grueling tug of war with my terror. I had a headset and microphone on to allow me to speak with the pilot, though most of my conversations at the moment were being held with our Father, not Father Scott.

Fortunately, unlike the eternal wait that accompanies my every flight to and from O'Hare, my fears didn't have long to percolate. Within minutes, we were streaking down the runway. I tried to stay perfectly still, given my hands and feet were mere inches from the yoke (what you cockpit neophytes call the steering wheel) and other instruments that needed to be safe from my oafish touch.

Father Scott, in contrast, was as calm and unperturbed as Holy Water, expertly handling the takeoff as he's undoubtedly done hundreds of times before. Soon we were airborne, and minutes later we were flying over beautiful Nushagak Bay. We were bound for the village of Clarks

Point, a jutting sliver of land at the edge of Bristol Bay, the easternmost waters of the Bering Sea.

Clarks Point is like many on Father Scott's St. Paul Mission itinerary, a town with a tiny population of mostly native Alaskans and a place that can only be reached via air or water. The village's year-round population numbers approximately 60, though it too expands a little during the warm-weather fishing season.

Before COVID, Father's trips here were rather predictable. He would call ahead to let the parishioners know he was coming and what time Mass would be conducted. If a service was on the schedule, Father Scott would tuck his small Mass kit into the plane before takeoff, then set it up upon arrival.

During his first stint at Holy Rosary, Mass was celebrated at a church building not far from the water. But a previous flood pushed the majority of residents atop the nearby bluff. The old building remains standing, but nature's pernicious grip is taking hold of it in the absence of regular services.

Following the flood, subsequent Masses were held at a newly built community center protected from future high waters. However, the tribal council that runs Clarks Point had not yet resumed in-person gatherings in the village, which was true of most of the communities Father Scott serves. On the frontier that is Western Alaska, extreme caution is a completely reasonable stance.

When I arrived it had been more than two years since he offered Mass to the people of Clarks Point and most of the other communities and he had only recently resumed traveling to those places at all.

The exception to his schedule was the regular jaunt to King Salmon, a smaller town southeast of Dillingham. Every other week, Father Scott boards his plane to spend the weekend at St. Theresa, which sits about halfway between King Salmon and Naknek. Sunday Masses rotate between St. Theresa and Holy Rosary. He also offers a livestreamed service, done from St. Theresa while there and from the rectory at Holy Rosary. The broadcast gets up to 100 views per week. Internet connectivity is surprisingly decent in the area, so some of the village residents who haven't been able to attend Mass since the pandemic started still have some weekly access to the liturgy.

Still, without the opportunity to offer Mass in places such as Clarks Point, his ministry is less traditional parish priest and more door-to-door missionary, calling on the Catholics there as he finds them. That's what we did, landing at the Clarks Point airstrip and hoofing it in the circle around town, looking for any parishioners or potential parishioners who might like a few minutes with their pastor. His is a priesthood that demands a healthy set of legs and lungs. Fortunately, Father Scott has them to spare, having already completed three Caminos when we met, with plans for a 2023 sabbatical to Europe where he expected to engage in more.

In addition to pastor and pilot, Father Scott has still one more hat he wears – canon lawyer. When he enrolled in seminary, the archdiocese asked him to consider simultaneously pursuing a canon law degree. He did, beginning the process before ordination and continuing with two more summers of work in D.C. after. He devotes most of his time serving as the judge in annulment cases, though he previously did work as the defender of the bond. As with the livestreamed services, internet connectivity has proven extremely beneficial to his canon law work, allowing him to adjudicate the cases at the rectory in Dillingham rather than requiring a lengthy flight into Anchorage.

While those jaunts have little appeal, flying into towns such as Platinum or Togiak is another story, one Father Scott embraces even while knowing the risks that come with his vocation's helpful avocation.

"Every year someone crashes and survives or crashes and dies. It gives me pause, yes," he admitted. "I get a sick feeling in the pit of my stomach. I usually don't fly for a week or two because I'm trying to process through it."

Ultimately, however, he understands he will keep crawling back into the cockpit.

"I truly know in my heart that God has called me to do this. This is my mission. That's how I get back in that airplane."

Transfiguration

Blythewood, South Carolina

"He who knows how to forgive prepares for himself many graces from God. As often as I look upon the cross, so often will I forgive with all my heart."
Saint Faustina Kowalska.

It was appropriate that the fourth Sunday of April 2021, the Sunday after Easter, took me to Transfiguration Parish in Blythewood, S.C., home of Connie Turgeon. This was Divine Mercy Sunday, the day founded by then-Pope John Paul II to recognize the revelations experienced by his countrywoman, Saint Faustina Kowalska. And Connie Turgeon is the living embodiment of the grace that comes from mercy and forgiveness.

It was approximately 15 years earlier when Connie began experiencing a recurrence of arthritic pains, starting in her ankle and ultimately radiating throughout her leg. The devout woman prayed to God to relieve the pain without the need for surgery, which would have immobilized her for up to two months.

She was a busy woman, holding two jobs while helping a daughter prepare for an upcoming wedding. Being off her feet for an extended period of time was not, she thought, an option.

Leaving the church one Sunday, she turned onto the two-lane road and headed for home. Cresting a hill, she came upon two cars barreling in her direction, occupying both lanes. She swerved to avoid the driver in hers. Unfortunately, one of the young men drag racing had the same inclination, resulting in a horrific collision that sent Connie to the hospital.

The injuries she incurred were substantial. Among the awful consequences of an accident she had no part in causing was the amputation of her right leg.

"Lord, I guess you fixed this ankle. It wasn't really what I had in mind," Connie recalled saying to herself, and her Savior, upon waking.

"You have to be very particular about how you pray for something," she joked now.

But along with her leg, an even more peculiar thing was missing from Connie Turgeon after this horrific accident: anger. Not at God. Not at her misfortune. And not at the 17-year-old boy who had upended her life.

The boy's name is Antonio Davis, a young man from the area who was, in Connie's eyes, not a lot different than so many other boys his age. Or any age.

"This was two kids making a really stupid decision. It wasn't like they came after me with weapons. When you're a 17-year-old boy, you make a lot of dumb mistakes," she reasoned. "Quite frankly, I still made a dumb mistake when I was 55."

Her outlook wasn't shared universally. Her daughters wanted the young man to pay for his reckless actions. A mere slap on the wrist wouldn't suffice.

But Connie Turgeon couldn't look at it that way. Rather than seeing the damage, she opted to look at the bright side, the various what could have beens. "That road has a lot of kids on it. There could have been kids playing in that yard. It really could have been worse."

It was with this attitude that Connie took to the Richland County Courthouse for a pretrial hearing in Antonio's criminal case. She asked the assistant solicitor, the local version of a district attorney, for the opportunity to speak.

Inside the room sat Antonio, his attorney, and his mother. With a history of minor trouble in his past, Antonio was looking at the possibility of serious jail time for his near-fatal recklessness, and the fear showed on his young face. "I thought," Connie recalled. "You can't put this kid in the bad guys' jail."

Instead, she asked the assistant solicitor for a reprieve. His case should be moved to juvenile court, where he had a better chance to turn around his life, she pleaded.

The decision shocked everyone in attendance – the assistant solicitor, the defense attorney, the judge. But perhaps no one was more surprised than the young man whose life she saw as one worth fighting for.

More than a dozen years later, Antonio Davis still can't explain just what Connie Turgeon saw in him that morning that led her to such an uncommon decision. "To this day, I don't understand where it came from," he said.

Connie Turgeon did not abandon him while he was locked up at the juvenile detention center, either. She wrote him regularly, as did her daughter Diane. She visited him as well, which required her to disentangle from a considerable amount of red tape.

Since she was the victim in his case, and not a blood relative, Antonio was prevented from making contact with her. State lawmakers hadn't envisioned a scenario where the victim would be jumping through hoops to stay in touch with the perpetrator.

It wasn't necessarily a straight path to the straight and narrow for Antonio after the courtroom decision, some his own making, others a byproduct of an imperfect system, Connie Turgeon said. While not prison, the juvenile detention center had its own issues, and the rehabilitative aspects were often shelved in favor of control.

As an interested onlooker, Connie was appalled. "If there are other kids causing trouble in the juvenile block, the whole block gets shut down. They don't go to class. They don't get counseling. That juvenile block was shut down 50 percent of the time."

But he persevered, and 10 months later he was back home. And that was when he could fulfill the single request Connie made of him that day in court. When he got out of detention, whenever that was, she asked that Antonio visit her for a year, helping her with the simple chores that her new condition made more difficult. She wanted him to see the effects of his poor decision.

Antonio filled that request. It wasn't easy walking up the steps that first day to visit the woman he had injured so permanently. But he did so, and kept coming back. He would mow the lawn or hang some Christmas ornaments. Just as often, she merely wanted his company, to talk to him and learn what was going on in his life.

One year turned into more, the condition of release expiring but the connection maintained, the visits continued. They were not drudgery, the lingering remains of his sentence or a guilty conscience. Rather, this court-accepted obligation became the start of something bigger. A friendship. A relationship.

Antonio grew older and more mature, with Connie treating him with the same combination of love, respect, and toughness she supplied her three daughters when they were growing up. If he behaved in a way that disappointed her, the kind of off-hand, off-color remark that any young man at the edge of manhood might be guilty of, she let him know. She was there, in all ways, for him.

"She never turned her back on me," Antonio marveled.

In an instant one Sunday afternoon, Connie Turgeon's old life was shattered. She could have stewed in her horrible fate. She could have sought a pound of flesh from the person who harmed her.

Instead, she chose mercy.

And while it was not a choice anyone expected, including her family, to Connie Turgeon it was simply no big deal. In fact, the idea that her response was in any way extraordinary bothers her.

"Is that not such a sad commentary that I did this nothing thing, what any right-minded person would do, and it was such a big OMG. I just don't understand it," she said.

Her accident was transformational for Transfiguration as well. A member since almost the founding of the parish, her fellow church-goers were both inspired by her response and moved to prayer to aid her recovery.

Transfiguration is a relatively young parish, having been founded in 2000. It remains fairly small, with 100 in attendance for each Mass on the Sunday morning I joined them. The church is a product of its time, not ornately adorned, a nod to tight budgets and rising construction costs. What's most striking is its bucolic setting. It sits on more than 100 acres owned by the Diocese of Charleston.

The land includes a copse of towering hardwoods across from the entrance, where the undergrowth was cut back leaving an accessible area to both admire and stroll through. A similar grove is found at the rear of the church, where the parish has designed a walking rosary amid the woods.

The parish makes ample use of the beautiful exterior space and South Carolina's year-round temperate climate. The week before, on Good Friday, the outdoor Stations of the Cross were used as they celebrated Holy Week.

About the only thing missing from Transfiguration the morning I visited was Connie Turgeon. Connie Turgeon had been having difficulty with her good leg for about a month, an issue that kept her from Mass, to her enduring frustration. So, like Antonio Davis before me, I was called upon to visit her at her home.

She was, as expected, a warm and gracious host, a woman still teeming with the Holy Spirit. That was my expectation based on our history of exchanged phone calls and emails, and the more personal encounter didn't let me down. Struck as I was by her inherent concern and compassion, I even remembered to text her when I got home that evening, fulfilling the request she made of me when I left. I was dead set against disappointing her.

Connie Turgeon never questioned her choice of mercy in her dealings with Antonio and time has only reinforced the wisdom and righteousness of that decision. It didn't take long for her family to recognize it as well. Yet nothing made that determination more clear than the time Antonio introduced her to a friend as, "the woman who saved my life."

"I've never been happier with a decision I made," she said with well-earned pride.

Her decision is equally appreciated by Antonio Davis.

"Honestly, she's like my mom at this point," he told me.

They don't see each other as much any longer, as Antonio Davis has grown into adulthood. He got his GED, and has worked regularly ever since. When we spoke, he was working with Local 813, the Teamsters, involved with commercial moving. He was also pursuing an invention he devised, hoping to turn the concept into a commercial product. Now in his 30s, he's a responsible adult, growing into the future Connie Turgeon saw in him a dozen years earlier, long before he saw it himself.

Connie Turgeon chose to forgive. And as a result, God's graces have been bestowed on her, and on Antonio, time and again ever since.

Notre Dame of Bethlehem

Bethlehem, Pennsylvania

"No test has been sent you that does not come to all men. Besides, God keeps his promise. He will not let you be tested beyond your strength. Along with the test he will give you a way out of it so that you may be able to endure it."
1 Corinthians 10:13

Rev. Bernard Ezaki has only been serving at Kolbe Academy for a few years. But in many ways, his assignment there has been a lifetime in the making.

Father Ezaki has been a priest in the Diocese of Allentown for nearly 35 years. When he was ordained in 1988, he became the first legally blind priest in the diocese.

His blindness dates almost to birth, when he arrived to parents Dr. Toshio and Mary Ezaki 10 weeks early. His premature birth was treated, as had been standard at the time, with excessive oxygen, a regimen that led to the near-total loss of his eyesight. "I can see a little in my left eye, enough not to walk into any walls, but not enough to drive," he explained. He has no vision in his right eye.

Still, he approaches his condition with his chronic good nature, looking at the glass he can't see as more than half-full. "I think it's harder to have had good eyesight and lose it. For me, good eyesight is just a theory." The son of a physician, he threw himself into education, completing both undergraduate and graduate school degrees. While in grad school, he had a niggling feeling the priesthood was calling him, though he fought the urge for a while because he wondered if it wasn't just a desire for the church to take care of him.

"It took me a while to realize the call to the priesthood was separate from my blindness. I thought they were intertwined for a while," Father Ezaki said.

Once he disabused himself of that notion, he followed through, though he still had to convince others that a legally blind man could adequately serve God. Fortunately, he had two factors working in his favor.

For one, Father Ezaki's own father had operated on the parents of the priest in charge of vocations for the diocese, making the reverend more amenable to the prospect. Additionally, while the Diocese of Allentown had no blind clergymen, a trailblazing priest from the other side of the Delaware River in the Diocese of Camden, Rev. Cornelius Lambert, was showing that a sightless man could lead God's flock. There was a path for Bernard Ezaki to become Father Ezaki.

Not long after Father Ezaki's ordination, the self-described "professional student" was assigned to the role he would occupy for a quarter century, chaplain and teacher at Bethlehem Catholic High School. It was at Bethlehem Catholic where Father Ezaki first became acquainted with John Petruzzelli, a former principal there and the maiden director of Kolbe Academy.

Kolbe Academy is not your typical school. In fact, it's the very definition of atypical. It is one of just 45 recovery high schools in the United States and the only one of those 45 schools that's founded in faith.

The academy is the brainchild of Dr. Brooke C. Tesche, then-deputy superintendent for the diocese. While researching addiction, she came across the recovery high school model, a new type of educational facility for young people fighting addiction to drugs and/or alcohol. But as she learned about the models, she recognized the existing schools were lacking a key component of many successful recovery programs – the element of faith.

"It's not only about having quality academics and a really good recovery support system with clinicians who understand the disease of addiction and the different pathways to recovery. But also, as the basic 12-step fellowship model does, inviting your higher power in. When you invite your faith into the process, the research shows that makes all the difference in the world," Dr. Tesche said.

Thus inspired, she set out to create this new model, taking the idea to former Bishop John Barres and the board of education, both of whom gave it the thumbs up. Over the course of the next few years, during which time Dr. Tesche became the Diocese of Allentown's chancellor of education, she worked with others in the diocese to build the school from the ground up, putting together a curriculum committee, raising funds from major donors, marketing and designing a logo. The finished product, Kolbe Academy Recovery High School opened in 2018 in Bethlehem at the former St. Francis Academy for Girls. John Petruzzelli had already been appointed to serve as its first principal, a position he held for the school's first four years of operation.

After the conclusion of the 2021-22 school year, Kolbe Academy was on the move. The school relocated to the former elementary school building at Sacred Heart parish in nearby Bath. In conjunction with the move, John Petruzzelli stepped down as principal, giving way to Andrew D'Angelo. The timing was fortuitous, with the former director working on the details of closing operations in Bethlehem and the new principal handling the start-up responsibilities in Bath.

Though it tries to deliver a normal high school experience to the kids, the school is small by design, with a goal of accommodating no more than 30 students at a time. Putting too many children in the building would limit the ability to give the students the personal attention needed to help them beat their addictions.

"We're going to be there to help support them on their path. We talk about trust and honesty and how that's the foundation of why we're successful," John Petruzzelli said.

And at the heart of that success is the Catholic faith.

Before its opening in 2018, as Dr. Tesche was putting the finishing touches on the new academy, she reached out to John Petruzzelli with information she knew he would welcome.

"One day, I got a call from the chancellor. She said, 'I have some news for you and I think you're going to be pretty excited about it,'" he recalled. "She told me Father Ezaki was named chaplain. Our entire staff was excited. To have him here has been wonderful."

Chaplain assignments are made through the chancery at the bishop's office and the personnel board, attempting to match skill and experience, particularly in the schools. "Father Ezaki has 20-plus years of experience being a high school chaplain, and he himself struggles with a disability, so he has this personal identification with the students in addition to this amazing experience and expertise," she said.

John Petruzzelli said Father Ezaki has been a tremendous asset to the school, bringing his pastoral qualities of compassion, humor and deep faith to the position.

"When you're dealing with your own disability and you have this guy who has been a priest for 30 years dealing with his disability, it's hard not to be impressed and inspired," the former director said.

When he's not serving at Kolbe Academy, Father Ezaki is the associate pastor at Notre Dame of Bethlehem, working alongside Monsignor Thomas Baddick. Father Ezaki presided over the noon Mass at Notre Dame when I attended, showcasing all of his pastoral traits. He delivered an informative homily rooted in Catholic teaching, shared a few dad jokes at Mass's end, and profusely praised the performance by the music ministry that afternoon, which only confirmed the conventional wisdom that the loss of one sense heightens the others. The trio of father David Guro on piano, daughter Paula on trumpet, and son Matthew on violin was truly exceptional.

Back at Kolbe, Father Ezaki downplays his role at the school, noting he's only there once a week. Rather, he marvels at the work being done by the staff and the value in recovery schools in general.

"If you put a kid in rehab, and then he goes right back into the school, he has a really high rate of returning to his addictions. But if you go to a recovery school, the rate of success of keeping them clean to graduation is about 65 percent," he said.

The school has started small, with less than a dozen students in the first group. The students can arrive at Kolbe in a variety of ways, such as referrals from a treatment facility, on the request of a parent, or on the recommendation of a public school. The term at Kolbe is voluntary and can end at any time, though the staff believes the student is best served by seeing out the entire education at the academy, rather than returning quickly to the school environment where the problems often began.

"Many times people in recovery, addicts or alcoholics, think there's going to be a quick fix. 'Great, I've stopped drinking or stopped doing drugs,'" Dr. Tesche said. "But that's just the tip of the iceberg. Recovery is a process.'"

And the staff, including Father Ezaki, play an integral role in that process at Kolbe.

"He's pastoral, he's compassionate, he has a wonderful sense of humor. He relates well with adults and teenagers and kids," John Petruzzelli said. "He gets to know people by their voice and he gets to know them without seeing them."

And the kids, in turn, have no choice but to take notice.

"They're amazed by what he does and what he can do. They're impressed and amazed all at one time," John Petruzzelli said.

That, in turn, is helping the young people at Kolbe do miraculous things.

"These are not just troubled kids; these are kids fighting for their lives because they're struggling with the disease of addiction and caught in its grips," Dr. Tesche said. "And now they're clean and sober. It's amazing to watch the transformation and be a part of that."

The three current students I met at Kolbe Academy represented the fluid nature of life at the school. Pete, a junior, had been there since his freshman year. Matt had been there less than a year, and Gianni only a few months. That partially explained their outlooks. The two newer boys were not sure they would stay at Kolbe through graduation, but Pete was planning to see it all the way through.

"It's God's plan. I came here for a reason; I'm going to finish for a reason," he said.

Regardless of where they get their diplomas, the values of the school were already being imbued in the boys. Just two weeks earlier, Pete completed the RCIA program, fulfilling his journey into Catholic adulthood that had begun years earlier with Baptism and First Communion. On the night of the Easter Vigil at Our Lady of Perpetual Help, Pete was confirmed. His principal, Mr. Petruzzelli, was his sponsor. And sitting in the pews to support him in the attainment of the sacrament were his Kolbe Academy classmates.

"There is that openness to faith, which I'm really happy about," their former principal said.

St. Patrick

Nashua, New Hampshire

"Read some chapter of a devout book....It is very easy and most necessary, for just as you speak to God when at prayer, God speaks to you when you read."
Saint Vincent de Paul

Q: Where is St. Patrick located?
A: The parish, the first I visited in my yearlong trip, is located in Nashua, New Hampshire, just across the state line from Massachusetts. It was the first parish in the community, though now Nashua has seven other Catholic parishes. St. Patrick's pastor, Rev. Michael Kerper, said the church building is the best and most elegant in the area, a traditional facility that appeals to Catholics who value stability.
Q: OK, well Father Kerper might not be the most impartial observer. Is he right?
A: I can't compare it to all of the parishes in the area, but it's unquestionably a beautiful building. It's an imposing structure whose doors sit just feet from the street and the rear of the building wraps around the local Episcopal Church, from whom the land was purchased. The two parishes, fortunately, remain friendly neighbors in their mutual service of the Lord.
Q: When was it founded?
A: The parish began celebrating Masses in 1855 as a Catholic mission with Rev. John O'Donnell, V.G., serving as its first pastor. It was one of the only churches serving all of Southern New Hampshire's Catholics. In 1909, when the current building was constructed, Father Matthew Creamer changed its name from Immaculate Conception to St. Patrick. It was initially the parish church for the Irish Catholics in the area, while the French Catholics had a separate church and woe was to the Catholic who found himself

worshipping in the "wrong" space. That ethnic territoriality no longer exists there, thankfully.

Q: How big is the parish?

A: In terms of the church membership rolls, not very. At the start of the century, the parish had as many as 1,000 families on the books, but it's about half that now. Attendance is limited by a downtown location in a community where few people live downtown. "The downtown has become isolated from the part of the city that grew in the 1970s and 1980s," Father Kerper noted.

Q: As a "traditional parish," does it offer the Latin Mass?

A: It has been holding the Latin rite once a month for years, but many of the early attendees have moved to another local parish that's holding the form weekly. St. Patrick's continues to offer the low Mass on Saturday mornings, in part for Father Kerper's own sense of continuity. "I kept it. If you know how to do the Mass and you stop doing it, you forget," he said.

Q: Who populates those Masses?

A: As has been confirmed at other places I've visited, it's often made up of young people. "It's the older people who want *Be Not Afraid* and *On Eagle's Wings*. It's the younger people who want the Latin," Father Kerper explained. "The old people grew up when the Latin Mass was not well understood and was poorly celebrated. They rapidly became accustomed to the vernacular. The younger people sometimes feel deprived of the richness of the Extraordinary form. It's as if they were saying, 'Why were you hiding all of this stuff from us?'"

Q: Why is this formatted as a Q&A?

A: I'm glad you asked. In addition to shepherding the flock at St. Patrick, Father Kerper is known to Catholics all across New Hampshire as the author of Dear Father Kerper, a feature that appears near the front of every issue of *Parable Magazine*, the official publication of the Diocese of Manchester.

Q: How long has Father Kerper been doing this?

A: Since the magazine's founding. When the magazine was launched in 2008, Father Kerper was asked if he would contribute a column. He was already known locally for his lively work in the weekly bulletins of the parishes where he worked in Portsmouth. Moreover, he was a writer by trade before entering seminary when he was 29.

Q: What types of questions does he answer?

A: Questions centering around how issues in our daily lives can be viewed through the lens of Catholic teaching. Often, the question will deal with an issue being covered in the magazine. Through the years, he's written about big topics such as a Catholic approach to voting, the Church's position on cremation and, recently, executive orders during the coronavirus and whether it contrasts with religious liberty. He also covers smaller ones such as why parishes differ on holding hands during the Our Father or why is religious education or CCD now called "Faith Formation."

Q: How does he formulate his answers?

A: Much of the stuff he's already familiar with, the byproduct of decades as a parish priest and a voracious appetite as a reader. But he will have to check his responses based on scripture passages, Code of Canon Law, compilations of church doctrine, and the like. And before it's published, his column is run past a fellow priest, plus a professor at St. Anselm and the editors of *Parable*. "We want to make sure there's no conflict," he said.

Q: Where does he get the questions?

A: Sometimes he's given the questions by ordinary Catholics he encounters. Some come to him through the mail. And others he develops through observing the world around him. Occasionally, he and the editor of the magazine come up with a question. All are addressed through his learned, but kindly, style.

Q: How popular is it?

A: I'll defer to *Parable* Editor Kathryn Marchocki on that subject. When she assumed the role at the magazine, which publishes six issues annually, Father Kerper had already been writing for nearly 10 years. He offered to step aside and let someone else take the reins. That wasn't an appealing offer to the newly minted editor, who already recognized Father Kerper's contribution as one of the most popular and well-read features each issue. "He gets a lot of feedback personally, letters sent to me directly, some he sends to me. In speaking to people in my parish, and on the street and in the diocese, just Catholics throughout the state, I know he is one of our premier columnists, if not the premier columnist," she said.

Q: What makes it so appealing?

A: "He's a great thinker. He knows his theology. And he can write in a way that most average Catholics can understand," Kathryn Marchocki said. "He has the deep background of knowledge and theology, but I also find in him a very pastoral approach. I think he's someone who truly loves his Church."

Q: Do you have an example of the kind of question he answers?

A: Sure, here's an excerpt of one from the July/August 2019 issue of Parable:

Q: Dear Father Kerper: I have tried to deepen my prayer life during the last few years and sought direction from friends who seem to know about spiritual matters. Now I'm completely confused. Some push me toward specific devotions, like the Five First Saturdays, Nine First Fridays, Chaplet of the Divine Mercy, the Christmas Novena, Brown Scapular, Miraculous Medal and the rosary. I am told that these are truly traditional and are superior to other devotions. How do I decide which to do?

A: Bull's eye!

You have identified an experience rightly called "spiritual clutter," or "devotional overload." Here's what happens. In their sincere effort to enhance their spiritual lives, some people latch on to a variety of personal devotions. There is nothing wrong with private devotions. However, they can endlessly accumulate and, in extreme cases, actually destroy the person's life of prayer. For example, some people say to me, "I don't have time anymore to say my prayers." This usually means that "spiritual clutter" has won the day.

Jesus warned against this harmful tendency. He once said: "In your prayers do not babble as the gentiles do, for they think that by using many prayers they will make themselves heard. Do not be like them." (Mt 6:7-8)

He then gave them the words of the Lord's Prayer, the only prayer he ever passed on to us.

Jesus always commends forms of prayer marked by three traits: simplicity, brevity and rootedness in God's word. These qualities always exist within liturgical prayer, the official worship of the Church. Some private devotions, however, tend to be overly complex, long and – worse – disconnected from sacred Scripture.

The Church's public worship, notably the celebration of the Eucharist and the Liturgy of the Hours, must always hold center place in our spiritual lives. Unlike private devotions, liturgical prayer mystically unites the prayer of all baptized Christians with the unified voice of Christ. Moreover, this unity extends across time, embracing the prayer of the earliest Christians as well as our own.

While strongly emphasizing the supreme value of liturgical prayer, the Church also encourages private devotions, such as novenas, special prayers, and the use of religious objects like scapulars, medals, and so forth. These are "private" in that they exist beyond the realm of the Church's liturgical life.

By doing so, the Church affirms the uniqueness of each person, including his or her own spiritual life. Some people, for example, have a more emotional approach to God, while others tend toward the intellectual. Private devotions, then, accommodate the enormous variety of people within the Church. As to the spiritual life, "One size does not fit all." And private devotions vary greatly in their spiritual value.

Q: That's really interesting. How can I read more like that?

A: You're in luck. Father Kerper was asked to put together some of his favorites for publication. It's available in paperback and as an eBook, *A Priest Answers 27 Questions That You Never Thought to Ask*. You can find it on Amazon.

You can also read some of his previous replies in back issues of *Parable* at the website, https://www.catholicnh.org/about/stay-informed/parable/.

St. Patrick's

Newcastle, Maine

"It is not sinners, but the wicked who should despair; it is not the magnitude of one's crime, but contempt of God that dashes one's hopes."
Saint Peter Damian

On the surface, Deacon Robert Curtis and his wife Phyllis faced a conundrum. Several years earlier, the deacon had been asked to serve as the chaplain for the Maine State Prison, an assignment the clergyman readily accepted. However, the post wasn't at the correctional facility in Windham near his home in Southern Maine as he anticipated. Instead, he was dispatched two hours north to Warren, home of the main Maine State Prison.

For two years, the husband and wife team trekked up and back to Warren to bring Christ to the men of the prison, but the drive was beginning to wear them down. They had a choice to make; they could exit the ministry or relocate closer to the prison

There wasn't much to discuss. It was time to call the movers.

Such was the appeal of this accidental ministry that Robert and Phyllis Curtis would upend their existence rather than give up serving the spiritual needs of the state's incarcerated population. "We moved so I could do more prison ministry. After we moved, I was in the prison about 30 hours a week, all as a volunteer," Deacon Robert explained.

Besides his work in chaplaincy, Deacon Curtis serves the parishioners of All Saints Parish, a collection of seven churches on the Mid-Coast of Maine. Those include St. Patrick's, the oldest Catholic Church in New England and the place I worshipped when I visited Maine in late-spring 2022, with Deacon Curtis assisting Rev. Peter Shaba.

The original church, constructed in 1807, is no longer the primary worship space, giving way to a beautiful sanctuary with a window behind the altar that highlights the area's abundant greenery. But the original remains standing, and will be back in use for Stations of the Cross and other small-congregation affairs when long-needed reconstruction that began in 2021 is completed.

Most of the interior work done over time was of the patch-up variety, which the current renovation will rectify. But the ongoing restoration marks the first exterior work done to the building, a structure listed on the National Register of Historic Places, in 214 years. The church windows were shipped off to a restoration company in New York while the bricks and mortar repair work was taking place.

On weekdays, Deacon Robert joyously exchanges the newly power-washed walls of St. Patrick's for an entirely different set of walls, those confining Maine's prisoner population. He wasn't always so enthusiastic about the prospect.

About 25 years earlier, a gentleman he met at a Cursillo was prodding him to attend a Kairos prison ministry meeting. Not yet a deacon, the Catholic man consistently resisted those entreaties, only yielding on the promise that if he went once, his friend would finally relent. The friend agreed.

Deacon Robert entered the ministry with the same preconceptions many of us have of the incarcerated: these were bad men who had committed horrific crimes and they ought to be locked up for good. But his perspective quickly changed. "It had to be the Holy Spirit, because it surely wasn't me," he admitted.

Now, he sees the incarcerated not as society's worst, men best kept away from the good people on the outside. Instead, "they're my grandfather, my father, my sons. I see God in their eyes. I see God in their face. I hear God in their voice."

His wife has had similar experiences.

"They tell me things they can't tell anyone else. They couldn't talk to the guards because it could get them in trouble. They couldn't talk to fellow inmates because they could blackmail them. So I was it. They called me 'Mom. And I love it. They all became my kids," Phyllis Curtis said.

While Deacon Curtis holds the highest role in the Church's service of Maine's incarcerated, he is just one of many Catholic men and women who have devoted portions of their lives to this important ministry.

They do so in a variety of ways and a variety of settings, but with a shared desire to demonstrate the love of God to people who much of society has forgotten, men and women who all too often were raised with the absence of familial love.

Frederick Prince entered the ministry with much the same skepticism as Deacon Robert. He was similarly disabused of his notions in a hurry when a man sitting across from him challenged him with this, "'When I was 14, my mother died and my father threw me out on the street. Where were you?'"

"That's when I realized what a hypocrite I was," he recalled. "I didn't know these people at all. I had a very blessed life. That's how I got into it," said Frederick Prince, who has been working in the ministry for the past quarter century in the Cumberland County Jail.

Many of Maine's prison ministry volunteers are introduced through the Kairos program, which is conducted in a similar fashion as Cursillo. Teams of a dozen volunteers spend a weekend inside the prison once a month, talking with up to 24 inmates in small groups. "It's a retreat about Christ, about Christ's love," said Dick Marchi, a leader in Kairos of Maine. "The idea is to get them to listen to one another, share with another. What begins to happen is those barriers get broken down and that love starts to come through."

Roger Lavigne has been active with Kairos since the beginning, believing his own struggles with addiction would make him capable of relating to the men inside, as drugs are often part of the reason for their incarceration. He's found the experience beneficial not just to the inmates, but to himself as well. "The camaraderie and sharing the struggle help both sides," he said.

That we're all sinners and we share that message with the men and women who are incarcerated is powerful. "You have to be able to give your testimony so they have a sense we're not all perfect. Just because we're here and giving you this sacred time doesn't mean we're a perfect vessel," said Blanca Trigueros Lytle, who joined the ministry after completing her own 12-step program for addiction.

The Curtises are always looking to grow the ministry, serving as many individuals as possible. Kairos programs for women have been conducted at Windham. And in the past, they've held weekends for women who had husbands, fathers, brothers, and others on the inside, serving their unique needs. "They're lives are awful," Phyllis Curtis said. "Some of them wouldn't go out of the house. They were afraid of being recognized."

They also try to involve former prisoners, or residents as Dick Marchi always calls them, to serve alongside, knowing that none of the volunteer ministers can be as powerful an advocate for the strength of God's love as someone who once shared a cellblock with them.

For those without a criminal record, the ability to relate to the prisoners is perhaps the quickest way to clear the communication hurdles. Deacon Robert recalled an instance when a particularly imposing inmate approached him with a provocation. "Do you know what I did?" the man asked. "I killed five people."

Much to the inmate's shock, and mine many years later, Deacon Robert responded, "No big deal, I've got you beat. I killed 35 and almost went to federal prison for life."

In Vietnam, Deacon Robert Curtis was Aircraft Commander Robert Curtis, leading a unit that responded to enemy gunfire in a no-fire zone, wiping out almost three dozen Vietnamese combatants. Without the intervention of a two-star general, the deacon may have been on the other end of the prison ministry relationship.

"He knew right then I wasn't going to be intimidated. We had a good conversation and he ended up being a model prisoner," Deacon Robert recalled.

And when you're dealing with someone like that incarcerated killer, looking past whatever crimes put a man or woman in there is imperative to effective ministering. "I say, 'I don't care what happened in the past. I'm here to help you figure out what you are going to do to make tomorrow a better day to give yourself a better life,'" Deacon Robert said.

But you can't force it. Frank Ober, a convert to Catholicism, has been involved in ministry at the jail level for years. He said for every trip inside that was seemingly unproductive, there was one that would result in incredible encounters. One thing he learned was not to go inside with the expectation of immediate, tangible outcomes. "You can't look for answers or results. You have to leave that to the powers that be."

The ministers must also be flexible, willing to explore new avenues to reach the men and women they serve. Frederick Prince recalled an experience with Lewis, who was sullen and uncommunicative when they first met. Trying to break the ice, the minister asked Lewis about the food. It was rotten and the quantities were small, Lewis responded with characteristic bitterness. Frederick Prince asked him to try something: thank God nightly for the rotten food and the small portions. It took time, but ultimately, the inmate's attitude toward the food, and his overall experience, had improved. "Nothing changed at the jail. They didn't hire a five-star chef. All that changed was he changed," the longtime prison minister said.

Prison or jail can become a truly positive life event for prisoners, he reasoned, because it's an opportunity for God to enter their lives.

The service can come in many ways. Sister Courtney Haase of the Companions of Clare began teaching prisoners how to knit in exchange for work done on the home where she lives in Skowhegan. She ended up going for 2 ½ years, to her surprise working almost exclusively with men.

In her dealings with the men, she didn't try to actively convert them to the Catholic faith, but merely acknowledge the role Christ has played in her life. "When I talk to them about Jesus, I speak to them as he is my spouse and he is my best friend. That was a different perspective for a lot of them," she said.

Deacon Robert said the work of the ministers is aided by supportive individuals above him, both inside and outside the prison. The commissioner of the Maine Department of Corrections, Randall Liberty, has the best of intentions, wanting the prisoners to serve their time productively, get an education as needed, and put themselves in a position to re-enter society with a new focus. And prison leadership values the role the ministers play in that process.

"The prison wants us there. They've seen what it has done over the years, how much it has changed things," said Phyllis Curtis.

Likewise, Deacon Robert's boss, Bishop Robert Seeley of the Diocese of Portland, is extremely supportive of the prison ministry, having served in it himself back in Massachusetts.

This kind of backing is a must, because most of the men and women incarcerated will one day walk out of the state's jails and prisons.

"There is light at the end of the tunnel, even if you're in prison. But you have to look for that light and you have to want to be a part of that light," Deacon Robert said. "That's the biggest thing I've found is trying to create that atmosphere where they want to be a part of it."

Creating that atmosphere demands treating the incarcerated with the same love Jesus would. "They are not ferocious creatures," Sister Courtney said. "They are people of God."

St. Rita

Nānākuli, Hawaii

"Don't you long to shout to those youths who are bustling around you: Fools! Leave those worldly things that shackle the heart – and very often degrade it – leave all that and come with us in search of Love!"
Saint Josemaría Escrívá

THEY ARE THE BRIDGE THAT CONNECTS THE FAITH WE WERE RAISED in and the one that we pass down to our children, a crucial span for keeping Catholicism in the U.S. thriving. Despite this, they too often go overlooked and underserved. They are young adults.

On Oahu, Hawaii's most populous island, Kainoa Fukumoto found that very problem. Attempts were made at his home parish, Our Lady of Sorrows in Wahiawa, to create a ministry for young adults, but those efforts fizzled out. Yet there remained a core group of young Catholics thirsty to belong to something bigger, to grow their faith through fellowship and study with their peers.

They were still meeting, informally, to celebrate through music and other low-key events. The young men and women discussed their faith and their experiences, both shared and unique to each friend. Out of that, a new, stronger young adult ministry was born.

"It almost organically evolved. They wanted to have a formal ministry like we had before and they asked if I would be the one to lead it," recalled Kainoa Fukumoto, who served as the first president and remains a director of the nonprofit organization. "I prayed about it and this was where God was leading me."

He was leading him to the organization he founded in 2013. Searching for a name, they hit upon one both easy to remember and difficult to deny: Ever Present in Christ, or EPIC for short. "We thought that was a good embodiment of who we were as young adults," he said.

EPIC's makeup covers the wide range of young adult experiences and situations. Young adults comprise established workers, recent college graduates, grad students, single men and women, and married individuals, some of whom have already expanded their families with children. That presents both a challenge and an opportunity.

"When you have that kind of demographic, you can't just do one thing," Kainoa Fukumoto said. "We have done things from sporting events, big social gatherings, Bible studies, prayer services, adorations, and retreats. We try to touch on as many different things as we can.

"A lot of it is founded on the idea, 'How do we make the faith relevant?'"

The members soon realized that EPIC wasn't going to thrive and grow simply as a parish ministry, particularly given how many of its members were coming from outside Our Lady of Sorrows. They decided to become a young adult community, welcoming fellow twenty and thirtysomethings from the area. EPIC became a chapter, with another parish, Resurrection of the Lord in nearby Waipahu serving as its second home.

Each month, the group engages in mix of events, rotating between the two locations. On the first week of the month, testimony is given, either by a group member sharing or through the invitation extended to someone in vocations. The following week is turned over to catechesis. Scripture is discussed at the third meeting and the final one is a community or fellowship night.

Additionally, other events are planned throughout the year. A few years back, a handful of members of the organization made a 12-day pilgrimage to Rome.

EPIC's Executive Director Malcolm Zara came to the ministry through his parish, Resurrection of the Lord. He believes that reaching and activating young adults is imperative for the health of the church. "I'm not trying to downplay the importance of ministering across all age ranges, but if we're trying to pull society out of where we are now, it has to start with young adults. Our job is to get well-formed Catholics into the world so they can teach their families and lead and guide their families away from this moral ambiguity in the world. If you get the families right, then you can get everything else."

The two men initially split leadership duties, with Kainoa Fukumoto responsible for the business side and Malcolm Zara handling executing the group's mission. He speaks regularly across Oahu, and even island hops to spread the word. In 2018, Malcolm Zara spoke to a group of Catholics on the island of Maui, a talk that inspired Cecilia Jacinto and Pua Kaialiilii to create a ministry at home. But when they had trouble getting their vision for a ministry off the ground, they opted instead to bring EPIC to Maui.

"We ran into so many issues, we started to realize we wanted to copy off their model because it's so successful and we were chatting with Malcolm so often anyway. We started modeling after EPIC and by the end of the summer we were gaining a little traction," Cecilia Jacinto said. That early traction led to the official creation of the second EPIC charter in early 2019. Yet even though the EPIC foundation is there, the Maui chapter is not an exact replica. The chapter exists as more of a vicariate effort, compared with the parish focus on Oahu. Additionally, whereas the Oahu chapter started with faith sharing, Maui built from small groups on up.

Malcolm Zara has no issue with that. While he's delighted that EPIC has expanded its ministry to another island, his talks with young Catholics are not about building the brand, but promoting the cause. "It's more than just do you want EPIC ministry to grow, we want the larger young adult Catholic community to expand and we're trying to do our part for that," he said.

One of the challenges the young leaders of EPIC face is one that often plagues young adult ministries, the unavoidable aging process. Kainoa and Malcolm and Cecilia and Pua will not be young adults forever. To develop a sustainable organization, new leaders must continually be developed.

"If you have a leader in place, and it's a good leader but that leader leaves, the ministry tends to fall apart. We've seen that time and time again," Kainoa Fukumoto said. EPIC took the next step with the appointment of Dallas Carter as the new president of the organization.

A longtime friend and colleague of Kainoa Fukumoto's and Malcom Zara's, his appointment aids that continuity EPIC seeks.

With the members of EPIC representing so many different parishes on Oahu, including the newly formed third chapter that covers the Windward section of the island, I had my pick of places to visit for Mass. On the recommendation of Dallas Carter, I opted for St. Rita on the north shore. The trip to St. Rita allowed me to experience the bilingual Mass – half in English, half in Hawaiian – that's offered on the first Sunday of every month. Once again, the Holy Spirit had me in the right place at the right time.

It was a lovely Mass in the small parish a few hundred feet from the Pacific Ocean. The songs were done in Hawaiian, the homily in English and readings were a lively mix of the two. The Mass as practiced here has its own joyous traditions. A lei is used during the Gospel reading and after the consecration of the Eucharist, its scent symbolizing our prayers being sent to God, among other meanings. A quilt sits behind the altar, and pre-COVID was used to cover the altar when the Mass is over. That use comes from the Hawaiian tradition of covering beds with quilts, not to be slept on but to be removed and folded when it's time to rest. "When the altar is not in use, it's so sacred you don't even want to touch it," said Rev. Alapaki Kim, pastor at St. Rita.

And when the Eucharist is distributed to the ministers who will take Communion to the homebound, each Sacred Host is put inside ti leaves. Those plants are legendary in Hawaiian culture, being used to ward off spirits, preserve food, and cure illness, making them the "perfect vehicle for those who are sick and receiving Christ," said Karen Victor, the parish's director of religious education.

Seeing these small customs being executed, then learning the meanings behind each rite, is always a treat. But my time spent with the community after Mass was equally pleasing. The people of St. Rita were not just open and welcoming to the traveling writer, but also made my entire family feel quite at home.

All in all, the parish was an inspired choice by Dallas Carter for my stop in the Aloha State. But before serving as my travel guide, the new president of EPIC was instrumental in steering the entire organization through a period that easily could have doomed it.

EPIC is based heavily on fellowship, with small group sessions and other in-person activities serving as the backbone to the ministry. Those activities grinded to a halt in COVID, particularly in Hawaii where state mandates were much stiffer than on the mainland. Thus, EPIC's focus temporarily changed direction, becoming a group that served to address issues caused by the pandemic.

"I wanted to put my efforts into solving whatever problems were arising at the time," said Dallas Carter. "With the support of EPIC Ministry as a sponsor, and using the 5013c status of EPIC, we were able to collect funds and create an organization called Kupuna Needs." In Hawaiian, Kupuna means "elder."

In short order, Kupuna Needs was able to build stockpiles of food. The ministry not only made that food available to those who required it, but also built a delivery system to take it to those elderly neighbors who were homebound during the pandemic.

A volunteer force of 130 to 140 young adults was assembled, creating a daily delivery outreach around Oahu. "We had so many donations that it was a 9 to 5 job just receiving the food, storing it, bagging it, and taking phone calls. And that went on for months," he recalled.

In approximately eight months, the group executed more than 100,000 food deliveries on the island. But that wasn't all they supplied.

For many of the men and women Kupuna Needs served, food wasn't the only basic necessity they were lacking. Widows and widowers abounded, many with children far removed. In those cases, the young men and women from the ministry would simply sit and talk, providing them the human contact they so desperately craved.

"There were a lot of times where we'd follow protocol and make sure we weren't putting them at risk, but we'd stay outside with masks on and just talk," Dallas Carter said. "Sometimes I'd go into a garage and see a stacked refrigerator. They were just calling us because they wanted to talk to someone."

But it was a wonderful blessing to the young adult ministers, who had a unique opportunity during the early days of the pandemic. They were an age cohort the least at-risk from the dangers of COVID, while many of them found themselves without work responsibilities and other activities tugging at their time.

"It ended up being this great thing," he said. "I wish that period on no one ever again, but in retrospect one of the graces of it was being blessed with the ability to minister to people and be there for people when no one else was," Dallas Carter said.

It merely reinforced the importance and relevance of not just EPIC Ministry as an organization, but the role that young men and women play in the Church's continued vitality.

The next step to strengthening that role, the organizers know, is forging solid relationships with youth ministries. They must reach today's teenagers, the next wave of EPIC Ministry members, encouraging them to continue their commitment to the faith beyond Confirmation and into high school and college.

Building another bridge, as it were.

St. John the Baptist

Cabot, Arkansas

"No human tongue can enumerate the favors that trace back to the Sacrifice of the Mass. The sinner is reconciled with God; the just man becomes more upright; sins are wiped away; vices are uprooted; virtue and merit increases; and the devil's schemes are frustrated."
Saint Lawrence Justinian

On the Sunday I attended Mass at St. John the Baptist parish in Cabot, Ark., the DeLuca family woke up early, as usual, to embark on the 90-minute, one-way drive to get to the church on time.

The night before, the McDonald family of Houston, Texas, curtailed the drive home from Wisconsin to stop in Central Arkansas, determined to grab a front pew seat for the 8 a.m. Low Mass. They had originally planned to stop in Tyler, Texas, to experience the liturgy at a Latin Mass parish there, but were glad they could be in Cabot to support this growing parish community.

The Turrietta family needed not take any excessive preparations to make the 10 a.m. High Mass that day. Of course, that's only because several years earlier the entire family relocated from Missouri specifically to join the St. John the Baptist community. Family matriarch Rose and sister Frances road-tripped across the country, visiting 15 or so parishes, looking for one where the Latin Mass was well done and the community was strong, a parish where the form wouldn't be abandoned anytime soon. They found that in Cabot.

Such is the appeal of the Latin Mass to the parishioners of St. John the Baptist, where the devout will take extraordinary measures to observe the extraordinary form.

St. John the Baptist is one of two Latin Mass parishes in the Diocese of Little Rock, the other being found in Springdale in the northwest corner of the state. The parish is an apostolate of the Priestly Fraternity of St. Paul, a clerical society of apostolic life of pontifical right, which was canonically erected by Pope Saint John Paul II in 1988.

For a parish devoted to celebrating the centuries-old form, St. John the Baptist is in its infancy.

The parish has been in existence for less than 25 years and has called Cabot home only since 2017. In 1993, a decade after then-Pope John Paul II's letter, Quattuor Abhinc Annos confirmed the idea the ordinary and extraordinary forms were two expressions of the same rite, a group of Little Rock Catholics began pushing to celebrate the form in the Natural State's capital city. Five years later, that permission was granted by Most Rev. Andrew Joseph McDonald, then the bishop of the Diocese of Little Rock.

The parish moved around the diocese for years, including a stay in a chapel at the diocesan office. The chapel, named for St. John the Baptist, gave the fledging parish its name. Some of those early parishioners from the parish's nomadic days, such as Janie Elsinger and J. Fred Hart Jr., remain part of the congregation today.

Janie Elsinger speaks for many when discussing the pull of the Latin form. "It's the reverence. There's so much more peace, not as many distractions," she said. "The Latin Mass seems more sacred and less secular."

The paths to St. John the Baptist vary for many of the long-time parishioners, but the sacredness of the liturgy is at the heart of most of their stories. "There's something special about it. There are rubrics that go with the Mass, this etiquette and reverence you don't find everywhere else," said Charles Turrietta, an altar server who served as Master of Ceremonies at the High Mass I attended. "It's more of a prayer."

For the Harmon family, converts to the faith, the appeal of the parish is how inherently Catholic the Mass. The family felt their previous parish hewed a little too close to the Protestant church they left. "I wanted something a little more Catholic," said Scott Harmon, who serves on the parish finance council.

Rev. P. Jared McCambridge, FSSP, has been pastor at St. John the Baptist since 2017, his arrival coinciding with the parish's move to Cabot. A graduate of the U.S. Naval Academy, Father McCambridge's pursuit of religious life began during his time in the Navy, spurred by a fellow pilot who noticed his devotion to the faith and asked if he'd ever considered the calling. "I went to eight years of Catholic grade school, four years of Catholic high school, helped chaplains when they needed it. And no one in all of those years ever suggested considering the priesthood."

His first steps toward the priesthood went poorly, coming away uninspired by his visit with a vocations director in his native Illinois. A short time later, he was introduced to the Latin Mass by a friend. "I didn't know they still existed," he admitted, though it was in the extraordinary form he found his place. He entered seminary through the Fraternity of St. Peter, which celebrates the traditional form of Mass and places the sacraments at the heart of its charism.

Every day, that celebration takes place at St. John the Baptist. On Sundays, the day begins at 8 a.m. with the Low Mass, the quieter form where the priest's words are almost all you hear. The High, or Sung Mass, follows at 10 a.m. It's a fuller form of the liturgy, with multiple altar servers and a robust choir. If the parish had additional staff, such as a deacon and subdeacon, St. John could conduct the Solemn High Mass, the most perfect form of worship in the Latin tradition, Father McCambridge acknowledged.

That the first two types of Masses are offered is a concession to reality of a small, though growing, parish community.

"Every true Eucharistic liturgy is the representation of the sacrifice of Christ on Calvary, but in an unbloodied manner. Intrinsically, they're the same and capable of infinite grace. But we ourselves are not capable of receiving infinite grace. Extrinsically, our dispositions limit how much of the infinite graces we capture in offering and praying Mass. If we were freely able to do a Sung Mass, but 'It's too long, let's get it over with,' we would still have the same graces available to us, but choosing to do less would necessarily limit the graces we receive," Father McCambridge explained.

He also recognizes the Low Mass appeals to some of his parishioners for a variety of reasons. One of those parishioners drawn to it is Samuel Rinaldi. "We only had the Low Mass during COVID, and because of the silence, I am able to unite my heart more to what the priest is doing."

Julie Kozlowski agreed. "Music can touch the heart, and there are some really good Novus Ordo songs that bring me to tears. But the silence I get at the Low Mass is just beyond. We live in such a noisy place, so it's nice to go to a quiet place and listen to God."

The High Mass also has its adherents. Among them is David Sonnier, who serves as choir director. "To some people, it's about the music or Gregorian chant or about the homilies. But to me, it's the entirety of it all."

The form is particularly popular among the younger families of St. John the Baptist, of which there are many. Perhaps the most unpredictable aspect of the revival of the Latin Mass across the United States was how it resonated with so many people who hadn't grown up with it. Frank Barry, who matured before Vatican II, serving as an altar server in his native New York, is surprised by the makeup of the parish community. "I look around the church and see these people and their families. I'm just amazed how many young people are drawn to it."

That attraction is not slowing down. St. John the Baptist's original home in Cabot, where I celebrated both forms, was in a former Protestant church the parish community purchased. But within three years, the community had already outgrown the modest building, leading to the acquisition of another former church building in the community. In March 2022, on the Feast of St. Joseph, Bishop Anthony Taylor from the Diocese of Little Rock blessed the new property, a mere half-mile from the previous worship space.

That rapid growth is a testament to how strong the appeal of the Latin Mass is to many Catholics, young and old.

Despite that appeal, or perhaps in some ways because of it, their preferred form of the liturgy is at risk. On the week before I attended Mass in Cabot, Pope Francis issued Traditionis custodes, a Motu proprio dealing with the use of the Latin form. He pulled back the Summorum Pontificum, the Apostolic letter written by Pope Benedict that allowed for the Latin Mass to be said by any Catholic priest. Under the newer letter, the bishop has "the exclusive competence to authorize the use of the 1962 Roman Missal in his diocese."

Father McCambridge acknowledged the significance of the letter from Pope Francis, but remains faithful to the idea the form will not disappear. "I pray God's will be done. My hope and trust is in God's providence that the traditional Mass will continue to exist."

Longtime parishioner J. Fred Hart Jr. wonders if the two forms will not only continue to co-exist, but evolve into something even greater, more complete. "We are still on a journey. There's no reason to believe it won't continue to develop, and will help each other, so that what finally emerges is neither the Latin Mass nor the vernacular, but something in between," he said. "We may still be in the early stages of the Church."

Until then, the community at St. John the Baptist will continue to enjoy the Mass in the form it was delivered for centuries, where they will find joy in the solemnity, power in the silence, and reverence and beauty in the words of a language few people speak.

St. Rose

Belmar, New Jersey

"Know that even when you are in the kitchen, our Lord moves amidst the pots and pans."
Saint Teresa of Avila

IN RETROSPECT, THE VALUE AND UTILITY OF ST. ROSE'S FROZEN FOOD ministry seems quite obvious.

Yet, while countless churches and organizations offer food pantries or free meals for the less fortunate in their communities, the ongoing service provided by the parishioners of St. Rose remains rather unique to this oceanside community.

It was approximately 17 years ago when Carol DeBartolo hit upon an idea. She had already been a volunteer with the parish's Society of St. Vincent de Paul when a mother in the parish was diagnosed with cancer. During the mother's ultimately successful bout against the insidious disease, the parishioner found many nights when the chemotherapy being used to attack her carcinogenic cells left her incapable of preparing meals for her young family.

Carol DeBartolo, who has since retired as the parish bookkeeper, saw this as an opportunity to serve. Already known to cook for the equivalent of an army at home, she realized she could set aside her extras and deliver them to the struggling mother. When chemo knocked the mother off her feet, her children could simply pop the pre-made meals in the microwave. Out of that kind response to hardship, a new ministry was born.

"That's kind of how it started," Carol DeBartolo said. "Soon, we put it out to the whole parish, to put a leftover meal and freeze it and we would give it out to people in need in the community."

In short order, the ministry took shape. The parish received a donation of a standup freezer to put in the community room. And, as the meals kept coming, they put in another. It wasn't long before the meals weren't just some families' leftovers, but parishioners were preparing the food specifically for the frozen food ministry.

Today, anyone who comes to the pantry can get 8 to 10 meals at a time, to be taken back home and heated up. The meals are perfect for older residents, often living alone or in rooming houses with either limited opportunity, or ability, to cook. The parish covers them all, no questions asked.

Occasionally, those without access to a microwave will come in and the volunteers on site will heat the meal up and serve it there. But most of the meals are handed out, to be heated and enjoyed over the course of the next week.

"It has really worked out. It's brought our parishioners together," said Carol DeBartolo, noting how the nature of the ministry allows people to contribute when it's most convenient. Older parishioners who might not want to come out later in the evening can instead drop off meals in the afternoon, to be distributed as needed. "It makes them feel a part of the community."

And it's not just the parish's older members who have participated. The ministry truly took off when students began to get involved in food preparation.

A few years back, Carol DeBartolo asked others in the parish to contribute and Italia Testa jumped at the chance. A member of St. Anthony of Padua Secular Franciscan Fraternity in Middlesex, Italia Testa was already committed to "helping the poor, the marginalized, the forgotten in our society." She enlisted the help of her children to begin preparing weekly meals when it dawned on her that she could tap into the healthy supply of young people in the parish to stock the refrigerators.

She launched Club Faith, a youth ministry beginning with middle school kids but eventually moving up to the older students. Each month, Italia Testa and her sister Rosanna Ayers would welcome in a dozen or so kids from the community to cook the meals for the pantry. The sisters and her children would do the prep work, then the other kids followed to cook, package, and clean over the course of several hours.

Pre-COVID, the students would come from all over the area. Some Catholic school students at St. Rose grammar and high schools and others in the region, but also from the area public schools. The students earn service hour credits for their schools or religious education programs, but it's more about what they're giving than what they're receiving.

"They feel they're doing something for those who are suffering in difficult moments. They're happy to be able to give back," Italia Testa said.

And it isn't just the kids getting something out of it. "It's very rewarding for me. I feel like this is what I was called to do. I have this opportunity where I'm able to teach something to the kids where they have these memories and maybe this will trigger something as they get older and they do other service," Italia Testa said.

She uses the experiences in the kitchen with the religious education department, explaining who the clients are, what their needs are, and how the students can be grateful for what they have. "They have a refrigerator to open any time when they want something to eat. Our clients, some are people living in boarding houses, living in motels day to day, or from off the streets," she said.

The kitchen's limitations, coupled with the challenge of working with students of varying levels of cooking experience, meant Italia Testa and Rosanna Ayres had to be inventive and adaptable. They had to come up with ideas for meals that are conducive to the kids, that keep both occupied and safe, yet produced a meal worth sharing with others in the community.

And the meals are not just sustenance, but also a path to healthier living. Rather than subsisting on a nutritionally scarce diet of fast foods that some guests would typically choose, they're getting more balanced, healthy meals through the pantry. Additionally, when the staff knows of existing health conditions, such as diabetes, among its regular visitors, it can tailor what it provides to best meet their dietary requirements.

"We do a lot of healthy choices – chicken, meatloaf, vegetables. Some people will bring in pasta, but a lot of the older people shouldn't have that many carbs," Italia Testa said.

Meals are provided twice a week at the church's community room. They're packed in material purchased through a restaurant supply house. The ministry doesn't use Tupperware and ask for it to be returned due to the difficulty in sterilizing the containers after each use.

The parish is consistently looking at ways to expand their services. One of the more recent developments was to begin delivering the food to those who couldn't get to the church, either due to illness or the absence of transportation. "We take great pride in offering that. It's very rare that food pantries deliver," said parishioner Dominic Guglielmi.

Stephanie Gaines came to the parish more than six years ago. When she arrived, she was hoping to start a young adult group, though the absence of many men and women her age served as an impediment. Instead, she simply began cooking for the frozen food ministry, inviting others to join her.

It has worked out exceedingly well. Once a week, Stephanie Gaines and Michelle Robbins shop for food, then dole out responsibilities to the young adult volunteers who join them, people with varying degrees of proficiency in the kitchen. "Michelle would usually have some kind of chili, so there could be a lot of chopping involved," Stephanie Gaines explained.

The evenings in the kitchen have proved to an exceptional experience and not just for stocking the freezers. The time together allows for wonderful opportunities to talk and share, much the same way a traditional young adult ministry operates.

"It's nice, because while you're cooking, you're talking about your life and faith things and depending on what time of the year it is, you could talk about Lent or Advent. And we always start and end with a prayer," Stephanie Gaines said.

On top of that, depending on what is being prepared, the young people can often step away from the kitchen to participate in adoration.

The cooking invites not just the small cadre of young adults from St. Rose, but from neighboring parishes as well. "Half the people here are not even from the parish. People like to go and visit other parishes. If there's nothing going on at your parish that night, you might as well check out something at another parish," said Patrick Burney, who spoke to me between kitchen duties. He was joined by his brother Jack, friend Patrick Byrne and sisters Ivory and Pearl Thrush. "It's great being with other Catholics."

For Stephanie Gaines, one aspect of the pantry that deviates from some other ministries she's been involved with is that the work is all done behind the scenes. "I know sometimes when you're volunteering, you feel good about what you're doing because you're physically seeing it. But it's also nice to be hidden and behind the scenes and trust that it's helping somebody and you're not seeing that person," she said.

And like so many ministries undertaken, this one has tangible spiritual as well as nutritional effects. Many of the individuals who have been served by the pantry have responded by getting more involved in the parish. "Recently one young man who had been estranged from his mother came for food. He was so moved that he called his mother and they got back together," Carol DeBartolo said. "We've met some wonderful people we've met through this ministry, people whose lives we've touched."

Some of the folks they serve keep coming back. "We've had quite a few people who, because of them reaching out to us for assistance, they have come back and said, 'I would like to join your church. I would like to become Catholic,'" recalled Dominic Guglielmi, who believes that should be one of the objectives. "That's always a consideration. If we don't do that, we're just social services."

The beauty of the frozen food pantry is just how many parishioners from St. Rose are involved, both in terms of doing the cooking and simply making it possible. The kitchen equipment was donated by the parish's St. Vincent de Paul Society and many of the profits from St. Rose's Selective Seconds Ministry were donated as well. "That's just a shining example of people within the parish and different ministries working together to help the needy," said Dominic Guglielmi.

Or, as Michelle Robbins summed. "As a community, the people of St. Rose are generous. A lot of people have a lot to give. Sometimes it's just their heart, sometimes cash, sometimes it's food. Sometimes it's space and sometimes it's time. Everybody has different talents they have to give, but we as a church come together and give what we can."

Holy Family Parish
Holy Trinity &
St. John Church

Middletown, Ohio

"Lord, if your people need me, I will not refuse the work. Your will be done."
Saint Martin of Tours

WHEN SHE WAS 15, KARA JACKSON HEARD GOD'S VOICE TELLING her what He wanted from her and she immediately began her plans to heed His call. It took her mother and father a little longer to get on board.

Lying in bed one evening, Jackson was informed that God wanted her to serve Mass in every state in the country. She had recently begun her duties as an altar server at St. John, her home church in Middletown, Ohio.

"I said I am your servant, I will follow you," Kara Jackson recalled. "He said to me, 'Believe in Me. Follow Me.'"

From that point on, Kara was determined to complete her mission. Her mother, in particular, assumed the role of Thomas, wondering whether such an undertaking was possible, whether the family could afford it, and the hundreds of other questions any parent runs through before finally saying, "Yes."

"You want to encourage your child, but you don't want to set them up for failure," Tina Jackson recalled.

But Kara persisted, and her mother eventually allowed Kara to pursue her pilgrimage, albeit slowly. Rather than dive in headfirst, the Jacksons dipped their toes in the water. In 2013, the family reached out to a parish in Richmond, Indiana, not too far from their Southwestern Ohio home. If the effort failed, they could return to normal life knowing they had at least let Kara give it a try.

Together they wrote a letter to the pastor there, the late Rev. Kevin Morris, asking if St. Mary would have an opening for the young woman to serve. By Friday, they had their answer. "Absolutely she can come," the priest responded. She was there for Mass that weekend.

Over the course of five years, the three-person Jackson family, including father Rick, regularly climbed into the family vehicle to set out for various parts of the country to complete their daughter's mission. Holiday and school vacations were no longer spent lounging around the home or frolicking on a beach, but crisscrossing the country picking up daily and weekend Masses wherever the opportunity provided. The workload was simple: Rick did the driving. Tina set up the Mass visits. And Kara served God.

It wasn't always easy. Some parishes do not allow female servers. Others didn't have opportunities for servers during daily Mass. But somehow, every issue had an answer, every detour offered an even better path somewhere else.

"You think you're in control, but you're not," Tina Jackson said. "God will choose you and direct you."

And so He did. Following the maiden visit across the state line, the Jacksons made their first legitimate road trip, a journey a few hundred miles east to Pittsburgh and the Church of the Epiphany. Then it was on to St. Francis of Assisi near the glitz of Las Vegas, Christ the King in the mountains of Cedar City, Utah, and beyond. Each Mass served offering a new opportunity, a new discovery, a new experience.

The conversation with God was not the first time Kara Jackson surprised her parents. Her very existence defied the odds in many ways.

The Jacksons had difficulty conceiving for many years before being blessed with Kara. But a neonatologist discovered abnormalities and informed the family their daughter would never lift her head up, never talk, never grow. The unfathomable, an abortion, was offered as an alternative, one quickly rejected by the devout Catholic family. So too was the idea of institutionalizing their daughter after her birth. Kara was their gift, and she would be treasured as one.

But it wasn't easy. After delivery, she spent time on a feeding tube, then more time on oxygen. But ultimately, she went home a wanted child in every way, the Down Syndrome she lives with just a small part of her character, one that neither defines her existence nor limits her ambitions.

By 2012, those ambitions included joining other children her age as an alter server. She took a flyer from the director of religious education at her parish and handed it to her mom, asking her to sign her up immediately. Tina Jackson was initially reluctant, worried her daughter wouldn't be able to handle the duties, always serving in the role of Kara's protector. But Tina's caution, however, has never been a match for Kara's persistence, so the young lady was there for the very first practice.

During that initial session, it became clear to everyone that Kara would have no problem shouldering the responsibilities. And, on retrospect, it was easy to see why.

"For the rest of the kids, they were getting pushed into it by their parents," Tina Jackson recalled. "It was my child pulling me into it."

Her experience at St. John convinced Rev. John Civille the Jacksons had little to worry about when it came time for Kara to serve elsewhere. "She's perfect," he said of her skills as a server. "When she serves, she's always there early and sits and waits. She's very serious about it."

He's also seen how she has grown through the experience of serving God. "She's very verbal now. It's given her a lot of self-confidence," Father Civille said.

She's still serving, though COVID kept her and others sidelined longer than she'd like. Yet the long delay didn't have any obvious effect on her skills, her service under Father Civille at the Mass I attended at Holy Trinity going off without a hitch. I suspect her years of work on her pilgrimage have fully ingrained in her all of the nuances of altar serving.

The trip itself was eye-opening, delivering so many moments of divine providence it was clear the Holy Spirit was the Jacksons' constant traveling companion. After serving Mass in Washington, D.C., a woman approached the family and marveled how she had been in Mass with

Kara just a few days earlier in her home parish in West Virginia, several hundred miles away.

When she served at St. Mary in Canton, N.Y., the Jacksons' visit was fortuitously timed with Rev. Bryan Stitt's annual pro-life homily, delivered on his 13th anniversary as a priest and her 13th state as a server. The visiting priest spoke of children such as Kara, whose very existence would have been imperiled in the womb had the Jacksons followed the advice of professionals rather than the teachings of the Church.

In Bowman, North Dakota, Rev. David G. Morman informed the Jacksons on arrival that Kara's service would not take place at St. Charles, but rather as he conducted Mass at a nearby nursing home. There she celebrated the 109th birthday of one of the home's residents, Irma Emma Deutscher.

And in Mississippi, she encountered a group of visiting Irish priests, one of whom asked her to come to the Emerald Isle to expand her efforts globally. The Jacksons had plans to follow through on the offer in 2020, though that experience was one of many casualties of the pandemic.

Kara's domestic trip wrapped up in 2018, with our 50th state serving as her 50th state. She concluded her pilgrimage at St. Augustine by the Sea in Honolulu.

As fulfilling as the journey was to Kara and her family, it perhaps had a greater effect on the people she encountered along the way. Such as the young father in Maryland whose life had gotten off track, but whose meeting with Kara led him to return to the Church to have his infant child baptized. Or the young girl whose own mother was reluctant to let her become an alter server until seeing and meeting with Kara. Those simple stories of renewed faith were omnipresent throughout the five-year experience, Kara Jackson's dutiful journey leaving her mark on many people along the way.

"I was very impressed with her. I remember when she came and she was very generous to help with the service," said retired Archbishop Roger Schwietz, O.M.I., who presided over Mass at St. Andrew in Eagle River, Alaska. "What impressed me was she really knew what she was doing and, in her own quiet way, was very professional."

"She was very sincere in her faith," said now-retired Rev. Peter Daly, who had been serving at St. John Vianney in Prince Frederick, Maryland. "She was an inspiring young woman."

Father Daly said there are lessons in an endeavor such as hers. "When you meet someone on a pilgrimage like that, you learn about them and you learn about your own faith. You realize maybe I should take risks for my faith," he said. And he did just that. Shortly after Kara's visit to his parish, he took sabbatical and went on a Camino.

Rev. Brian Hurley, then serving at St. Anthony in Temperance, Michigan, recalled taking Kara aside and asking the young lady for her story. "She was just matter of fact. 'I was talking to Jesus and He told me He wanted to serve.'

That was good enough for the priest. "If the Lord spoke to her, then He spoke to her," Father Hurley said.

"I was very moved by the spirituality of Kara. She was doing this because she wanted to be closer to God," said Rev. Henry Carmona, pastor at Holy Spirit Catholic Community in Pocatello, Idaho.

But perhaps no one was more captivated by her mission than Rev. Cornelius Onyigbuo, a native of Nigeria serving at Immaculate Conception in Cuba, New Mexico. "There is a spirit that lives in her, that allows her to serve" said Father Cornelius, who stayed in contact with Kara and the family with cards and letters years after her visit. "It got into my heart. She is a sign of hope for people who are depressed."

The capacity to generate such admiration or inspiration or hope explains perfectly why one evening a decade ago, God spoke to a guileless young woman in Ohio and asked her to serve Him. And just as she was finishing up, a much older man in Indiana was getting ready to embark on a similar pilgrimage, following in the footsteps of a girl he hadn't yet had the immense privilege to meet.

St. Rose of Lima

Newtown, Connecticut

"In my deepest wound I saw your glory and it dazzled me."
St. Augustine of Hippo

DECEMBER 14, 2012, BEGAN AS A JOYOUS DAY AT ST. ROSE OF LIMA Elementary School. The Advent season was in full flourish. A young boy, one who had not grown up Catholic, had met his obligations and was preparing to receive First Communion in front of his classmates. His parents were there, his younger brother nearby in the Pre-K classroom.

Shortly after Mass began, a teacher dashed into the church, informing the staff that a man with a gun had been spotted in the area. The facility went into lockdown mode, soon learning the building itself was incapable of being fully locked down, churches being designed to invite people in, not keep them out.

Minutes passed into hours. Teachers and administrators heard reports of a second shooter, of the school itself being the next target, that a shooter was inside a kindergarten classroom at St. Rose, the truth banging heads with rumor as so often happens in the midst of unfolding chaos. A religious instructor began saying the Rosary, only to be reminded there was no talking allowed during lockdown; even intercessory pleas to Mary had to be conducted silently. The children huddled inside the church and the school building both, frantic parents outside begging to be allowed in. Helicopters hovered overhead, their chopping blades a reminder of the ongoing danger.

It was an experience no Catholic school, no school of any kind, should ever have to endure, though one all too familiar across the United States.

Later, the parish community learned the awful truth. A young man, a one-time student at St. Rose, had gone on a murderous spree at nearby Sandy Hook Elementary School. He had shot and killed his mother before heading out for her place of work to unleash unfathomable tragedy on society's most vulnerable population: elementary school children.

In all, he took 28 lives that day at Sandy Hook. Twenty of those victims were children between the ages of 6 and 7. Many of them were parishioners at St. Rose.

"We were all preparing for the birth of Jesus, not the deaths of innocent children," recalled Mary Maloney, who had been working as principal at St. Rose when the shooting took place.

Eleven days before Christmas, Newtown, Connecticut, joined the far-too-long list of American cities and towns ravaged by inexplicable school violence. The people of St. Rose of Lima, from Principal Maloney to Rev. Robert Weiss, were charged with helping the community recover from the unspeakable horror.

That recovery started just a few hours later, when Father Weiss announced there would be a special Friday night service. All were truly welcome. And all came.

Two hours before Mass began in the heavily Catholic town, the church had already far exceeded its 600-seat capacity. Loudspeakers were erected outside, so the overflow crowd, a mix of Catholics and non-Catholics alike, could connect with the service.

Pam Arsenault, who spent 20 years directing religious education at the parish, recalled arriving at St. Rose for that night's Mass to find a local Protestant minister standing outside the church. He looked apprehensive. Pam Arsenault told him that he needed to join Father Weiss at the altar.

"But I'm not Catholic," he told her. "I said, 'At times like this, it doesn't matter,'" she responded.

Father Weiss had been summoned to the school during the event, then relocated to the firehouse where the Sandy Hook schoolchildren had been transported. He stayed with them until their parents arrived. And then he stayed with the parents whose children would never make it home.

He immediately called for the Mass, knowing the community needed a place to come together, to mourn and to pray. In some ways, it was an ordinary Mass, no different than any of the thousands he's said during his years as a parish priest. But it was also unlike any other. "The Mass was not a problem, but I didn't know about the message I had to deliver," Monsignor Weiss recalled.

The homily he opted to give spoke of finding light in the darkness, a theme that united the Christian holiday approaching and the Jewish holiday that had already begun. When Mass ended, the governor and the state's two Senators, among others, addressed the congregation, the first of many signs the world outside was there to support the small community of Newtown through its darkest days.

And St. Rose of Lima was there every step of the way.

Pam Arsenault believes the parish assumed that responsibility with the first Mass on the night of the shooting.

"I think that's what solidified the church's role in saying, 'We are here to heal the brokenhearted.' It wasn't just those families who lost their children or lost their teachers, it was everybody in the community. Everybody knew children in that school system. Many had children who witnessed the tragedy. There were varying degrees, but everybody was traumatized," she recalled.

The days and weeks that followed were a mixture of mourning and celebration. For a week straight, the church conducted funeral services for the victims – eight of the children were members of St. Rose of Lima. Wakes and funerals were held one after the other.

Before each funeral, the religious ed department asked each family to describe a son or daughter lost, that information relayed to Father Weiss to help him deliver personal homilies. And the families themselves typically chose to offer their own remembrances.

Pam Arsenault recalled one mother who spent the entire funeral Mass sobbing uncontrollably, but when it came time to speak, was suddenly able to offer a message of love that had parishioners laughing and crying in equal measure. "It was the grace of God; we all knew it," she remembered.

At the same time, the community continued its preparation to celebrate the birth of our Savior. The town initially considered taking its Christmas decorations down, but ultimately concluded that celebration, that light in the darkness, was never more urgently called for.

"The people needed Christmas, especially that year. We worked hard on providing some beautiful Christmas liturgies. The church was left open 24/7 for people to come and pray," Monsignor Weiss recalled.

The monsignor considered his role throughout the entire ordeal was to simply be a presence, to be there for those suffering unimaginable pain. Others believe he's selling himself short.

Michael Coppola spent much of the aftermath with the priest he still calls, affectionately, Father Bob. He marvels at the strength the pastor exhibited, serving the needs of the entire community.

"He was amazing for the families. He never said no to anybody. He was the calm after the storm for the entire community."

Mike Stutman had a similar assessment. He was stunned at how adroitly the parish, and its pastor, handled the dual challenge of mourning the lost and providing a source of hope for the community as a whole. "There was a lot of mourning to do; there was never an attempt to diminish that. But it was also about seeing that light through the darkness," he recalled.

And it all started with Father Robert Weiss, whose respect within the parish community is reflected in the gathering hall and the Garden of Peace, both of which bear his name in tribute. "He was the right man at the right time in an unfortunate place," Mike Stutman said. "He was the person our community needed to step up from a faith perspective and be that voice of strength and resiliency."

"Prayer, support meetings at the church, joining numerous committees to help others understand how to support the community, working with the selectman and following up with the families, particularly during the first year, was his gift to all of us at the school and community," Mary Maloney remembered. "He never put himself first."

As the rest of the nation's focus shifted elsewhere, pulled away by the onset of Christmas, the start of another year and new tragedies and triumphs, the heartache remained in Newton. The church and the school, among others, continued to lead the way in the healing.

At school, the teachers and administers at St. Rose had to assume an entirely new method of instruction and classroom management. The ABCs and times tables were supplemented by grief counselors and enhanced safety protocols. Expectations had to change; the immaculately tuned structure of a well-run Catholic school gave way to the understanding that grief was not interested in schedules, that teachers and administrators may have to talk less and listen more to meet the unique needs of the St. Rose schoolchildren.

Grants allowed the school to bring in counselors, not just for the remainder of the school year, but for the next two years. They spoke in groups with the kids, or in individual sessions, depending on the needs.

"If there's anything we can be proud about, it's that we did everything we possibly could have," said Mary Maloney, who later moved on to serve as president of Immaculate High School in nearby Danbury. "Attendance wasn't a big deal. If you were absent, that was OK. If you had a meltdown, it was OK."

The story was the same for the religious education program Pam Arsenault oversaw. "I tend to be intellectual and look at resources. But there's no book written on this. There's nothing you can do but to rely on the grace of God."

And that grace was everywhere. To Pam Arsenault, it was most reflected by Jenny Hubbard and Sandy Previdi, the parents of victims Catherine Violet Hubbard and Caroline Previdi. The two grieving moms were asked to speak at numerous events, and Pam Arsenault often accompanied them. The educator remains awestruck at their ability to deliver poignant and meaningful remarks each time they stood before a crowd.

"They would go to the chapel and ask, 'Lord, remove all my insecurities and worries,' and then they would get up and each and every word they said were coming from the grace of God," Pam Arsenault remembered.

Today, almost 10 years later, the effects of the Sandy Hook shooting continue to be felt, though the aftershocks are smaller. People move out, others move in. The visual reminders are still there in bracelets and car magnets, if slightly faded by time

Yet needs still exist, an undeniable reality of life with the post-traumatic stress the community undoubtedly suffered. Kids now in high school or college, parents of children lost can still be set off by events, either obvious triggers or seemingly mundane occurrences. And the church and school will continue to do its part, as long as those in the community require the kind of healing only faith can provide.

But there's also the inevitable scarring.

"I see the community is healing. We'll never accept it. We'll never understand it," said Mary Maloney. "But people are feeling as if they can move on."

That sense is palpable on the first weekend of June in 2021. Subtle hints of the tragic past were present on the beautiful grounds of the parish and school, but there was also an undeniable vibrancy before, during and after Mass. Theirs is a resilient and noticeably joyous community that stood firm in the face of the most unimaginable of tragedies. And a parish that continues to recover and grow stronger, one Sunday at a time.

Church of the Holy Name of Jesus

Providence, Rhode Island

"When you look at the crucifix, you understand how much Jesus loved you then. When you look at the Sacred Host, you understand how much Jesus loves you now."
Saint Theresa of Calcutta

IN DIOCESES WHERE PARISHES ARE THREATENED WITH CLOSURE OR consolidation, one bulwark against such a measure is the existence of a dedicated community worshipping at the space.

Church of the Holy Name of Jesus in Providence is double-protected.

The East Side of Rhode Island's capital city has always been a working class area and Holy Name was once the parish where the nearby Polish, German, or Irish immigrants worshipped. But changing demographics have altered the mix and now there's a heavy influx of African immigrants, primarily from Cape Verde, sitting alongside the older families of European heritage. These folks largely make up the territorial base of Holy Name, the people populating the pews at the 9 a.m. Sunday Mass.

An hour after they've recessed, a new mix of adherents enters the Basilica Church, as Holy Name's larger worship space is called. For more than four decades, the Latin Mass has been celebrated at Holy Name to one degree or another, and the rite continues to draw people from all over Rhode Island. At 11 a.m., the High, or Sung, Mass is celebrated.

Finally, at 12:30 p.m., in the smaller Lady Chapel tucked behind the Basilica Church, Holy Name's West African community celebrates a service that borrows heavily from the Catholic Mass traditions in Nigeria and neighboring countries.

All of these diverse populations, plus 4 p.m. vigil Mass and 7:30 a.m. Low Latin Mass communities, comprise Holy Name. "Basically, it comes to a point where you can almost say, 'If you don't find a home here, you're not going to find one anywhere,'" Rev. Joseph D. Santos told me in August of 2020.

None of the communities is terribly large, but each is fully committed to the faith. And the parishioners embrace and celebrate the other parishioners who share the Holy Name campus. On the Sunday I spent at the church, parishioners at the Novus Ordo celebration recommended I stick around for the next two Masses, and the Latin Mass goers insisted I attend the African Mass, suggestions that were welcome but not necessary. Still, it was heartening to find no Catholic provincialism in Providence.

"You don't get a sense of who we are unless you see all of us," said Jennifer Galipeau, who sang at both the 9 and 11 a.m. Masses the Sunday I was there. She has also spent time in the Gospel Choir, which performs at 9 a.m. the first three Sundays each month.

Two of her favorite times of the year are when the three communities join forces. The first is during Holy Week, when the three choirs perform a number of songs together on Holy Thursday. The other is on Corpus Christi, when First Communion and Confirmation candidates process into Mass as one. "Every day at Holy Name is beautiful, but I get choked up at those two," she admitted.

Richard Davis, who has handled many roles at the parish in the past two decades, credits Holy Name with bringing him back to the faith. And it's only gotten more special over the years.

"I've lived in Asia. I've lived in Latin America and I've been to Africa. I've never seen a parish the characteristics of Holy Name. It's so diverse," he marveled.

That diversity is appreciated.

"The people do make an effort to work together within the different communities. That's always a preoccupation when you have different groups; instead of working alongside together, they start working against each other," Father Santos said. "We have not had that problem."

Building a fully cohesive parish for the three communities was one of Father Santos' many objectives at the parish. Current parishioners and staff members confirm he had done just that by December 2021, when the beloved priest died after a month-long battle with COVID-19.

The parish was still mourning his loss when I arrived. A memorial event was scheduled for the following Sunday, which marked six months since his passing.

"He was extremely energetic and connected to a lot of people. His passing is very keenly felt, especially for the people who were closest to him, myself among them," said Mark Berardo, a parish trustee and the Master of Ceremonies at the Latin Mass.

Rev. Lazarus Onuh, who served under Father Santos for several years and has since been named parish parochial administrator pro tem, said the late pastor could relate to anyone in the community. "Father Santos was someone who could have a serious political discussion now and then speak with a child and have a conversation about cartoons. He was able to lift every person up. He's greatly missed."

That kind of ability was founded in a knowledge of a variety of subjects – both inside and outside the Church – that bordered on encyclopedic. Following his passing, fellow priest and former schoolmate Rev. Joseph Escobar cited that well-rounded knowledge. "He was kind of like Google for us. You could ask Joe any question, even an obscure religious thing, and Joe would know the answer," Father Escobar told local media.

Among the many accomplishments of Father Santos during his 17-year stay at Holy Name was a thorough remodeling of the Basilica church. The ceilings were repaired, interior repainted, floors redone, and more under his care, all taken with an eye on the returning the parish to the grandeur of its founding. "At his funeral, I said, 'We can't call this the church Father Santos built. But it's definitely the one he restored,'" Mark Berardo said.

His passionate work at restoration, and a similar push decades earlier, have made Holy Name the perfect setting for the beauty and tradition of the Latin Mass. The church building, dedicated in 1900, has the towering ceiling, high altar, pulpit, marbleized plaster columns, mosaic flooring, and intricate adornments reminiscent of old world European cathedrals. In fact, it was designed in a style similar to the Basilica of Saint Paul Outside the Walls in Rome.

In a way, misfortune paved the way to its current splendor. In 1965, much of the sanctuary was damaged by fire. The first restoration began immediately, with the church rededicated the following year. Shortly thereafter, the church building reforms that accompanied the Second Vatican Council swept through Providence and elsewhere. However, Holy Name didn't have the funds, or the will, to embark on another major construction project, leaving the space in its traditional form and the ideal location to revive the Tridentine Mass.

That revival preceded the formal Quattuor Abhinc Annos issued by Saint John Paul II. In 1978, former pastor Rev. Joseph Gallagher began celebrating a solemn sung Latin Mass in the new rite and that continued to be offered. Upon release of Ecclesia Dei, Holy Name became the logical choice to offer the Tridentine Mass.

The push to expand the parish to include a third community came under Father Santos. Though a native of nearby Bristol, Father Santos was ordained at the Cathedral of Braga in Portugal, where he served for 10 years, giving him a deep appreciation for the world outside the States.

As Providence's population of Catholic immigrants from Western Africa expanded, the faithful was looking for a single parish to worship as a community. They arrived at Holy Name a few years earlier and they've been an integral part of the parish trinity ever since.

This unique blend of communities could have been threatened with the loss of its pastor, but Father Lazarus has ably stepped into the void, including quickly becoming adept at presiding over the Latin Mass. He had already been saying Low Mass to satisfy his own natural penchant for learning as well as to fill in for Father Santos when the pastor was out of town. Father Lazarus was the priest at all three Masses I attended, shifting comfortably from the Novus Ordo to the Sung Mass to the African Mass in short order.

Mark Berardo and others at the parish are both thoroughly impressed and a bit concerned. "While we very much appreciate him, we're a little worried because he's one man trying to do the work of two. Father Lazarus has been nothing but generous in keeping things going, and we've been nothing but supportive of him, or at least we're trying to be."

Shortly after presiding over the Latin Mass, Father Lazarus was next door in the Lady Chapel to lead the African community in prayer.

Much smaller and more intimate, the chapel too is the fitting home to the worship taking place there.

On the surface, the two services couldn't be more different. The Latin Mass is quiet, even the High Mass, with all attention focused on the priest and the centuries of tradition behind it. The African Mass is a boisterous affair, evidenced by Father Lazarus inviting replies from parishioners during his homily, the long line of parish children delivering self-written calls for intercession during Prayers of the Faithful, and the lively music that makes sure every verse is sung (and clapped and swayed to).

One striking moment, though one I didn't quite comprehend as it was taking place, involved the offertory. After parishioners dropped off their cash donations in the basket, they proceeded to deliver ordinary household items as gifts, including a value pack of toilet paper and a case of bottled water. To my untrained eyes, it seemed a strange occurrence.

But this exchange traces back to Africa, where the worshippers would give the priest fruits and vegetables they had picked from their own gardens. In urban Providence, where gardens and farms are not quite as plentiful, these dry goods and other supermarket finds substitute for the fresh produce of their homeland.

As with many of the worshippers, Father Lazarus is a native of Nigeria, which is how he landed in the parish to begin with. After the departure of the former African community priest, Father Jude, the parish reached out to nearby Providence College, a Dominican university, and asked if the school could make an educational opportunity available to a Nigerian priest who would also be able to serve at Holy Name. Father Lazarus, who was then serving as secretary to the archbishop of Abuja, was tapped to come to the U.S. He's been here ever since.

In addition to saying Mass, he and others assist the community of immigrants, many of whom have come alone, in acclimating to their new home. "Without support from their family, without support from people who have been here it becomes very challenging. We provide that kind of support to help them with basic needs," Father Lazarus said.

Of course, sharing a faith plays an outsized role in easing the transition, particularly when they are able to celebrate the Mass in a way that's familiar.

Whatever differences exist between the multiple communities at Holy Name, they also share a far more important commonality: an overriding zeal for Church teaching.

"That's the thing that unites us. Regardless of what Mass you attend, you get Catholicism," Mark Berardo said. "If you want to send your kids to CCD, and one of the African community members is teaching, you can have confidence if you're a Latin Mass goer that kid is going to get the solid Catholic faith."

Or as Father Santos explained to me: "The liturgy may have certain differences, but the faith is the same. There's no discussion about what the faith stands for, where we're going with it."

Our Lady of Guadalupe & Shrine of St. Jude

New Orleans, Louisiana

"I feel that our souls are moved to the ardor of piety by the sacred words more piously and powerfully when these words are sung than when they are not sung, and that all the affections of our soul in their variety have modes of their own in song and chant by which they are stirred up by an indescribable and secret sympathy."
Saint Augustine

In the city of New Orleans, born during an early plight, you will find the Shrine of St. Jude, where music and faith unite. Our Lady of Guadalupe, as the church is also known, taps on NOLA's music talent to praise God each Sunday morn.

New Orleans' Catholic heritage is undeniable. The city is a place where its Catholic cemeteries are destinations; its biggest celebration begins after Epiphany and ends right before Ash Wednesday; and where its football team is named after the Church's greatest servants. Heck, the counties in Louisiana are called parishes.

And with apologies to Nashville, it is also America's most important music city. New Orleans is the birthplace of jazz, the backbone of rhythm and blues and soul and a leading figure in Gospel music. If it can be sung, blown, strummed, or banged, someone in New Orleans is doing it at this very moment, from the sidewalks to the barrooms and, most definitely, to the places of worship.

At Our Lady of Guadalupe and parishes throughout the Archdiocese of New Orleans, this marriage of devout faith and glorious music is carried out every Sunday. And once a year, as was the case when I visited the parish with my entire family, that music is incorporated into the liturgy to celebrate the birth of our Savior. We attended Christmas

Mass in 2021, closing out that extraordinarily difficult year with a stirring and cathartic exultation of our Lord's nativity.

Our Lady of Guadalupe, also known as the International Shrine of St. Jude, is the oldest church building in the famed city. It was constructed in 1827 to hold funerals for victims of Yellow Fever, the first pandemic to ravage the town.

Nearly 200 years later, Our Lady of Guadalupe is home to far more joyous celebrations, Masses that lean heavily on the city's great musical traditions to glorify the Lord. The 9:30 and 11 a.m. services are the parish's jazz Masses, fitting for a church on the edge of the city's famed French Quarter.

The band, a seven-piece unit that Christmas, performed the standard nativity songs, including resounding versions of *Come All Ye Faithful* and *Joy to the World*. All of the group's songs hit the proper balance between showcasing exceptional craftsmanship while also inviting the congregation to exuberantly add their voices to the mix.

The jazz Masses are under the direction of Stephen Lee, a convert to Catholicism who has been playing and composing music for more than 40 years in a variety of settings. He first came to New Orleans in the 1970s to study music therapy at Loyola University, working in hospitals and other settings. "I started sensing a call to study church music formally," which he did at the Interdenominational Theological Center. He returned to the city in 2014, following his son to the parish then slowly involving himself in the music ministry.

Now, most of his musical attention is focused on his role at the church. "St. Jude gets my full, active, conscious participation," he explained.

Stephen Lee said his role is to invite the congregation to experience the grace of the Mass through song. "There is an element of gathering each individual into the community of faith and making something beautiful."

The nature of Our Lady of Guadalupe, Shrine of St. Jude, makes that experience even richer. The parish is a diverse mix of people, with local folks of all races intermingling with a steady stream of outsiders who descend on the city year round. "You have this home base there every Sunday who are ready to activate the spirit, but then you have these wonderful visitors who come from all over the world. Many of them are blown away because they've never experienced the liturgy the way we offer it up, not only through the music, but Father Tony and the other ministers and the ushers and hospitality ministers. There's something very dynamic about St. Jude," he said. Rev. Tony Rigoli, OMI, is pastor, continuing the century-old tradition of the Oblates ministering to the parish.

The musicians under Stephen Lee's orchestration have taken different paths to Our Lady of Guadalupe, though all are sown from the community's rich crop of musical talent.

Take Percy Williams. He has been playing professionally for decades, in recent years traveling the world as a horn player for Irma Thomas, the Soul Queen of New Orleans. Williams is a relative newcomer to church music, but is quickly discovering it is more fulfilling than what he plays on the secular circuit.

"I'm finding my satisfaction musically at the church," he said. "I feel really comfortable there."

That didn't happen immediately. Initially, he held back, not playing the "licks" he would were he blowing his horn in a club or concert. But he's overcome that, to the point where he's perfectly at home playing a solo verse of *Silent Night* on his trumpet before the vocals kicked in at the Christmas Mass.

While Percy Williams was invited to join the ministry by a previous music director, drummer King Rowe's entry was more organic. Following his completion of the RCIA program, he was determined to continue his involvement in the faith and he could think of no better way than offering his talents as a percussionist and vocalist.

"They asked, 'How do you want to serve in the church?'" he related. "Automatically my spirit knew it was going to be the music ministry. That's where my roots are."

A member of the musician's union, King Rowe plays in clubs and bars, but now infuses all of his playing with the Gospel.

When he's not playing on Sundays, he'll make time for the 7 a.m. daily Mass. He appreciates the opportunity to simply sit quietly in the pew, taking a break from the challenge that Mass playing demands, when thoughtful contemplation and prayer collide with concerns over missing a cue.

For Kesha McKey, another vocalist at the jazz Mass, singing provides her a more complete Mass experience. "It's like giving yourself permission to fully open yourself to the Spirit coming in," she explained. "Getting up and being a part of the ministry is like, 'Use me Lord.'"

A lifelong Catholic, Kesha McKey was initially just a parishioner at Our Lady of Guadalupe, but was always interested in joining the music ministry. A breast cancer diagnosis was the impetus she needed to follow through. "It was time for me to do this," she said. "I needed it for my soul."

Fellow vocalist William Willoughby began his participation in the music ministry slowly, coming in on invitations from time to time in the mid 2010s. The transition to church music was an easy one for William, who said, "Anywhere you can put music, I'm there."

And one of the places you're going to find the best music is in the city's panoply of churches, both Catholic and Protestant. "New Orleans is a real gumbo. If you go in one part of town, it's a little different than another. But there is respect for everybody and their own music," he said.

That varied musical flavor is even present within the parish. The 6 p.m. Sunday Mass, also guided by Stephen Lee, is the Gospel Choir, with singers no less enthusiastic though not as versed in singing harmonies.

Before Stephen Lee assumes his responsibilities, the Saturday vigil and Sunday 7 a.m. Mass, are under the direction of Shirley Stewart, a fixture at Our Lady of Guadalupe for more than 50 years. She sings a range of traditional church songs with a pianist accompanying her.

Shirley Stewart's musical CV is extraordinary, covering both the secular and spiritual sides of song. She has performed with the New Orleans Opera since 1974 and sang in the choir at Saint John Paul II's visit to the city in 1989. She's even married the two traditions, lending her voice to gospel legend Mahalia Jackson's funeral in 1971 and performing *I Want Jesus to Walk With Me* on popular musician Aaron Neville's album, Midnight at St. Jude's, recorded right there at 411 North Rampart.

"Being in church music has allowed me to do things I never thought possible," she said, reciting experiences singing around the country as well as at Fatima and Lourdes. And after singing for him when he came to New Orleans, she met the late pope on a subsequent visit to Rome. "How many people can say they sang for and talked with a saint?" she asked. "You can't beat God."

Every weekend, Shirley Stewart is doing her part to serve the Lord. For her, one of the most important aspects of the role of director involves selecting the proper music for each Mass. "Every time I go to select a piece, I'm looking at those readings. If you're doing something that has nothing to do with the sermon and no connection to the theme of the Mass, what's the point? This is not a concert," she argued. Rather, it's an integral part of the liturgy, ideally one that invites the entire congregation to join in.

While Shirley Stewart and Stephen Lee's musical styles differ, they see their roles similarly.

"The whole idea is to enhance the prayer life," Shirley Stewart said. "This is a part of my prayer life that I hope to transfer to them."

He concurred. "We are to engage, to enliven, to enable the prayer of the assembly through song, through instrumental music as well as vocal music. Whether it's using contemplative music or celebratory music, it's done to enrich the prayer."

For all of the musicians, one idea resonates over and over, the beat that compels them to perform each and every Mass. It was in a message given to Percy Williams in his early days at Our Lady of Guadalupe, at a time when he was struggling to find his place in the ministry.

"I told the choir director at the time that I was having a hard time expressing myself through the music," he recalled. And she responded flatly, "'That's the gift that was given to you. Just play.'"

By tapping into those considerable gifts, each member of the music ministry at Our Lady of Guadalupe, Shrine of St. Jude, is capable of delivering a hymn of joy every weekend.

St. Francis of Assisi Mission

Yellowstone National Park, Wyoming

"I want creation to penetrate you with so much admiration that wherever you go, the least plant may bring you clear remembrance of the Creator. A single plant, a blade of grass, or one speck of dust is sufficient to occupy all your intelligence in beholding the art with which it has been made."
Saint Basil

MAN HAS CONSTRUCTED SOME GLORIOUS SPACES TO WORSHIP THE Lord. Notre-Dame in Paris, St. Patrick's Cathedral in New York, Las Lajas Sanctuary in Colombia, and so many more are marvelous feats of architecture and artistry, amazing locations in which men and women come together to pray.

Yet, for all of our advancements in design and engineering, none of our human-made creations will ever match those of the Creator. And His work is rarely as breathtaking as what's found in Yellowstone National Park, which makes it a spectacular place to enjoy a Sunday Mass.

But don't take my word for it. Listen to Rev. Rick Malloy, S.J. The Philadelphia-born Jesuit was serving at the St. Stephens Indian Mission at the Wind River Reservation when he filled in for the first time at Yellowstone in the early 2000s. Captivated, he made it clear if the park's summer priest position ever opened up, he was interested in filling it.

"Around Dec. 27-28, I got the greatest Christmas present ever. Rev. Vernon Clark (the now-retired priest from St. Anthony of Padua in Cody, Wyoming), called and asked if I could come do it. I've been out there ever since."

For 15 years, Father Rick has been leaving the East Coast to venture to Wyoming's northwest corner for the summer months. The attraction of the position is the warm and generous people of Cody and the park community combined with Yellowstone's natural beauty. Its unmatched fishing opportunities are also a lure to the avid angler. "The last time Jesus was here, he appeared to a bunch of guys on a fishing trip. You can look it up," he said, pointing to John 21.

Masses at America's First National Park have been offered for almost 100 years, all of them through the commitment of St. Anthony of Padua, the not-really-nearby parish in Cody. It is approximately two hours from Cody to the park, which makes the church's St. Francis of Assisi Mission an invaluable resource for all who populate Yellowstone during its busy season.

During the summer months, there are four separate places where Mass is offered at Yellowstone, two indoors, two outside. On Saturday afternoons, a vigil Mass is conducted at the Canyon Outdoor Amphitheater, usually said by Rev. Charles Heston Joseph, who comes up from St. Anthony of Padua while Father Malloy takes his place in Cody. Vigil Mass attendance is often the largest, drawing 40 to 60 parishioners on any given Saturday.

Father Heston, who became pastor at St. Anthony upon Father Clark's retirement in 2021, enjoys the opportunity to lead Mass at the park for a variety of reasons, including the opportunity to meet people from around the country and the chance to worship in a setting built by God Himself.

But the primary appeal is the faith of the parishioners who take time off from their holiday to make time for Christ. "Even on vacation, the spiritual thirst people have makes me happy," he said.

On Sundays, there's a 9 a.m. Mass at the Old Faithful Lodge, offered in the employee recreation area. On the morning I was there, Mass kicked off approximately 15 minutes after nearby Old Faithful's most recent release. Each Mass attracts a mix of tourists and park hands, almost all of whom have come to this remote area of Wyoming from somewhere else. Worshippers at the 9 a.m. Mass near Old Faithful included the visiting Turner family, where mom and dad were accompanied by their two daughters, the Young Faithful.

Kyle Turner, who works as director of university ministry at Regis University, a Jesuit school in Denver, said the family always tries to carve out time for Mass when on the road. "We do try to seek out a liturgy somewhere close. If we're not able, we'll often watch a livestream or do a small Liturgy of the Word ourselves."

Upon arrival at Yellowstone, he was delighted to discover Mass being offered at the park, particularly when he realized its location at the Old Faithful Lodge was "literally across the geyser from where we were staying."

Next up on the Sunday schedule is the 11 a.m. service at the Lake Lodge, with beautiful Yellowstone Lake and other examples of God's creation serving as a chronic source of distraction. A lone bison caught wandering eyes during my Sunday visit.

Park worker Julia Devalk tries, though not always successfully, to save her appreciation of the environment until after the service has concluded. "It's a beautiful moment to walk out of Mass and you're like, 'there's the lake and there's the mountains.' It's gorgeous."

Sue Llibre was there to greet the parishioners at the Lake Lodge, a duty her engaging personality is tailor-made for. For her, the casual/not casual nature of the people who worship at the park is what stands out.

On the one hand, the uniform for all of the Masses at Yellowstone tends toward T-shirts, shorts, and sandals rather than button-downed shirts and dresses, an inevitable byproduct of a congregation filled with vacationers and park workers. However, these are also serious Catholics, men and women who don't believe a week off from work provides a dispensation from our weekly obligation to the faith.

"The people who show up went out of their way to stop their adventure to attend Mass and be spiritually lifted and thank God for being here," she said. The Llibres, Sue and John, have been spending summers at Yellowstone for five years, with John serving as one of the captains on the Lake Queen boat. The Florida couple finds this part of the country so appealing they've purchased a second home in the area.

The final weekend Mass is offered back outside at the Bridge Bay Amphitheater. Attendance varies considerably here, depending on the number of campers staying in that section of the park on a given weekend. The flooding that ravaged parts of Yellowstone in early spring spared all of the areas where Mass is said, though it seems to have dampened overall attendance levels for part of the summer of 2022.

Because people are coming from all over and resources are limited, Masses follow a simple formula. Volunteers are solicited to handle readings. The same three songs are sung, typically acapella, though a pianist accompanied the Mass at the Lake Lodge I attended. *Here I am Lord*, *Amazing Grace*, and, fitting for the surroundings, *America the Beautiful* are rendered. These are standards known to most everyone, at least the U.S.-born guests. Father Rick insists the final song is performed at the Yellowstone Mass like nowhere else.

Irene Jervis was spending her first summer in Yellowstone when we met. The retired nurse sold her home in Upstate New York and is now traveling the country in a camper, bouncing from park to park. She works 32 hours per week at Yellowstone, which gives her time to pursue hiking and photography, two of her favorite pastimes. She's also able to attend Mass regularly.

Finding a new place to worship has been a common occurrence for her, having spent the last 19 years of her career as a traveling nurse. Being Catholic helps in that regard. "One of the best advantages of being Catholic is you don't have to find a church to go to. It's relatively easy," Irene Jervis said. "I've met other nurses who take forever to figure out where they were going to go to church on Sundays."

Julia Devalk is another park employee who makes sure to reserve time each week for Mass. A recent graduate of the University of Iowa, the existence of the Saint Francis of Assisi Mission helped tilt the scales toward Yellowstone when she was choosing a summer work location. Other parks, such as Crater Lake in Oregon, require a two-hour drive to the nearest Catholic Mass. "There are some sites where the distance makes it so much more difficult, especially with not knowing what my weekend schedule is going to be. My mom found there was Mass in the park, and I was like, 'Perfect.'"

For years, the Morris family was helping make the experience for Yellowstone Mass goers even more perfect. The couple, Pat and George, became fast friends with Father Rick through their mutual East Coast roots and the passion for fishing George and Father Rick share. Soon, they began joining him on his weekend treks to Yellowstone, where Father Rick provides the Eucharist and the Morrises deliver a more secular kind of feast.

For years, after helping Father Rick set up the altar and benches for Mass, usually at the Lake Lodge, the couple would supply food for a post-Mass picnic with the staff members and visitors who chose to stick around. "Everybody loves everybody at these Masses. Nobody is shy. Father starts the Mass by asking people where they've come from and that kind of breaks the ice and gets everybody into that community-type feeling," said Pat Morris.

Even though there are opportunities for Mass four times a weekend at Yellowstone, that doesn't completely prevent lapses. Well-intentioned tourists will occasionally misjudge the length of time it takes to get around the park or find themselves stuck in a "buffalo jam" that snarls traffic. Father Rick keeps extra consecrated hosts for that family of four who comes charging up to him after Mass has concluded.

And for full-time employees such as Julie Devalk, the Masses may not always fit neatly into her weekend-heavy work schedule. Before arriving at the park, she shared her worries about that possibility with her uncles, both of them priests. They suggested she take in a weekday Mass or watch a Sunday Mass online to fulfill her obligation. And then they provided her with a most salient piece of advice.

"You're in some of the most beautiful areas on earth," she was told. "Just say a Rosary and appreciate it."

Yellowstone is indeed a perfect location for quiet or prayerful reflection, a feeling that permeates the park. When I was traveled across it, I heard no yelling at Yellowstone. The hundreds of onlookers did not erupt when Old Faithful did. Rather, they watched in muted appreciation. They spoke infrequently and when they did it was mostly in hushed voices.

It was as if we were in a cathedral.

Ellsworth Air Force Base

Box Elder, South Dakota

"God sends us friends to be our firm support in the whirlpool of struggle. In the company of friends we will find strength to attain our sublime ideal."
Saint Maximilian Kolbe

IN THE SPRING OF 1996, DAVID BUTLER AND HIS WIFE WERE HAVING some marital problems, the kind common to many young couples. But unlike most spouses, David Butler was preparing to leave home, a requirement of his position as an enlisted man in the United States Air Force.

Before he left, wife Tammy was determined to send him off with protection, the minor squabbles not affecting the love and concern she had for her spouse. She had a St. Christopher's medal for David, a convert to the Catholic faith, and drove off the base in New Mexico into town to have it properly blessed by a local priest.

He put that medal on ahead of his deployment to Saudi Arabia. And it was that medal he credits for keeping him safe on June 25, when a truck bomb planted by Hezbollah forces detonated outside Khobar Towers, killing 19 members of the United States Air Force's 440th Wing and injuring 498 air personnel and civilians. The Air Force had been using the facility as living quarters during Operation Southern Watch.

"If I had been one place or another, it would have been so much worse. I swear that medal she gave me put me in the right place I needed to be," said David Butler, who 25 years later, is still overcome with emotion at the memory. "That was a powerful moment for me."

For the Catholic men and women of the Armed Forces, those potent occurrences are plentiful, an inevitable consequence of routinely putting oneself in harm's way in defense of the country. And parish communities such as the one I visited at Ellsworth Air Force Base play an instrumental role in supporting and complementing that service. David Butler is perfect example of that.

Though he is long retired from active duty in the Air Force, his commitment to his country has never wavered. He currently serves in the family advocacy program at Ellsworth, working with active duty airmen and airwomen and their families on the domestic violence problems that are just as common to military families as they are in the civilian world.

As with the case for those who pursue religious life, David Butler felt called to return to the base to help airmen and airwomen navigate the unique circumstances of military existence. "It's good to help these young kids. You've been through this stuff, you probably know what you're talking about," he reasoned.

Bernie McFarling is in a similar position. A few years back, she had been serving in active duty with her husband, a fellow service member. They, along with their two daughters, had just located to a base in Okinawa, Japan, when she pursued and was offered a position as a sexual assault response coordinator with the Air Force. Hoping for somewhere warm to be assigned, the McFarling family instead was sent to Ellsworth.

Hers is a particularly challenging position, dealing with one of the worst crimes that happen on a base, a role that often leaves her emotionally spent. In 2020, during the height of the pandemic, she was also struggling with the racial upheaval in the United States that followed the murder of George Floyd in neighboring Minnesota. The combination of events left her temporarily drifting from the Church. "Because I was the only person who looked like me, I felt like nobody could understand what it's like to be me and my family," she explained.

But, as she's experienced many times, the faith intervened at the most opportune time. As she was home lamenting her withdrawal from participation in religious life, Rev. Gerry McManus, pastor at the base, knocked on her door, wondering about her absence.

"We talked, and I felt like he was really trying to understand. I felt a true effort on his part," she said.

She was at Mass the next day, and has been a regular ever since. "I don't think I would have lasted in this job, hearing the things that have happened to other people, without being able to come here and get support," she admitted.

Father McManus has been dealing with these types of situations for much of his life as a priest. Ordained at his home in Pennsylvania, he first served with reserve units before going on active duty in 1992, receiving five different deployments until his retirement in 2015. That retirement coincided with the departure of the priest serving Ellsworth.

If no active duty chaplains can be found, a base hires a civilian priest to provide the ministry, which is how Father McManus wound up working in Box Elder. "I'm no longer a chaplain. I'm a contract priest," he explained.

He said many who serve as chaplains describe their work as a "vocation within a vocation." It is not a job for every priest, as the circumstances surrounding parish life are so different.

One aspect of this double-vocation truly distinguishes chaplains from their peers in the neighborhood parish world. "In general, they're not unlike their civilian counterparts, but there is a whole other layer of responsibilities, of requirements, that are placed on them, because they raise their right hand and pledge to support the Constitution," Father McManus said.

On the positive side, the chaplain doesn't have to worry about how he's going to afford to replace the air conditioning unit that just blew out or what to do about the custodian who isn't getting the job done. The government owns the worship space and everything around it. That leads to such unique conditions as the existence of a cover for the Cross, or having the statues built on a swivel. Those are both features at the Black Hills Chapel, necessary oddities since the worship space is not limited to Catholic services. Each base chapel, as well as all Navy ships, must also have a place for a Blessed Sacrament. "That must be there, somewhere in the chapel, and it cannot have a dual purpose," Father McManus said.

On the other hand, the base chaplain is dealing with a unique parish community. It's a place where the wide-eyed country kid from Mississippi comes together with a fast-talking city kid, both of whom may be getting their first taste of freedom. It's a closed society unlike that which is found anywhere else.

But that closed society has its benefits. The communities that develop around the parish become true families, a development that occurs whether the base is located in small-town South Dakota or in a major city overseas.

"We share two bonds, our faith and our military background," said Irene Skroch, who lost her airman husband several years earlier but retains her bond with the Ellsworth parish community. "The things that everybody has to go through – the separations and all that. It's that common support you can give, even if it's just listening."

And sometimes it's more than that. In his long Air Force career, one that took him all over the world, Carl Landreneau and wife Sarah spent many a Sunday or holiday inviting single men and women, or even young couples, to join them for dinner after Mass. "We're away from home, they're away from home. We're away from our extended families. We can be miserable apart or we can come together."

Dennis Wier comes together with the community on weekdays, returning to his home parish of St. Patrick's in Wall, S.D. on weekends. He spent 27 years on active duty and now works as support coordinator for the base, overseeing all of the various helping agencies, such as the ones David Butler and Bernie McFarling manage. "My friends are jealous because I get the blessing of coming to Mass every day of the week," he said. "The times we haven't had a priest, you start to realize how it becomes a habit, that half-hour reprieve."

When the parish is between priests, which happens with greater frequency on bases, the Catholic community is even more dependent on Deacon Raul Daniel. The deacon's duties include overseeing the religious education program and serving as community coordinator, handling many administrative responsibilities. He joined the parish after first serving at the Cathedral of Our Lady of Perpetual Help in Rapid City. He's grateful that his service took him 12 miles east.

"This is where I got a chance to really know people. It's been a much more rewarding experience within diaconate life than it had been at the Cathedral," he said. "I don't want to speak ill of the Cathedral, but it was just so big. It's like the difference between if you want to live in New York City or Rapid City."

While small, Western South Dakota can be every bit as unfamiliar as any big city. In early 2021, Chris Soliz was assigned to Ellsworth, his first after completing basic training. A native of Corpus Christi, Texas, Soliz found himself 1,500 miles away, far removed from the family and friends he'd grown up with. Finding a faith home was crucial to navigating this new experience. "In the Church, I feel a little piece of home," he said. "After a stressful week, I just sit back and say, 'I can't wait for Sunday. That's the part where I feel really comfortable.'"

Unlike most jobs, serving in any branch in the military is a 24-hour commitment. When I'm not at work, I'm just a husband and a father. But being an airman or airwoman isn't a punch-the-clock occupation. Chris Soliz understands that, and calls on his faith to assist him in his perpetual state of service.

"When you're in the military, 100 percent of the time you're an ambassador of the Air Force. How you portray yourself, how you walk, how you talk, how you do your job really reflects the Air Force," he said. "So using my faith, what I mainly do, every time I try to pray for me to be the best I can be."

Faith and prayer carry these men and women long after their time in the Air Force has formally ended. Like many retired military personnel, Doug Heiser followed up active duty life by taking a job with a military-adjacent operation, in his case a contractor doing reconstruction in war-ravaged Liberia.

Doug Heiser's role in the company was installing generators at a hospital built to replace the one destroyed through the nation's bloody civil war. Soon after the main generator was installed, the engine blew, resulting in the smaller generator being forced to handle all the power needs for the lone healthcare facility in the area. Fixes for problems such as this, in places such as Liberia, are not as easy as they would be back home. For more than a year, the hospital had to rely on the smaller generator to keep the lifesaving equipment running while the workers begged for the necessary replacement parts.

Every night for a year, Doug Heiser prayed the lights would stay on. When the new generator finally arrived, he took apart the old machine that had been working overtime for some desperately needed service.

"There was just bare wire. It shouldn't have been running" he said, choking back tears at the memory. "Miracles happen."

Holy Trinity

Washington, D.C.

"Justice, and only justice, you shall pursue, that you may live and possess the land which the Lord your God is giving you."
Deuteronomy 16:19-21

Holy Trinity was not among the parishes that were traumatized by the clergy abuse scandals that did so much damage to the Church. But the parishioners of the comfortable Washington, D.C. parish still wanted to be part of the solution.

"If not us, who?" asks Chris Hannigan, president of the parish council. "It wasn't our priests; this is a systemic problem. But if a parish with these kinds of resources, with this kind of intellectual and political firepower is not part of the response, then who is going to be?"

Holy Trinity, a Jesuit parish in the Georgetown section of the nation's capital, has long been linked with America's most prominent leaders and its history. It's original chapel, still standing, was the site for the first Catholic Mass in the District of Columbia. Abraham Lincoln attended a funeral there and the church was used as a hospital during the Civil War. The nation's first Catholic president attended his final Mass there before his assassination.

Being so persistently connected to history made the parish uniquely well suited to address the issue, which hit closer to home in 2018 when former Archbishop Theodore McCarrick was first removed from public ministry, then removed from the priesthood seven months later.

"For a lot of our parishioners, there was shock and disgust with first the Pennsylvania grand jury report, then the McCarrick report and the public revelation of allegations against then-Cardinal Ted McCarrick," recalled Rev. C. Kevin Gillespie, S.J. Though the parish hadn't been a location where abuse had taken place, Holy Trinity and its parishioners had worked closely with the defrocked McCarrick.

Rather than recoil from the revelations, or simply be privately thankful the horrific acts had all taken place elsewhere, the parish community dived headlong into the issue. To do so, the parish called on the Jesuit teaching at the heart of life at Holy Trinity.

Among the many pursuits ongoing at Holy Trinity is a Restorative Justice ministry. The ministry is headed up by a group of parishioners who have been educated through both secular and Catholic-affiliated groups on corrective measures.

The idea behind Restorative Justice is that both those who do harm, and those who have bene harmed, come together for dialogue and remediation, and healing emerges from the process. In the traditional application of Restorative Justice, it would bring together a perpetrator and a victim. Here, it was modified to simply invite parishioners to come and respond to the crisis "in both an emotional and spiritual sense," said Chris Hannigan.

Holy Trinity's efforts were set off by the release of the original grand jury report from Pennsylvania. The parish scheduled two listening sessions, or circles, to address the topic. The plan called for capping registration at 25 people per session, but more than 70 parishioners signed up for the initial sessions, demonstrating the demand for participation was even greater than imagined. Ultimately, Holy Trinity conducted more than two dozen circles, giving voice to victims of abuse at some point as well as parishioners who simply wanted to express their feelings or offer their suggestions to ensure the Church never experiences anything like this again. Though the parish itself escaped the scandals, some of the parishioners at Holy Trinity were victims of sexual abuse, including at the hands of church employees and even priests at other parishes.

"It was very powerful stuff," Chris Hannigan recalled. "People were hurt, angry, disgusted."

It was almost exclusively a laity-driven endeavor, with groups occasionally broken down into like segments, such as one for parents of Holy Trinity Elementary School and another for the parish's men's group.

A few of the sessions were attended by priests of the parish or from outside, but when they participated, they maintained a low profile. "People feel more comfortable expressing what their responses are, particularly to the clerical involvement in all of this, if there's not a collar in the room," Chris Hannigan explained.

The only person of authority in the sessions was a trained facilitator from the Restorative Justice ministry, known as a circle keeper, whose function is limited to keeping the sessions flowing.

That so much of the effort was driven by the parishioners was entirely consistent with a Jesuit parish, said Father Gillespie. "We're unique in training lay people to give spiritual direction."

When the sessions were finished, the Holy Trinity staff transcribed and anonymized the recordings, organizing and cataloguing them into different categories. The complete report of the sessions was posted to the parish's website. Holy Trinity compiled more than 60 pages of comments, thoughts and recommendations from the attendees at the sessions, suggestions that covered the emotional and spiritual side to specific actions that should be taken.

After publishing the initial responses from the various circles held, the parish scheduled a large public gathering to take those various concerns and recommendations and turn them into concrete action. They called this phase the Season of Discernment, one founded in the Ignatian tradition that examines how the spirits are moving within us. "A lot of folks, when they heard the term 'discernment,' their minds go with the idea that this is about thoughts and prayers. But action is part of the discernment process," Chris Hanigan said.

Ultimately, these forums led to the creation of multiple measures that were required to both correct the problems of the past and ensure the safety of the future generations of Catholics. The items were separated into various buckets, with one focusing on the structure and organization of the church, another on the role of the laity, a third on support for survivors and families, and so on. All this was undertaken with the understanding that as "passionately as people felt, they weren't necessarily educated enough to advocate for best practices in child protection," he said, noting that improvements in "self-education" were required to fill those gaps.

As with any effort, the initial results were mixed, with some successes and other areas where the push fizzled out. However, the subsequent release of the McCarrick report served to re-energize the parish's work.

With ample material already compiled in its earlier phases, the parish began working with various agencies, tapping resources at nearby Georgetown University and meeting frequently with the archdiocese to advise on many of their finding and recommendations. Again, that theirs is a parish of well-connected people in the nation's capital doesn't hurt.

Hanigan isn't certain how much influence they ultimately had on the archdiocese and beyond, given other groups were also serving as pressure points in the push for change. But he knows Holy Trinity's work was successful in another regard. He would routinely receive calls and emails from other parishes around the country, seeking their findings and their materials because nothing like that was taking place in their dioceses.

"If the correspondence I got is any indication, maybe we were able to set off a bunch of little sparks in places that maybe don't have the resources we do," he said. "Our efforts did a lot to inspire and motivate people in other parishes."

Additionally, the parish is now much more educated on both how church governance works and about proper child protective measures than it was two years prior. "We led them through an exercise of discernment. We went through the cycle, from experiencing consolations and desolations, then a time for action and a time for reflection," he said. "And now we have a new child protection policy that we've implemented, which our research has shown that a lot of what we were doing was already best practices."

The effort on behalf of the victims of sexual abuse is just one example of Holy Trinity's commitment to serving those in need. It has numerous ministries reaching out to and serving all of the needs of the nation's, and the world's, vulnerable people, from aiding the impoverished in the nation's capital to an extensive LGBTQIA+ ministry. Yes, the parish has occasionally been questioned by the archdiocese for being "too liberal."

Most recently, in the wake of the coronavirus, the parish created Cura Virtualis, a separate page on its website devoted to "Virtual care of the whole person at Holy Trinity." The idea was to develop a digital space for the parish to come together when such physical opportunities were off limits.

"Celebrating the Eucharist is the source and summit of all we do, and suspending Masses was the most difficult decision for us to make. But perhaps this time of crisis may also be a period of *Kairos* – this time can be sacred, whereby new revelations of God's providential care for the entire human and global family may be discerned and discovered," the page informs.

This ongoing push to innovate in the ways it serves the community, and beyond, has attracted many Catholics in the D.C. area, men and women who share some of the parish's priorities and have found their way to the Georgetown area. Several parishioners I spoke with after Mass acknowledged they had come to Holy Trinity from elsewhere in the Beltway, drawn by the parish's efforts on social justice and community outreach.

It even lures people to the faith itself. Peggy Asante-Spitzer had extensive experience with the Church growing up, attending Catholic universities for both her undergraduate and graduate degrees. But she and her husband initially worshipped at a non-denominational Christian church after getting married. However, that church's seeming indifference to the world outside its walls, particularly any events taking place beyond the United States, had the couple looking for a parish that instilled in their young children the concern for the wellbeing of all the planet's inhabitants. They knew those values were shared at Holy Trinity.

And on very rare occasions, the pull to Holy Trinity comes in reverse. Linda Wiessler-Hughes and her family were looking for a new church home when they attended one Sunday Mass at Holy Trinity. During the service, their son blurted out, "Can this be our church?"

I think all parents can agree on this: If a 7-year-old boy ever stakes a claim on a parish he wants to call home, that's the next best thing to a command from God Himself.

They've been parishioners ever since.

St. John the Baptist

Laughlin, Nevada

"I will go anywhere and do anything in order to communicate the love of Jesus to those who do not know him or have forgotten him."
Saint Francis Xavier Cabrini

A WRONG TURN ON THE WAY TO THE DOWNTOWN HOME OF Laughlin's St. John the Baptist will take you to the dazzling lights, pinging slot machines, boisterous craps tables, and the rest of the sensory overload that is a Nevada casino. No, you want the slightly more subdued Don's Celebrity Theatre, otherwise home to tribute bands and touring comics. This will not be an ordinary Sunday. St. John the Baptist is no ordinary Catholic parish.

The parish was born in the early 1990s, when local Catholics convinced the Diocese of Las Vegas to grant them a parish to call home. The nearest Catholic Church in the state was 80 miles away, though there were closer options in Bullhead City, Ariz., across the river, or Needles, Calif., a little farther south.

Laughlin sits astride the Colorado River in a sliver of land between Northwestern Arizona and Southeastern California. Until the 2000s, there wasn't even much of a Laughlin in Laughlin, the town not a lot more than a way station for gas and gambling. Even after its boomtown phase, its population still doesn't dent five digits. But the community wanted a Catholic Church, even if it had no place to say Mass. The bishop agreed, sending Rev. John McShane to establish the church in the southern outpost. And the town's primary industry was there to provide a home.

The parish initially celebrated Mass at Sam's Town Gold River Casino, then moved to Riverside Casino in 1996. Holding Mass at these facilities made sense, and still does, as most of the Catholics in

Laughlin on any given weekend will be found in one of those river-hugging gaming palaces.

"A lot of people came to Laughlin on bus trips or flew in on junkets, so they didn't have cars. If they were anywhere in one of the casinos they maybe couldn't get the five miles up to church," said Rev. Charlie Urnick, the pastor at St. John the Baptist.

Thus, even after the parish's growth led to the construction of its own church building in 2003, the Masses at Riverside remained. Each weekend, the parish conducts two Masses at the parish church, and three others at Riverside Casino, where Father Charlie offers Communion in front of the theater stage and poker chips are among the donations found in the collection box.

Attending Mass in a casino is undoubtedly uncommon, and can take some getting used to.

"I wondered, 'Is this really a church?'" said Jo Anne Saunders. "But the minute you walk in, despite the stage, the heavy curtain, the heavy props they might set up, they have the altar set up right in front of the Mass and you know you're in God's house. There is no doubt."

"I was hesitant to go to Mass because it was in a casino. But for some reason, I was there, it was a Saturday and I went. It was the best Mass I'd ever been to in my life," said Ed Fryke. "You know how when you fall in love with something, you know right away it's a good thing. That's how I felt."

Father Charlie feels equally comfortable in either location, whether he's worshipping beneath the cross at the parish church or standing before a giant Elvis poster at the casino. "I have to tell people, we're here to worship The King, not that King," he joked.

Like virtually everyone at St. John the Baptist, Father Charlie is from somewhere else. "I haven't met a native Nevadan," said parishioner Tony Arcuri, himself a transplant from South Carolina who has been a member of the parish since 2019. The parishioners at St. John the Baptist are a lively mix of snowbirds, retirees, travelers, and others who have found themselves in what Father Charlie regularly refers to as "paradise."

Father Charlie was born and raised on the other side of the country, in New Jersey, but the desert was never far from his mind. He and his mother made regular trips to Las Vegas, and occasional detours to Laughlin, where he stayed and prayed with Father McShane.

He had long planned to retire to Nevada, but in 2008 he realized he didn't want to wait. He would rather make the move to the desert when he was still a working priest, finding a parish out west to serve. He sold the archbishop in Newark on his idea, then received similar approval from the bishop of Las Vegas.

Three weeks before his departure from the Garden State, Father Charlie got the word: he would be assigned to Laughlin, the wonderful little town he'd first visited in 1991 when local Catholics were in the process of collecting signatures for the creation of their own parish. "I didn't know it would be available," he recalled. "I said 'I would love Laughlin.'"

And Laughlin loves him back.

"He's been a Godsend for everybody here. Everybody who has a friend who has fallen away, they say, 'Go listen to Father Charlie, it will bring you back,'" said parishioner Bobbie Kitto. "He makes you want to be there."

"Father Charlie makes it stand out. I'm a lifelong Catholic. I've been in nine parishes. This guy is probably the best pastor I've ever been associated with," said Tony Arcuri.

The love extends beyond the parish itself to the entire community. For Laughlin, Father Charlie is one part spiritual leader, one part cheerleader. No one in the community has done more for the Food Bank than he has. And when a weekend gathering of motorcyclists hits town, Father Charlie will don the fake tattoo arm sleeves and go mingle with the bikers. He feels at home with everyone and makes everyone feel at home.

"He's been the Man of the Year in Laughlin, at least once, and nominated three or four times" said parishioner Tom Strauss. "He's the key that holds everything together."

The kindly priest had a rich life even before arriving in Nevada. He served in the Air Force and worked as a chaplain on a cruise ship, among other adventures. But the desert kept calling him westward.

Interestingly, it was not the roulette wheels or craps tables that kept Father Charlie coming back to Sin City. Nor was it, obviously, the sin.

Rather, it was Father Charlie's interest in one of the Strip's longtime sideline attractions – magic. Father Charlie would come out for shows and immerse himself in the world of magic and its practitioners. Not as a performer; rather as simply an admirer of the craft. "I'm a great audience member. But if you watched me, you would know I'm not good at misdirecting people."

In some ways, he sells himself short. For Father Charlie is inherently good at an entirely different kind of sleight of hand. At the ambo, he will dazzle his parishioners with amusing anecdotes, fascinating asides, and even the occasional prop. His penchant for penguins is known across the parish. With Father Charlie delivering the homily, parishioners' eyes and ears at St. John the Baptist are routinely directed elsewhere, captivated by his cheerful manner and anything-goes approach.

And then, POOF, Father Charlie will strike you with the Word of God. He has found his own brand of prestidigitation – driving home Christ's enduring message, regardless of whether you were ready for it.

"When Father Charlie talks to you, he doesn't start with the message. He starts out with how his weekend was, then all of a sudden he hits you with the Gospel message. You don't see it coming," said Bobbie Kitto.

"He does have good homilies, but sometimes he's very entertaining. He's entertaining you before he gets to the real Gospel stuff," said Linda Wisch.

"Father Charlie has a way of bringing his message every week into our daily lives. He's able to make us relate to the message to what we live, rather than just preaching," added Lori Fonzi, who has been attending St. John the Baptist with husband Ron since 2007.

Though Masses continues to be held at the casino, and likely always will, the parish is steadily building a wonderful community up the hill, where many of the year-round residents worship.

"The actual church is beautiful. It's small but it's very beautiful," said Melissa LaCaze of the parish church that overlooks the river. "It's not like a cathedral, where you get the overwhelming awe. But it's sweet. You feel really close to God when you go into that church."

And St. John the Baptist is continuing to expand there, trying to build that full parish community. On the weekend I attended Masses in both venues, the parish dedicated the new Garcés Center, a large parish hall where meetings and other events will be held. It was clearly a passion project for Father Charlie in more ways than one.

The building is the first in Nevada named after Francisco Garcés, the first priest to visit Nevada. The Spanish Franciscan friar and explorer ventured into Laughlin in 1776, crossing the river he gave name to in the process. Five years later, he and three fellow friars were martyred in an uprising involving Native Americans, a tragic end given his success establishing warm relations with many of the indigenous peoples of the West.

Father Charlie has become an avid student of Father Garcés's life since following his footsteps to Laughlin. The reverend believes Father Garcés's martyrdom makes him a strong candidate for canonization and is interested in aiding any effort. Beyond that, his research into the life of the Spanish Franciscan simply suggests the pair would have become fast friends had they not been separated by 200-plus years of existence. "The more I read about him, the more I got interested. He liked chocolate, he loved the Native ceremonies. He liked being out with people. I would have enjoyed hanging out with him."

This connection to Nevada's first Catholic is just one more thing that keeps Father Charlie tethered to Laughlin, his paradise before Paradise.

St. Ann

Charlotte, North Carolina

"The important thing is to do charity, not to talk about charity. We must understand the work with very poor people as God's chosen mission."
Saint Dulce of the Poor

ST. ANN ON CHARLOTTE'S SOUTH SIDE HAS UNDERGONE NUMEROUS transformations in the course of its 65 years. But the church found itself by embracing the traditional.

Today, St. Ann is a church that's not huge in terms of the number of families, but makes up for it in the size of the families who belong. The parish is home to a preponderance of large families, with minors making up 31 percent of the congregation. The parish has the highest average family size in the Diocese of Charlotte.

At any given time, there are dozens of pregnant mothers among the congregation, enough so that when one expectant mom went into labor during a Mass, it was more of an inevitability than a surprise.

Founded in 1955, St. Ann was nearly an afterthought to the school being designed around it. The perception the parish was merely a sidekick to the school suffered no penalty when, during construction of the planned church building, the parish was split in half, with a mission parish founded three miles away. For years, the parish languished financially. And aesthetically.

At its founding, a lower church was built, with plans to construct a larger upper worship space above it. Funds were raised and drawings made, but the split cut off the collections, and the upper church went unbuilt. The end result was a building that was called, even by those who worshipped inside it, "the ugliest church in Charlotte."

"For the longest time, we were known as the basement church," said longtime parishioner Jeff Rothe, who has chronicled the history of St. Ann in several photo directories.

The halfway nature of the church was everywhere. An impressive entranceway led nowhere. To enter the church, you had to go around back and walk down into the low-ceilinged basement.

Over the years, capital campaigns to erase the unfished nature of the church were launched under the direction of the presiding priest. But just as headway was being made and monies being pledged, the former pastor would be replaced by a priest with an entirely different vision, dooming the newest iteration to the same fate as the last. The political and social changes that characterized the latter half of the 20th century also played out at St. Ann, ultimately resulting in a stagnation of the parish's growth.

That changed with Rev. Timothy Reid. The pastor of St. Ann, now in his 14th year, set the one-time "liberal" parish on a more traditional path, in all fashions.

"We've had some very liberal pastors and more conservative pastors, and Father Reid is by far the most conservative pastor we've had. I know there are a lot of people who left because of him, but even more have come because he speaks the truth," Jeff Rothe said. "It's created a parish of really strong believers in the Catholic faith, and created a community of people strong in faith and the nuclear family."

Among the developments included the offering of the Latin Mass on top of the Novus Ordo liturgies. It has led to a vibrant liturgical and musical life in the parish, Father Reid said.

Though the extraordinary form is only used in one of the four weekend Masses at St. Ann, the influence is felt throughout the parish. St. Ann is comfortable using Latin in any service, is partial to Gregorian chant and restricts altar service to boys – the girls have a separate ministry.

But the adoption of the traditional has led beyond the liturgical into the architectural. The new St. Ann would not be a contemporary worship space that some of his predecessors had envisioned, but one that called up the look of the historic cathedrals and churches.

Work began on the project in September of 2008, and the new building was dedicated in December 2009. That was just the start of the transformation, as the physical change is an ongoing process.

"It went from being the basement church to one of the most beautiful in the country in the span of 12 years," Jeff Rothe said.

Apropos of a parish with a strong connection to the past, the physical metamorphosis did not begin with a teardown of the old basement church. Rather, the builders removed the 12-foot ceilings and stretched upward. The original floor and pews were retained, and the new building emerged from it. It's been adorned with spectacular stained glass windows and art commissioned specifically for the new church. The artwork includes life-sized statues of the saints and a 400-square-foot mural.

And the parish community isn't resting. During my visit, St. Ann's Monsignor Allen Center, which serves as an activity center shared by the school and the church, was undergoing a renovation while the construction of a new grotto to Our Lady of Fatima was taking place just outside the doors. The $3 million project was undertaken without a formal capital campaign, just the enduring generosity of its hearty parish community.

The result of all of the work is a parish that is no longer an eyesore, but one that inspires. "It's gotten a lot of attention for its artwork and architecture. People come here because it's a pretty place," Father Reid said. "My thought as a pastor is the beauty of the building mirrors the beauty of the people here."

During Father Reid's time at St. Ann, the people have included a special group of young men. In 2016, St. Joseph College Seminary was founded to serve as a home for the men of the diocese pursuing the vocation of the priesthood. From its inception, the men were housed at St. Ann, first in an unused convent and then in nearby buildings as enrollment grew. In 2020, the college opened its seminary in nearby Mount Holly, though the seminarians maintain a presence on campus through the opening Mass and hosting Solemn Vespers on Sundays. St. Ann is still the home parish for the seminary and the people of St. Ann welcome their presence.

"It was great having those guys here, and the parishioners fell in love with the boys. They got very interested in their lives and the discernment process. They were really moved by the piety of the seminarians," Father Reid said.

Undoubtedly. Among the first five classes to enroll at St. Joseph, five of the men came from St. Ann. Their presence spurred an interest in vocations, Father Reid said. By the spring of 2022, when I attended Mass at St. Ann, there were nine men from St. Ann in seminary, seven in the diocese and two more in religious orders. There were more men pursuing the priesthood from the parish than from some dioceses.

While the parish is committed to helping develop the next generation of priests, it also maintains a deep connection to another group of religious men, the Missionaries of the Poor. The global monastic Order of Brothers is dedicated to joyful service with Christ on the Cross, pursuing that aim by serving the poorest of the poor around the world.

MOP has a presence in North Carolina, in nearby Monroe, allowing the parishioners of St. Ann to work with the Brothers both home and abroad.

Father Reid, whose relationship with the Brothers predated his assignment to St. Ann, has led more than a dozen mission trips, accompanied by parishioners who have discovered the unmatched gratification that comes with praying and serving side by side with the Brothers. They have worked with the Missionaries of the Poor in Jamaica, Haiti, and India.

Though the pandemic curtailed the trips for two years, that didn't stop St. Ann from aiding the Brothers in India. With time and talent put on hold, they opted for treasure alone, sending enough money to build a chapel at the site, something St. Ann's missionaries recognized was desperately needed from their very first visit to the country.

Lucie Tonon has been on multiple trips, the first prompted by her own health crisis. "I had breast cancer. It was not severe, but it caused me to pause in my life and say, 'Why did God put me on this earth, and have I been fulfilling my purpose?' I felt like I needed to reach outside for that."

She did, eventually participating in trips to all three countries. Each experience was amazing in its own way.

Fellow parishioner Terry Alderman has also made three trips, though all to India. Father Reid determined that with so many U.S. parishioners participating at the much closer locations in Jamaica and Haiti, the Brothers in India were more desperate for the assistance.

Wherever they are, the Brothers are truly inspirational. Their faith is boundless, rising in the pre-dawn hours for morning Mass, praying the Liturgy of the Hours, and holding adoration during the day. All done with unbridled joy and enthusiasm that quickly spreads to the American guests.

"From my experience, the closest I've felt to Christ is when I'm around them, because of their prayer life and what they do for other people," Terry Alderman said.

For Chris Brunhuber, it's in the people the Brothers serve where our Savior is most evident. "We see Christ in these people. That's where I learned to start seeing that," she said.

The people the Missionaries tend to are a country's most disadvantaged, young and old people alike who suffer from disease or illness or are disabled in some way. Many have been abandoned on the streets by their families.

Their lack of family, health, or wealth doesn't dampen their spirits, however. "It's amazing how happy the people are who don't appear to have anything," Terry Alderman marveled.

And they embrace their American visitors, even in the many instances when they share no common language. "The people there just want to be loved, recognized. They've been abandoned by their families and their country doesn't do much for them," said Steve Brunhuber, Chris's husband. "Anything you can offer up, they appreciate it."

Chris Brunhuber saw the quintessential experience on her first trip to India, when fellow St. Ann parishioner Marla Walsh approached a man with leprosy and shook his hand. "My first thought, was, 'Should we do that?' she recalled. "But then I thought, 'Why not?' This man has probably not been touched by anyone other than the Brothers for years."

Their responsibilities are not overwhelming. They're not asked to build bridges or find new sources of potable water. Rather they're tasked with small acts of kindness and service: help clean or apply lotion, provide basic healthcare services, or simply join the children on the floor to draw in coloring books. Many of the tasks involve touching the people, creating an intimacy and connection that bridges the language barrier.

Ultimately, the parishioners who have been on the mission trips reach a common conclusion about the experience.

"When you go on these mission trips, you think you're going to go and do something for the poor and you're bringing all these supplies with you," Lucie Tonon said. "And then you get there and you realize how much they renew your spirit."

Terry Alderman agrees. "You totally get more than you give," she said.

St. Michael

St. Michael, Minnesota

"It is right that you should begin again every day. There is no better way to complete the spiritual life than to be ever beginning it over again."
Saint Francis de Sales

From the moment I pulled up to St. Michael for Sunday Mass, I sensed this was a parish willing to buck the status quo. The church, the fourth building in the city outside Minneapolis that bears its name, features three large domes, not what you expect to find on a Roman Catholic church in the United States. That's not an accident. When the parish had outgrown its downtown facility and was looking to relocate onto a larger piece of land, the newly appointed priest, Rev. Michael Becker, expressed his disappointment at the staid designs for the new building. He wanted, in his words, a truly Catholic Church, one that followed the ongoing push from Saint John Paul II to unite the Eastern and Latin rites at the dawn of the 21st century.

The result is a spectacular structure that marries elements of both in one welcoming church, while also serving as a model for the approach the entire St. Michael community takes to the faith. St. Michael is a parish not afraid to break free from the way things have always been done.

Perhaps nowhere is that attitude more prominent than in the parish's youth ministry program, long under the direction of John O'Sullivan. From its convention-defying approach to religious education to its ambitious summer camp program, St. Michael is embracing new methods of instruction and engagement that are paying spectacular dividends.

Religious educators across the United States are intimately familiar with the Confirmation conundrum. For too many young people, attaining the sacrament of Confirmation signals the end of their Catholic instruction. They don't see its realization as the deeper calling to be missionary witnesses of Jesus Christ in our lives, which the sacrament asks of us.

St. Michael once faced that issue. But now the parish has moved away from the traditional Confirmation process followed in so many religious education programs in hopes of forging that deeper, longer lasting commitment.

John O'Sullivan said the transformation was due to the simple realization the old way of instruction wasn't working. "I'd describe it as, rather than doing the same thing and expecting a different result, we're striving to do something new."

St. Michael no longer ties Confirmation to a specific grade level. Instead, the parish invites teens in grades 8 through 12 to discern the sacrament while encouraging their participation in the parish's discipleship groups.

Each teen involved in the youth ministry is now linked with a willing adult as part of these discipleship groups. "From a big picture perspective, our goal is to have every youth in our parish have an adult who knows them, who walks with them, who is praying for them to be disciples," O'Sullivan said. The parish typically brings about 100 kids into discipleship groups. As an unexpected blessing, the groups have also served as an evangelizing tool for the adults as well. Dave Ferry is both a parent of a teen involved in youth ministry and a discipleship leader, so he's experienced the value the exercise provides from two separate perspectives.

"It's beautiful when it works, but it can be messy. You're talking about things that people get antsy about, meeting with other teens and adults and talking about relationships and their lives. It requires a lot of time and attention, but their retention rates have been phenomenal," he said.

O'Sullivan said the retention rate is, by one measure, 60-70 percent of the teens. However, looked at another way, it's 100 percent, "because we have adults praying for all of these kids, even if they're not coming anymore."

At the heart of every effort in the youth ministry program are five basic biblical principles: fellowship, worship, service, evangelization, and discipleship.

All of those traits, plus a whole lot of fun, are on display during the parish's Extreme Faith Camp, another O'Sullivan creation and one I had the immense pleasure of witnessing in the summer of 2021. The camp is a weeklong exercise to build stronger relationships with Christ among the teens of the parish. To describe it as a resounding success is a massive understatement.

The camp is broken down into two primary group. The junior high kids represent the campers, those being brought to a stronger relationship with Christ. And the students in grades 10-12 serve as their counselors, the older peers showing them the way. Adults and college-aged young adults are also there in various capacities.

Finally there's another group that stands alone, quite literally. Rather than move from campers to counselors over the course of one summer, the freshmen on the trip spend the entire week on the Prayer Team, where they participate in perpetual adoration. In 2021, camp organizers turned a garage into a chapel, and the ninth graders spent almost the entire week there, strengthening their prayer life.

Emma Thorp has been through the entire process, from camper to counselor. As with many others, she cites her time on the Prayer Team as one of the most powerful experiences at EFC. "It's a good transition year where you're going from middle school to high school and maturing. Prayer Team was a good chance for that maturity to build because you're spending so much time with the Lord, you can really build your faith."

Each year, more than 200 teens from the parish – a cluster which also includes its neighboring parish cohort at St. Albert – attend the event. The camp is led by the parish's "core team," the name given to the teens who form the foundation for the youth ministry. Those core team members return to the parish and work to evangelize the community kids, the parish teens whose commitment is not as strong. The hope is to turn them into core team members.

This ongoing cycle of developing core team members who then work to evangelize their peers is "the engine that's kept it going and growing and going and growing," O'Sullivan said.

Bob Swift, the parish's director of evangelization and faith formation who oversees the adoration chapel, believes the faith of the counselors really drives the success of St. Michael's youth ministry program. "Relationships will be established at the camp environment, but they'll see them and minister to them throughout the school year. It's one of the secrets that make it so powerful."

The original installment attracted approximately 70 to 80 kids from three separate churches. In 2021, there were six separate weeks of the camp, attracting teens from 43 separate parishes in the Twin Cities area.

Dave Ferry, the parish's business administrator, has sent six children through the parish's youth ministry program. It didn't take him long to recognize how successful Extreme Faith Camp was becoming in the community. His oldest sons, now in their late 20s, were confronted with a conflict when the camp butted up against the high school basketball camp organized by the varsity coach. They chose EFC.

"That was my first 'ah ha' moment. You don't skip your coach's basketball camp unless you're really compelled by something," Dave Ferry recalled.

Ferry wishes every adult at St. Michael would just spend a few hours at Extreme Faith Camp, watching how the kids celebrate Mass, spending hours in adoration and engaging in numerous other spirit-filled exercises. "You come back thinking, 'This is what faith should feel like.'"

Jerry and Karen Polaschek are a testament to that. The parents of four children who went through St. Michael, the Polascheks have been serving at the camp for years, starting with their two youngest children. They admit to getting as much out of the program as the generation of kids they've seen come through the camp.

They feel it wasn't enough just enrolling their children in the parish's youth ministry program; they needed to be present as well. At the camp, Karen helps with the Prayer Team and Jerry leads some fishing expeditions. But they feel their primary role is merely as an example. "We're not natural teachers. If we can just show them what a proper married couple looks like, that's kind of what we bring," she said.

Extreme Faith Camp's effects are undeniable. It's been a contributing factor in the discernment process of many Twin Cities priests, such as St. Michael's alum Rev. Paul Shovelain, now the pastor at St. John the Baptist in New Brighton. "For me, Extreme Faith Camp is an extremely important part of my vocation story. It built on the foundation that had been established between my Catholic education, my parents' faith-filled home and their faith they instilled in me," said Father Paul, who still attends camp each summer. "Extreme Faith Camp helped me develop my relationship with the Lord and feel more of the Father's love in my head, but also something in my heart."

Rev. Andrew Zipp has a similar story. "My first thought about the priesthood and joining the seminary was after my freshman year in high school," said Father Andrew, who currently serves at St. Vincent de Paul Parish in Brooklyn Park. "At Extreme Faith Camp, serving on the Prayer Team, spending a week in adoration, that's where I really heard the call for the priesthood and started to think about it."

As with all things at St. Michael, resting on laurels is not an option. In 2021, Extreme Faith Camp underwent a change when it partnered with the similarly successful Damascus program. The Catholic camp program was looking to expand its model outside its Ohio home and found the perfect partner in the Archdiocese of St. Paul/Minneapolis. Unlike EFC, Damascus owns the campgrounds where it holds events, which allows it to conduct year-round programs, not just in the summer months. The hope for Damascus is to deliver that model to the Twin Cities, allowing St. Michael and other parishes to expand their successful programming to the school year as well.

"We're very open to evaluating, looking at our strengths, looking at our weaknesses to see how we can improve, to see where the Lord is taking us. In the end, we're always remembering our primary mission is Jesus' mission of the Church – to go make disciples," John O'Sullivan said of the youth ministry's steady evolution.

"If we're not doing those things, then we're failing."

They aren't failing.

St. John Chrysostom

Atlanta, Georgia

"The light of the East has illumined the universal Church, from the moment when 'a rising sun' appeared above us (Lk 1:78): Jesus Christ, our Lord, whom all Christians invoke as the Redeemer of man and the hope of the world."
Saint John Paul II

SITTING ATOP A HILL IN THE EXCLUSIVE ATLANTA NEIGHBORHOOD of Druid Hills, in a place built by a soda pop magnate, you'll find St. John Chrysostom Melkite Catholic Church. The church is among the many places in the United States where Catholicism is practiced according to its Eastern traditions but in full communion with Rome.

St. John Chrysostom is one of 45 Melkite churches across the United States. Its roots date to Antioch, one of five patriarchal sees founded by Peter before he left for Rome.

The Melkites have a long winding history, both globally and here in the States. Though rooted in the Middle Eastern countries of Syria, Lebanon, and others, the Church's reach extends across the world, driven by an immigration process that was equally the product of the pursuit of opportunity or the escape from conflict.

Though individuals who adhered to the Melkite tradition began arriving in the U.S. in the middle of the 19th century, it wasn't until 1889 when the church had its first priest in the States. But growth was modest, hampered by the deliberate nature of the Vatican.

"Rome acts slowly," said Most Rev. Nicholas J. Samra, who serves the U.S. churches as the bishop of the Melkite Greek Catholic Church Eparchy of Newton in Massachusetts.

Evidence of that snail's pace was in the emergence of the eparchy. The first request for a bishop to serve the Melkite Church in the U.S. was made in 1921, seen as necessary to stave off the inroads being made by Orthodox churches with the arriving immigrants from the Eastern world. Though the request was supported by a Roman Catholic bishop who had come to the States to investigate the need, the first U.S. bishop wasn't appointed until 1969. "If a bishop was appointed in 1922, we could be triple the size we are today," Bishop Samra lamented.

But that isn't the only factor holding it back. As immigration has taken place beyond the coastal or largest U.S. cities into more locations, the need is there for more Melkite mission churches to serve them. Yet they are limited by the same factor seen in the domestic Roman Catholic Church – a shortage of qualified priests to serve them.

That could change, however. In 2014, Pope Francis reversed nearly 100 years of rule when he determined Melkite and other Eastern priests could once again be married, as they had been since the beginning. In that time, the U.S. Melkite Church has ordained more than a dozen married priests, giving some hope the pipeline will be easier to fill in the years to come.

"All of the married guys were well accepted by the other clergy, at least publicly" Bishop Samra said. "I wish some of my celibate priests had the same gumption as some of my married priests."

Rt. Rev. Archimandrite John Azar, who entered the priesthood long before Pope Francis's decision, is one of those priests who has accepted the new order. "For those entering now, as vocation director I give them the option. When I interview any persons who are interested in the priesthood, we tell them it's an option and it's perfectly legitimate," he said. "I don't think it's going to be an overnight rush to the door. It's going to take time for people to get used to it."

The Melkite Church came to Atlanta in 1955, when a small but ambitious Melkite community purchased Coca-Cola founder Asa Candler's former home, then owned by the American Legion. In 1957, it was dedicated as St. John Chrysostom by Bishop Francis Hyland of the Diocese of Atlanta.

The parishioners and clergy of St. John have carefully renovated the Candler Mansion, as it was known, into a beautiful worship space. It is noteworthy for its brilliant gold colors at the altar, consistent with its Middle Eastern origins. And when the spectacular leaded glass ceiling was beginning to show its age, with glass crashing to the floor below as the lead began to shrink, the parish didn't just fix the dome, but improved upon it with the inclusion of icons into the glass. Iconography is the way of the Melkite Church; you won't find statues anywhere in the worship space.

St. John Chrysostom's membership rolls have risen and fallen through the years, part of the challenge all Eastern Churches face in the predominantly Roman Catholic Western Hemisphere. Parishes such as theirs have to contend with the ongoing forces pulling its parishioners away from the church.

First-generation Catholic Syrians or Lebanese who come to the U.S. find comfort in the church so far from home. But as these families become assimilated into the U.S. culture, it becomes easier to drift away from the Melkite Church into a Roman parish or beyond the Catholic Church altogether.

The nature of the communities works against them in some ways. Atlanta is an enormous metropolitan area with an unenviable traffic reputation. As families move in and around the city and into the suburbs, it becomes more challenging to drive 45 minutes to Divine Liturgy when there's a Roman Catholic parish in the neighborhood. Or having young Melkite Catholic children enrolled in a Roman Catholic school may result in a similar shift from their native tradition.

"Once they become fed there, they are going to stay there many times," said Bishop Samra.

Father John Azar sees that happen. And he knows the distance and traffic make holding events throughout the week, something that can and does happen at more geography-based parishes, not really available to the Melkite Church. That's also why the parish does its best to make Sunday a meaningful occurrence.

"I would hope that because they're only able to come once a week, generally, that they would look at Divine Liturgy as something very, very special. That's it's not just an ordinary thing," Father John said.

The typical Sunday at St. John Chrysostom begins with Orthros, a prayer service at 10 a.m. That's followed by Divine Liturgy at 10:30 a.m., a service that can run nearly two hours as it follows the Byzantine traditions and incorporates both English and Arabic into the prayers. The mix of language may be dependent on the makeup of the church. English will be favored in parishes where fewer and fewer of the parishioners speak Arabic, which happens the longer a parish is in existence.

There are other differences, both inside the liturgy and in its exercise of the sacraments. During Divine Liturgy there is an extensive commitment to the Holy Trinity, with the clergy and parishioners making the Sign of the Cross dozens, if not hundreds, of times during the course of the service.

The Church explains: "The cross is the concrete expression of the Christian mystery, victory through defeat, of glory through humiliation of life through death."

And there are differences outside the liturgy proper. Perhaps most notable, and one that can lead to confusion when Melkite children attend Roman Catholic schools, is each child baptized in the church is also given the Eucharist and Confirmation at the same time. It can't be done again.

Following Divine Liturgy, a coffee hour follows in the parish's cultural center. It's a laid back affair that gives the members of the congregation the opportunity to connect again before they spread back out around the metropolis.

The challenge of finding a Melkite Church service can be a lifelong experience for a U.S.-raised adherent. There is no better example of that truism than longtime parishioner Vic Maloof.

The son of first-generation Lebanese immigrants, Maloof grew up in rural Tennessee, where it wasn't just impossible to find a Melkite Church, but any Catholic Church. The only way the community could even celebrate Mass was when his or other Lebanese families in the area would host visiting priests in their homes.

It wasn't until he went to study at a Benedictine-run boarding school in Alabama, St. Bernard Abbey, when Maloof even realized that his faith tradition was outside the Roman Catholic Church. That was likely a product of his family's insistence they were Americans first, where Arabic wasn't spoken in the home. "That was the first time I realized there were 20-something rites of the Catholic Church, and the Latin rite was just one. Though here in America, that was all we knew," Vic Maloof said.

He and St. John Chrysostom landed in Atlanta at roughly the same time, with some of his relatives among the early parishioners. Even still, his faith life bounced between the Melkite and Roman churches, owing to his and his wife Sue, an enthusiastic Catholic convert, building a home on Lake Lanier in Gwinnett County.

At the time the Maloofs moved there, Gwinnett County had no Catholic churches of any kind. But they had some land, a 1956 gift of wealthy businessman Bona Allen to honor Leo Lawler, a long-time devout Catholic employee of his. Allen put in one stipulation, that a Catholic Church had to be built within 20 years or the land would revert to his family trust. Thus, on Christmas Eve 1975, shortly before the deadline, the dozen or so Catholics of Gwinnett County celebrated Mass at the newly christened Prince of Peace Church in a building designed by the group's resident architect, Vic Maloof.

Today, the since-relocated Prince of Peace counts more than 4,000 families as parishioners, including one Melkite Catholic, Vic Maloof, who still attends Mass there a couple of times a year.

To him, this movement between the Melkite, Roman, and even the Maronite Church, to which several of his family members belong, is completely natural and healthy. "We're Catholic; that's all there is to it."

While the threat of parishioners lost to the Roman Catholic Church or others is ever-present, the Melkites are boosted by the reverse shift as well. John Chambers is just such a parishioner, one of the men and women who grew up in Roman Catholic parishes but have found themselves drawn to the Melkite Church, its tradition and worship service.

John Chambers, who has also attended a local Maronite Church, was originally attracted by the music, as he found himself pushed away by the contemporary Christian-style music being played at some Roman Catholic parishes. Over time, he became immersed in the entire tradition. "Going to Eastern Catholic churches, even with the translations, the language seemed more poetic than the English. Some of the prayers in the Maronite and Melkite churches, they're much richer and probably closer to the Old Testament and Psalms."

But he's quick to point out, particularly to those friends and family members who question his subtle shift, "I have not left the Catholic

Church. These churches are in communion with Rome," he said. "Otherwise, I wouldn't go."

Christ Our Hope

Seattle, Washington

*"If you do not find Christ in the beggar at the church door,
neither will you find him in the chalice."*
Saint John Chrysostom

THE GRAND ROOM JUST A FEW FEET FROM THE CORNER OF STEWART and Second streets in downtown Seattle was once where presidents and performers and ballplayers ate in style. The New Washington Hotel was the glamour spot in the fledging city in the Pacific Northwest, and the dining room was no doubt the site of many sumptuous feasts.

Today, however, that same room is used for a much more nourishing and fulfilling banquet. It is where Catholics from all backgrounds come together to celebrate the Eucharist. It is Christ Our Hope.

As a Catholic parish, Christ Our Hope is in its infancy stages, its founding dating back to just 2010. The path taken to get there is a little more winding.

By the 1960s, the New Washington Hotel was long past its glory days when the Archdiocese of Seattle purchased the building. The intent was to use it for Catholic seniors living downtown and that was its function for several years. But as seniors began to move away from the city center, the facility was transitioned into low-income housing operated by Catholic Housing Services, the building christened The Josephinum.

After the turn of the century, things changed again. The Congregation of the Most Holy Redeemer operated Sacred Heart of Jesus parish near the Space Needle and also held Mass on occasion at the Second Street site. The Redemptorists were considered pulling out of both, though the order ultimately opted to maintain their presence at Sacred Heart.

Enter Rev. Paul Magnano. Serving at the time as vicar of clergy for the archdiocese, he asked then-Archbishop Alexander Brunett if the see could take over The Josephinum site to be used as a parish church. The archbishop told Father Paul if the priest could raise $1 million, the request would be granted and Father Paul could serve as its founding pastor. The reverend presented the archbishop a check the next day, a generous gift from a parishioner he knew from a previous assignment.

After holding Ash Wednesday distribution services in 2010, Father Paul and his band of volunteers closed the parish to begin renovations, toward which he ultimately raised $7 million. The work included the first floor worship space, the pastoral center, plus upgrades to the basement and mezzanine levels. By August of that year, the now-retired archbishop was back to dedicate Christ Our Hope.

Father Paul's vision for Christ Our Hope is captured in its mission statement, which reads:

> "Christ Our Hope in Downtown Seattle is a beacon of life where all are welcome to growth in faith, hope and love through vibrant celebrations of the liturgy, programs of faith formation, evangelization and compassionate outreach, and responsible stewardship."

The first part of that mission is perhaps the most notable aspect of the parish community. Church leaders and lay people alike reiterate the importance of becoming that beacon calling all people inside. And some take that message very much to heart.

"I like to let people know they're welcome," said Sacristan Irene Mitchell, who demonstrated that very fact by introducing herself to me moments after I took my seat before Mass. "If you want to go to church and not talk to anyone and don't look left, don't look right, just say your Rosary and say goodbye, that's not me."

As founding pastor, Father Paul was given the opportunity to name the new church. He chose Christ Our Hope for several reasons, most prominently because that was the name Pope Benedict used for his pilgrimage to the United States, which Father Paul attended with some Seattle seminarians.

The archbishop was initially perplexed by the name, joking to Father Paul that "it sounded Lutheran." "We'll call it Christ Our Hope Catholic Church," Father Paul quickly responded.

A few years ago, Father Paul, approaching his 75th birthday and 50th year a priest, decided to step down from his duties at Christ Our Hope.

Since then, he has returned part-time to Skagit, Washington, where he helps two other priests serve 13 weekend Masses in the area. He also still serves the Tuesday Mass at Christ Our Hope and works as an advocate for Catholic Charities and in the Downtown Seattle Association, suggesting he doesn't really do retirement very well.

Father Paul's replacement at Christ Our Hope was Deacon Dennis Kelly, whose own attitude toward active Catholic service fit perfectly with the mission at Christ Our Hope. He sees Christ Our Hope as the embodiment of Pope Francis's concept of the church as field hospital. In 2013, the pope said the church needed the ability "to heal the wounds and to warm the hearts of the faithful. It needs, nearness, proximity."

Proximity is what Christ Our Hope is all about.

I attended two daily Masses at Christ Our Hope, the 7 a.m. Mass on a Wednesday and the 12:10 p.m. service the following day. Once again, the Holy Spirit was at work, delivering me to the corner of 2nd and Stewart at the most opportune time – when the Sacred Encounters ministry was going to be fulfilling its calling. Deacon Dennis welcomed me to join the participants in their ministry, an invitation that did not need to be repeated.

Each Wednesday at lunch time, the ministers from Sacred Encounters set out with bags full of sandwiches, bottles of water, snacks, and whatever else can be carried by hand. Their mission is to share those goods with the destitute in Seattle, a city with one of the highest rates of homelessness in the country. Finding people in need is not difficult.

Sacred Encounters is an outgrowth of MercyWatch, the nonprofit Deacon Dennis runs in Everett, a city north of Seattle. That all-volunteer organization provides street medicine to the unhoused in Snohomish County. When he was assigned to Christ Our Hope, he brought the non-medical side of the MercyWatch program with him.

"We have an amazing team here," he said of the Christ Our Hope group. "We truly see Christ in those encounters."

Before we embarked, Deacon Dennis reminded us of the need to stay careful and vigilant, as the streets of Seattle can be problematic. We needed to work in groups, with one of us constantly aware of all of our surroundings. This is not a ministry for the timid.

Alas, about the only deference to caution made by Sacred Encounters missionaries Barbara Ivester, Jillian Jacobson, and Mike McKasy was to steer clear of "Stab Alley." For the rest of the two-hour walk, their call to serve tended to win out over their desire for self-preservation. When a person who might be in need of assistance was spotted, my friends in the ministry would make a beeline there, determined to offer both corporal and spiritual gifts to the city's most troubled population.

Doing so can be difficult. Seattle's sizable unhoused population consists of some combination of the mentally ill, the drug-dependent, and the simply impoverished. Those suffering from mental illness or long-term drug use may have difficulty communicating clearly, or at all. Yet these seasoned missionaries were steadfast in their service. They seemed to approach each encounter with the zeal of John, the patience of Job and the heart of Jesus.

As we ambled along the downtown sidewalks, Jillian Jacobson remarked to me, "When I used to see the homeless, I would ignore them. Now, I run up to them."

My experience with Sacred Encounters was not the first time Christ Our Hope welcomed strangers to join in its engagement with neighbors. Before the pandemic shut things down, the parish operated an Immersion program, where students from local schools were invited to Christ Our Hope for a day of activity centered around Catholic service.

The students would arrive in the morning, where they'd receive a talk from one of the staff members on the church's mission and how it relates to Catholic social teaching. From there, the kids would be sent out to work in any number of downtown settings – homeless shelters or soup kitchens or even at The Josephinum. Upon completion, they'd return to the church and share lunch with the residents, an experience that can be transformative. There, the students wouldn't just do dispassionate good works, but would sit down and talk one-on-one with The Josephinum's inhabitants, providing a glimpse of life outside the students' often-insular world.

"That conversation and that story that happens is something you just don't get when you're folding socks in a supply closet. Which is important work, and if people need them to do that, they do that," Deanna

Tighe said. "But the meals offered an opportunity to share bread, which is just like the Eucharistic. It's our faith written all over it."

Like so many other church programs around the country, Immersion was a victim of COVID-19, though Deanna Tighe and others hope it can be revised in the years to come.

But the parish does not just step outside its walls to serve the people around the downtown area. It also invites them in. All of them.

The parish is immensely supportive of the residents above, and invite the men and women to worship, dine, and otherwise engage with the people of Christ Our Hope. On the Sunday before I arrived, the parish held a resource fair for the 240 residents, inviting them down to gather toilet paper, toothpaste, and other essentials that had been skyrocketing in price during the inflationary days of early 2022.

Michael Drummey's work at Christ Our Hope is largely in service of those residents. The retired business executive is the point man in the lobby, making sure The Josephinum's residents are safe and well cared for. Like Father Paul, he finds tending the needs of The Josephinum's tenants a more fulfilling way to spend retirement than chasing around a golf ball. "You get to know people. It's really rewarding. I'm just a common guy trying to do a great job for folks I know are having a tough time."

In addition to many programs involving and including the residents of The Josephinum, Christ Our Hope invites others in the community who want to experience God's love. That attitude of inclusion is evident in many ministries, but most exemplified by the Choir of Hope.

When Dr. James Savage retired after 30 years as liturgist at Cathedral of St. James, he wanted to stay invested in the Church in a more voluntary capacity. He came to Christ Our Hope to help start a new type of choir, a no-audition music ministry that invites downtown people from all walks of life to come and share their gifts, meager as those talents might seem to the cynical ear. It's where Pope Francis wants the Church to be, on the margins, where people need church more than ever.

When I visited, Deanna Tighe was just months away from becoming the pastoral coordinator at Christ Our Hope, with Deacon Dennis returning to Everett to focus on MercyWatch. The parish's leadership went from a priest to a deacon to a layperson, but both Father Paul and Deacon Dennis are confident the parish is in good hands.

"The strength of Christ Our Hope is the lay leadership," said Father Paul. "It's a church that has very competent volunteers."

Deanna Tighe plans to call on those volunteers regularly. Though she believes the parish community is excited about the prospect of a lay leader, she will need their commitment to keep the parish moving forward. "I said to everybody who said, 'Congratulations,' 'I'm not doing this alone. If we want to be an example of a lay-run parish in the archdiocese, I need people to help.'"

Paradoxically, the growth and health of the parish can be limited by the nature of the community it works so hard to serve. In 2022, sister parish St. Patrick was scheduled to close, but there was no guarantee any or even most of the parishioners there would choose Christ Our Hope as a replacement. The homelessness, drug use, and crime facing the downtown also keep some cautious Catholics from the area altogether.

"The rate of homelessness and crime has skyrocketed since pre-pandemic. And people are frightened," Deanna Tighe said. "At the same time, we're still ministering to the people who are smoking heroin. It's a tension."

On the other hand, the downtown is an ever-evolving neighborhood, with residents turning over more rapidly than elsewhere. Many have joined the parish since the pandemic, which means they haven't experienced Christ Our Hope at its best.

"A number of people have never seen us in the way we really are, how we truly share meals and support our residents and support our downtown community," said Paula Holmes, who has been a parishioner since its founding. "That's going to be super exciting to see."

St. Gianna's Maternity Home

Warsaw, North Dakota

> *"For this reason I kneel before the Father, from whom every family in heaven and on earth is named, that he may grant you in accord with the riches of his glory to be strengthened with power through his Spirit in the inner self, and that Christ may dwell in your hearts through faith; that you, rooted and grounded in love, may have strength to comprehend with all the holy ones what is the breadth and length and height and depth, and to know the love of Christ that surpasses knowledge, so that you may be filled with all the fullness of God. Now to him who is able to accomplish far more than all we ask or imagine, by the power at work within us, to him be glory in the church and in Christ Jesus to all generations, forever and ever. Amen."*
> Ephesians 3:14-21

TUCKED AWAY IN THE CATHOLIC CORNER OF NORTH DAKOTA, NOT too far from the Canadian border, women are committing to life in the most meaningful way possible.

These women, who can range in age from the preteens to their 40s, are the residents of St. Gianna's Maternity Home. They come here alone, often fighting the forces that encourage them to take the easy, sinful, way out. They come to give their unborn children a chance at life. They are, in small ways, the living embodiment of Gianna Beretta Molla.

In 1962, the Italian mother was expecting her fourth child with husband Pietro when an examination revealed a tumor on her uterus. Doctors recommended a hysterectomy or abortion. She refused both, opting to have the fibroma removed to spare the life of her unborn child. That child, Gianna Emanuela, was born on April 21st. One week later, Gianna died from septic peritonitis. She was beatified April 24, 1994, and canonized 10 years later by then-Pope John Paul II, her husband and children there for her elevation to sainthood.

Her legacy lives on in Warsaw, North Dakota. For more than 20 years, her namesake home has been providing at-risk women a loving environment to give birth and raise a young child. They do it by living out the home's motto: One Mother, One Baby, One Family at a Time.

The women can come to St. Gianna's from anywhere, though most are from North Dakota and surrounding states. Some find the home on their own, while others are referred to the facility by pregnancy help centers or women's shelters. Women of all faiths, or no faith, are welcome, though they will share a Catholic life upon arrival.

That includes attending Sunday Mass, plus prayer before and after meals. They also pray each evening. Regardless of what kind of role religion played in their lives before arriving, most embrace the Catholic environment at St. Gianna's. "It's amazing how women who don't have faith, how hungry they are for it," said Mary Pat Jahner, the home's director.

That describes Jessica Bercier. Now a mother of five who arrived at St. Gianna's in her teens, Jessica is one of the home's biggest champions. She often finds herself at abortion clinics, counseling young women that the home exists as a much better option. But ask her the greatest impact the home has had on her life, and she's quick to answer, "Finding God.

"I never prayed. I never knew anything about church," said Jessica, who as a child was shuffled in and out of foster homes, few of them worth remembering. "Now, when I have questions, I'll pray, and when I'm done praying, the answer has revealed itself."

At St. Gianna's, that faith in God is presented as part of daily life, a necessity as the women will be returning to the outside world within a few years. The staff is not training the woman for religious life, but it's still crucial to show how God exists in the everyday.

"We live a Catholic life here. We don't just talk about it. We don't segregate it. We don't pigeonhole it," said Rev. Joseph Christensen, FMI, the spiritual director and chaplain who lives in a friary just a few hundred feet away. He established the Third Order Franciscans of Mary Immaculate in 2011. "It's not something we do here personally and do something different publicly."

Still, most of the typical day is spent engaged in routine activities that will aid the women when they leave the home – education and chores and simple, respectful fun, the foundations of a healthy family life. Education can involve attending the local school system for the teenage girls to securing a GED for the older ones. Some of the young women have left the home with certificates in cosmetology, massage therapy, and medical coding, giving themselves a leg up when they re-enter the secular world.

A key element of the program is simply getting the residents accustomed to a regular schedule and proper nutrition. Many of their residents have a history of couch-hopping from one friend to another, staying up late in the evening, sleeping in and eating foods that aren't on any dietician's recommend list. Drugs and alcohol are an all-too-often crutch, regardless how old the mother is upon arrival. Developing structure that can carry them forward is imperative.

At the same time, every woman who comes to Warsaw has a different story, and thus no two residents have the same needs. A teenage, first-time mother is going to demand a different approach than an experienced mother in her thirties coming out of an abusive relationship.

At St. Gianna's, women are welcomed at any point during pregnancy up to a few weeks after the birth of the child. They can stay at the home up to two years after child's birth, though they tend to leave after a single year.

The staff would prefer they stay longer, as it enhances the odds the change in lifestyle and approach that are at the heart of the St. Gianna's experience will take root. "It's hard to change their lives completely in six months or a year and a half," said Father Joseph. "We try to guide them to a better place, but many times they go back to the same place, and they just fall into the same way of life."

Ke is an example of that. She was the sole mother at the facility when I visited, there on a special dispensation from the board as her son was a little over the age of 2. She had come to St. Gianna's during her pregnancy, when she was only 15, but soon returned to the dysfunctional homelife she knew before. Back home, her mother died, and she found herself using heroin and methamphetamines, neglecting her young son the same way she had been neglected. To her, that was the way things worked.

Fortunately, she entered a drug treatment program, getting herself clean and determined to do better for her son. "I came to realize I was treating my son the same way my mom and dad treated me. I didn't realize it at the time. I thought that was normal," she said.

Her post-residency experience is the one area of the home's mission that Mary Pat Jahner would like to be able to strengthen. "We do what we can, but more is needed," she conceded.

She dreams of a full-time employee handling post-residency care, but the home doesn't have the resources yet. And the challenge of follow-up assistance is further burdened by the tendency for the house mothers to turn over, meaning today's employees don't have the relationship and trust built with the women who have previously lived in the home. And trust is crucial to the experience, as the women who come to St. Gianna's have been let down by so many of the people in their lives that faith in others is not granted easily.

The maternity home has the space to accommodate up to six women at once, though the staff prefers to cap the number living there at one time to four. More than that makes it difficult to provide the kind of one-on-one work that is fundamental to the process.

Besides Mary Pat, Father Joseph and Brother Nicholas, a Franciscan novice, the staff includes an assistant director, office manager and two live-in housemothers. And in recent years, Mary Pat has broken down and added a dog. "I'm not an animal lover, but I see what it does for them. It took me many years to give in on that," she said.

The housemothers work shifts during the day, and each is guaranteed eight days off per month. To Mary Pat, the housemothers – women who come to St. Gianna's from all over the country – don't just serve a domestic role through their day-to-day work, but as devout women for the residents to emulate.

That's how Rachel Juve sees herself. Rachel began working as a housemother after spending a year with NET Ministries. She saw St. Gianna's as a chance to serve people more directly, in a different way, than her work with NET.

But she sees her chief responsibility to simply serve as a model for the residents, who tend to be close to the housemothers in age. "I want to be an example, like a witness. They need someone to look to for how they should live their life, but in a way that isn't telling them what to do, but by example. By living as faithfully as I can and loving them as well as I can so they can do that in return with others," she said.

One trait the housemothers must possess is patience, said Morgan Christensen, who has been with the home for six years and now serves as Mary Pat Jahner's assistant director. There is a desire to jump right in and help fix these women, many of them severely broken by years of abuse or neglect. It's not that simple.

"The hardest part for me is trying to change something that someone is not ready to change. You can show them the better way or the benefits of doing so, but they have to want to make that change," said Morgan Christensen, Father Joseph's niece.

There aren't many volunteers who work on site. It's not because they don't have individuals willing to assist, but because of the commitment Mary Pat Jahner demands. She doesn't want people coming in and out of the facility, giving of themselves one Saturday afternoon and then not being seen again. That isn't good for their residents, who need to see the same faces day after day to help rebuild their faith in the reliability of others.

There is no counselor on staff, but the home will arrange sessions with nearby professionals if one of the residents has such a need. All of it is done with the same aim, to create the greatest opportunity for the young mothers to succeed while recognizing their inherent worth. "In the end, we want them to be joyful, happy, and healthy. When we feel joy is when we feel loved by God and others," Mary Pat Jahner said.

The home was founded in the early 2000s, when the former Catholic school teacher Mary Pat Jahner and some other local supporters took on the challenge of developing a home for pregnant women and their unborn children. The process was daunting, but the group, persevered, aided greatly by their namesake. "We went around telling her story, and people were so moved, so touched, they wanted to do something for the unborn," said Mary Pat Jahner.

Naturally, the group hoped to land a wealthy benefactor that would set them up for years. Instead, it accomplished its aims through a bevy of small donors, individuals who would become the St. Gianna's family, supporting the home and the mothers year after year. "I attribute all of that to St. Gianna for touching the hearts of so many people," Mary Pat Jahner said.

Their contributions are rewarded with every birth. And every evening, the women who come to St. Gianna's free of charge thank the donors while praying the Liturgy of the Hours.

Mary Pat Jahner has been approached about expanding the model elsewhere, but she's rebuffed those entreaties. She has no interest in creating St. Gianna's 2, though she has assisted other groups who are pursuing similar efforts. To her, the maternity home that's been built in Warsaw is a unique experience that can't be duplicated, nestled as it is in the largely unspoiled land in the Upper Red River Valley. "We're a remote village, and I think that's part of our charm and our advantage. There's not a lot of craziness or outside influence, which gives them time to reflect and make changes that will change their whole lives."

In many ways, Father Christensen believes his presence, and that of religious candidates such as Brother Nicholas, serve as an important guidepost for the young mothers and mothers to be. Many of the women have been damaged by the men in their lives, including their own fathers and the fathers of their children, leaving them leery of the opposite gender. Seeing men who are committed to living an honest and godly life can serve as a necessary counterbalance to these impressions. "We're not looking to get married, but we can be a male example for them, what they should look for, what they should insist on when they're dating."

And the examples can come in so many ways. When Jessica Bercier came to St. Gianna's the first time, she actually left the home six days before her child was born. She considers it one of the biggest mistakes she's ever made.

But out of that mistake came a lesson that she never anticipated, in part because it was one she had never experienced. Despite walking away from the home, she was shocked to discover Mary Pat and the others on staff didn't turn their backs on her.

"She stayed in my life, even though I made a wrong decision," she said. She was forgiven. She was loved.

And she still is.

52 Masses

Daniel Markham

Tri-Parish West Virginia St. Patrick

Bancroft, West Virginia

Holy Trinity

Nitro, West Virginia

Christ the King

Dunbar, West Virginia

> "I charge you in the presence of God and of Christ Jesus, who will judge the living and the dead, and by his appearing and his kingly power: proclaim the word; be persistent whether it is convenient or inconvenient; convince, reprimand, encourage through all patience and teaching."
> 2 Timothy 4:1-2

IT IS DIFFICULT TO DETERMINE WHETHER IT WAS REV. JOHN CHAPIN Engler's path to the priesthood that was more unconventional or the road he's traveled since then.

Each Sunday, Father Chapin presides over approximately 150 parishioners, total, in Masses in three separate churches in rural West Virginia – Holy Trinity in Nitro, Christ the King in Dunbar, and St. Patrick in Bancroft. And each week, he reaches up to 100,000 people on the television program and web show he's been overseeing for approximately a decade.

"In a million years, I never aspired to be on TV," Father Chapin recalled. "The Holy Spirit is an amazing thing."

His program, My Daily Living, is broadcast on a number of stations in and around the Wheeling-Charleston area, plus an increasing number outside the state. And for those who can't see the program over the air, it is broadcast over the internet at www.mydailyliving.com.

If you're looking for high-tech graphics, sweaty shouts of "Alleluia" or promises for immediate healing, all for a nominal fee, you've come to the wrong place. Rather, My Daily Living is just Father Chapin and the Word, the good-natured pastor explaining how the Gospels relate to the lives of the ordinary people who tune in each week. It is his response to what he sees as a fundamental absence of the Lord in many of those lives.

"There is a tremendous number of people who believe in God. They don't know him, but they know about him. They profess themselves as Christians, but they don't take the time to read the Bible," he acknowledged. Father Chapin attempts to frame those stories, those lessons, in ways that resonate with his hungry audience. And from emails and letters he receives, his efforts are paying off.

"I can't tell you how many letters I get from elderly people, who say, 'I've been going to church my entire life and I never understood why the elder son was out of line in the Prodigal Son. I thought he was the good guy and got the short end of the stick. You finally made me understand the older brother was the pharisee who feels entitled,'" he related, though he's also quick to reject credit. "I'm not stupid enough to think it's me. I try to put the Gospels in a palatable way, spoon-feed it to people who have never heard it before and the Holy Spirit does the rest."

The programs generally run about 28 minutes, or quite a bit longer than his typical Sunday homily. He films each episode about a month before it runs. He then takes the message delivered in My Daily Living and distills it for Sunday Mass.

But you won't hear the same one twice. At the vigil Mass on Saturdays at Holy Trinity, Father Chapin will include much of the message, allowing the congregations to tell him, through their responses, the parts that are working and which ones need to be left out of Sunday's sermons.

Sunday, 8 a.m.

He begins his day at St. Patrick in Bancroft, the smallest of the three parishes. The crowd numbers 25 when I'm there, which was not much more than it did at the height of the pandemic. The St. Patrick crowd is a small but hearty bunch, who blanched at the rules prohibiting post-Mass gatherings during the pandemic by taking the weekly fellowshipping just outside the church.

At St. Patrick, the homily is the shortest, a concession to the tight schedule facing Father Chapin. He's already in his car, in his vestment, heading for Nitro long before the parishioners at the Bancroft church have dispersed from their weekly reunions, which they were kind enough to include me in.

Writing the message is actually a collaborative affair, undertaken between Father Chapin and his brother. Their partnership began while Father Chapin was in seminary, writing his first homilies. The two spoke on the phone, with the would-be priest explaining what subjects he was covering and his brother countering with improvements. Soon, it became clear to both men that Father Chapin's sermons needed his brother's special touch. For the past 20 years, the two have partnered on the pastor's homily every week.

Father Chapin's road to the Diocese of Wheeling-Charleston began, oddly enough, in Chicago, where he worked as a stockbroker for Merrill Lynch. A lifelong Catholic, he was beginning to feel "spiritually dry." But that barren sensation was short lived, his faith sparked first when he began serving as a cantor at the Cathedral, and again when he followed a girl he was dating to a Pentecostal church. "There's always a girl involved," he joked.

He was still attending services at both churches when the Lord spoke to him.

"He said, 'I want you to take the energy you see here in this carnival Christianity, with people waving their hands and all of the big screens and the singing. And I want you to wake up my people,'" he recalled. "It was clear as day."

Still, he didn't respond to this message immediately, waiting a full nine months to make sure the calling was genuine before enrolling in seminary.

Sunday 9:30 a.m.

Next up is the liturgy at Holy Trinity, the hyphen in the Tri-Parish community. All three towns hug the Kanawha River, with Bancroft to the north and Dunbar to the southeast roughly equidistant from the centrally located Nitro. That evocative name derives from nitrocellulose, the primary ingredient in the gunpowder that was once made locally to support the U.S. and its allies in the First World War.

Father Chapin had been the pastor of Holy Spirit for three years when I attended Mass there. That left him only 42 years short of the service of choir director Lou Kapicak, a fixture at virtually every Mass and funeral conducted at the parish during those four-plus decades.

Lou Kapicak said the thing that stands out about Holy Spirit is the level of hospitality, which he has a significant hand in providing. From his perch at the head of the choir just off the altar, he sees every unfamiliar face that enters the church and makes it a point to greet them. Often, one or more parishioners have already beaten him to the punch.

"We try to make them feel as if it's their home as well as our home," he said.

Father's homily at Holy Trinity is a little longer, as he continues to hone the message. Each is delivered not from reading or memorization, but rather a deep understanding of the subject and, as always, the guidance of the Holy Spirit.

Though he had heard the calling, his passage to the priesthood was strewn with obstacles, some of his own making. He was booted out of his first attempt at seminary and spent two years working in a homeless shelter, but the pull of the collar did not relent. He sought out West Virginia, believing the diocese was desperate enough to welcome a bit of a nonconformist such as him. "God draws straight with crooked lines," he said of his unlikely journey to religious life.

He has been assigned to various parishes in the Mountain State, now comfortably his home.

Sunday, 11 a.m.

Though under one umbrella and pastor, each of the three parishes has retained its own character. At Christ the King in Dunbar, the parish was unique in its approach to the pandemic, not just in West

Virginia but in other parishes where I worshipped. Months after some dioceses had lifted all requirements, the parishioners at Christ the King remained covidly cautious. Masks were still being worn and social distancing practiced by about 40 percent of the congregation. The parish accommodated that by sitting the masked on one half of the church, the full-faced members on the other. This wasn't segregation, but a sign of mutual respect and understanding.

The parish's sense of care for the entire congregation was evident again at the conclusion of Mass. Almost the entire assembly gathered at the baptismal font for a near-weekly communal anointing of the sick. Father Chapin said it's the first time he's encountered the practice, but would love to see it become commonplace.

The homily here is, in Father Chapin's estimation, typically the best version, aided by his ability to work out the kinks elsewhere and the fact he's no longer keeping one eye on the clock.

Shortly after taking his vows, Father Chapin made his broadcast debut, but again, it wasn't quite that simple. He started working on an AM radio station, playing the rock and roll of his youth, but delivering his hard-won, spirit-filled wisdom to his listeners between cuts from the Beatles and Pink Floyd. A listener advised him he ought to pursue television, but to "cut out all the music and do your homily and have fun."

And fun is just what he's having, which is evident in every broadcast. The show is shot in his tiny basement in the rectory. The entire set, including cameras and sound equipment, occupies only slightly more space than a confessional.

The show itself was initially supported by some wealthy benefactors, who helped him grow the ministry. After some time, they advised him to start asking the viewers to foot the bill.

Today, My Daily Word is supported by the many listeners from West Virginia and beyond. Supporters receive the weekly script before the program airs. Most of the financial support comes in small donations, with more than 50 percent of the money coming in checks of $25 or less.

At present, he averages about $3,000 per week, which goes to fund the program and make additional media buys in other markets. The money goes into a My Daily Living account at the diocese – Father

Chapin does not maintain a fleet of jets or own six homes like some of his peers in the world of broadcast faith.

If there seems to be some incongruity to the pastor of a tiny collection of parishes in rural West Virginia reaching thousands, it's not lost on Father Chapin. But that doesn't mean he's longing for the bright lights of a bigger market.

A few years prior, he was hit by a car crossing the street, an incident he takes full responsibility for causing. And it was a group of five nurses from the three parishes that cared for him, aiding his return to full health. It's that kind of responsiveness from the community that tells him he's found a wonderful place from which to reach the world with God's Word.

"Cluster parishes sharing a priest tend to resent each other. I've been on assignments where the churches didn't like each other," he said. "I don't have that here."

And that is just one of the many reasons Father Chapin feels at home with the wonderful people of Bancroft, Nitro, and Dunbar. "I've never been happier."

Daniel Markham

St. Christina

Chicago, Illinois

"Be merry, really merry. The life of a true Christian should be a perpetual jubilee, a prelude to the festivals of eternity."
Saint Theophane Venard

There was a time when the Catholic parish served as the unmistakable hub of a given community. When entire neighborhoods of immigrants – Polish or Italian or Lithuanian – had settled in a single location, the only item accompanying them from the Old World was their strong Catholic faith.

Those times are largely gone, unintended byproducts of the flight to suburbia, gentrification, marriage outside the faith, and a whole host of other societal trends that have defined American life these past 50 years.

You can still find, however, the occasional relic, that neighborhood that has maintained its ethnic and spiritual heritage against the tsunami of forces working against such shared experience, such homogenous communities.

St. Christina is one of those outliers. The working-class church on the Southwest side of Chicago still bears the hallmarks of the traditional neighborhood parish. Families in the area go to Mass there, send their kids to the elementary school, and engage themselves in a variety of parish activities over the course of the year.

And no time in the calendar is this more evident than March. The end of winter brings with it two of the major events in the community – the arrival of Lent and St. Patrick's Day, the religious and the cultural highpoints for the heavily Irish Catholic congregation.

In addition to Stations of the Cross, Eucharistic Adoration, the Boundless Compassion Lenten Retreat, and other occasions for prayer available at the church, St. Christina is the place to go on Friday nights as it delivers "the best Fish Fry on the South Side."

For decades, the parish has been serving up fish, French fries and spaghetti each Friday during Lent, a tradition that only COVID-19 could put a halt to.

While many parishes, particularly those in the Midwest, offer communal, meat-free meals on Fridays during the Lenten season, few do so with as much enthusiasm and professionalism as you'll find at St. Christina, the byproduct of years of practice and an endless sea of volunteers.

The tradition started small, as most do. But it grew over time, enhanced when a local red hot restaurant closed down and the parish picked up a wealth of commercial-grade equipment. On the day after Christmas in 1995, more than 50 parishioners arrived to help expand the kitchen to accommodate the new equipment.

"The volunteers just showed up out of nowhere," marveled long-time fish fry fixture Gary Nothnagel. It's a phenomenon that repeats itself on Fridays during Lent.

Each week, the parish serves hundreds of people from the area, the horde expertly tucked into the basement hall by the team of fish fry logistics experts. It's a true South Side crowd, evidenced by the large number of men wearing paddy caps, clothing with White Sox logos or, on occasion, White Sox paddy caps.

Tom O'Connell came to St. Christina, and the fish fry, through participation in the Holy Name Softball League, another area of life that unites that faithful in the neighborhood. The softball games are played on the parish's fields, once the home to the first iteration of St. Christina Church. "Holy Name is almost like a gateway drug. It started there, then I came here and it's such a terrific group of men and women you become a part of it," O'Connell said.

Volunteers at the fish fry span the entire St. Christina demographic. Students, from elementary through high school, walk the floor selling desserts and cleaning up. Their parents work the fryers and beer taps in the kitchen. And seniors check you in, find you a seat and deliver your meal. Yes, that's right. There's no self-service here. This is a top-shelf operation.

"I'm always impressed with the young kids helping out," said Tom O'Connell. "Some of them are getting service points, but then they've got enough points and they still keep coming out. That says a lot."

I attended separate fish fry dinners, made possible by the fact I don't live too far from the neighborhood. The first was one of the last before COVID shut things down in 2020 and the second was the triumphant return engagement in 2022. It was pretty clear that two years' worth of inaction couldn't derail decades of institutional knowledge; the event was as expertly run after the pandemic as it was before.

Remarkably, almost 700 were served on that first night back, suggesting a ravenous hunger for not just seafood and pasta, but the fellowship that had been so lacking from our lives for far too long.

The enormous crowd caught the fish fry team slightly off guard. No one knew quite what the response would be, or how many parishioners and community members might still be skittish about large, in-person gatherings. Thus, many of the food items were depleted long before the scheduled closing time, a shortage they were determined not to experience again in subsequent weeks.

A few weeks after that, I returned for Mass and the other great St. Christina tradition, the South Side Irish Parade, which takes place the last Sunday before St. Patrick's Day. So it's Mass and then a movement en masse a few blocks east.

Like the fish fry, the annual march down Western Avenue had been called off the previous two years, so the parishioners were eager for this tradition to return. St. Christina, of course, had a float, as it does every year. To be honest, I was focused on a different float, the one ridden on by wife. She was a first-time participant in the parade in 2022, a result of pandemic-timed appointment as a principal at St. Gerald, another South Side Catholic parish.

St. Gerald's counterpart in Catholic education, St. Christina School, was also present at the parade. That's not surprising, as it's a source of tremendous focus for the parish.

"St. Christina School has been an absolute anchor," said Rev. Tom Conde, pastor at the parish. "It really provides an alternative to the public schools and it provides a vehicle for evangelization."

The school is one of the larger ones on the South Side, educating just shy of 500 students from preschool through Grade 8. The public school students can enroll at the parish's religious ed program, which operates a unique scheduling system with other local churches. St. Christina offers religious ed on Sundays, while other parishes provide it on different days of the week. If a family has other obligations on a given day, it can send a child to a program at a nearby parish at a more convenient time, choking off one potential excuse for not availing themselves of lessons in the catechism.

All students, whether full-time at the K-8 parochial school or religious ed participants, stand to benefit from the planned expansion project at St. Christina School. The idea is to add on to the existing structure to create space for five new classrooms, all connected. Currently, the school uses the Homan Building across the parking lot for additional classroom space. A single school building would keep students from having to exit the building to attend classes, a major goal for Father Tom. "There was some terrorism stuff three or four years ago. It scared the living bejeebers out of me," he admitted.

If the plan is executed, the Homan Building, which previously served as the church building before the current worship space was constructed in the 1950s, would be leveled. But don't think that such a decision would find strong opposition among the parishioners of St. Christina. Father Tom insists that isn't a concern. The building itself has been remodeled numerous time since being decommissioned as a worship space to the point where its former self is barely recognizable. "The biggest initial question was, 'Who's still beholden to that thing?'" he asked, then answered. "There's no great love lost. There's no great sentimental value to it."

One woman who can remember the time it served as the worship space is Joan Stubenrauch, who joined St. Christina when she was a teenager, the oldest of 10 children in her family. Even then, long before fish fry dinners and parades, St. Christina was the fulcrum of the community. She recalled how the revered former priest, Rev. J.A. Rebedeau, would show movies in the church. "The whole town of Mount Greenwood would come," she said.

There's another possible reason why St. Christina remains such a magnet. It isn't just a faith and a zip code the people of the parish share. For a great many of them, it's an employer.

The neighborhood around the parish is the unofficial home to Chicago's first responder community, with police officers, firefighters, and EMTs finding the Mount Greenwood neighborhood the ideal place to raise a family. The city employee residency requirement, which demands workers live within the boundaries of Chicago, plays a crucial role in this occupational hegemony. The neighborhood is the last stop before the city ends, giving way to the rest of Cook County.

The overwhelming presence of first responders in the community acts as a bulwark against the sad trend dominating many South Side neighborhoods – out of control criminal violence. Chicago's recent spate of indiscriminate shootings, most in the southern reaches of the metropolis, has not really touched the residential area surrounding St. Christina.

The parishioners of St. Christina believe, with good reason, the Mount Greenwood neighborhood is a place where peace of mind is a way of life. As longtime parishioner Linda Dixon noted, "I've got eight coppers and seven firemen on my block." And lest you think that's some kind of anti-blue slur, be advised that's retired Chicago Police Department Detective Linda Dixon.

Now, the fact so many St. Christina's parishioners share much in common can be a cause for the occasional headache, as any work dispute or neighborly feud can conceivably carry over to the parish. But Father Tom realizes that's just a natural outgrowth of supremely close-knit communities.

"The reality is, we don't all get along all the time. Whether that's church or neighborhood or employers, it doesn't make a difference," Father Tom said. "But it's like a good family. You fight but you still love each other."

St. Augustine

Winnebago, Nebraska

"If we wish to serve God and love our neighbor well, we must manifest our joy in the service we render to Him and them."
Saint Katharine Drexel

IN WINNEBAGO, NEBRASKA, THE BOYS AND GIRLS ARE EDUCATED IN A school founded by a saint. And today, more than 110 years after St. Augustine was opened, the school is becoming the place where the superior Catholic education for Native Americans envisioned by St. Katharine Drexel is perfectly supplemented by the celebration and preservation of the culture of its students.

Indian schools have dotted the Western United States for more than a century, though they often have failed to live up to the holiness of its founder, who opened dozens of schools for underserved African American and Native children during her lifetime. Horror stories of abuse and neglect surround far too many Indian boarding schools, including those with ties to the Church.

St. Augustine doesn't have the sordid past that some schools have, though it's also not without moments where it didn't fully meet its mission. Like many schools of its day, the early years were marked by efforts to introduce the dominant Christian culture to the Natives. It was a goal not just from Church leaders, but the entire U.S. government. Religious groups were assigned to different tribes, all with the goal of assimilation, which included the eradication of all facets of Native life. It left scars, in Nebraska and elsewhere.

"There is some pain around the boarding school days. We still pray for healing for that," said Rev. Mark Beran, the pastor at St. Augustine. Though he grew up only 30 miles away, he had almost no exposure to the reservations. That lack of experience hasn't kept him from being warmly welcomed at events both inside and outside the church.

St. Augustine Indian School is located on the Winnebago reservation, though it serves Native families from two separate tribes, the Winnebago and the Omaha. Nearly all of its students are Native or have Native ancestry, continuing to fulfill St. Katharine's intentions for the schools she founded.

The Pennsylvania-born saint lived with Native families in Winnebago as the school was getting off the ground, always the humble servant. "If she was going to ask a woman to scrub the floor, she'd be right there with them," said Deacon Don Blackbird, the principal at St. Augustine Catholic School. "And she was very protective of trying to make sure the non-Native students didn't come in and take over, that the Natives would always have access to an education."

St. Augustine is more than just a place of employment for Deacon Don Blackbird. He is also a graduate of the school and the first Native to serve as principal. When he decided to pursue education he knew he wanted to do so in a reservation school, or at St. Augustine, his first choice. He taught at the school for a while before entering administration, which is where he's found his home. "I was offered a lot of tempting positions, but I made the decision to commit to here because that's what I felt I was called to do."

His commitment is needed. Over the years, the number of Indian schools has declined considerably, quite a few for good reasons. Today, there are fewer than 50 across the country. Many of them are associated with a religious order. Fewer are parish schools, as St. Augustine is.

To support the schools that are left, St. Augustine helped create the American Indian Catholic Schools Network at the University of Notre Dame. It was a way of expanding its advocacy for American Indian Catholic education beyond just Eastern Nebraska to the entire country.

St. Augustine began as an all-girls school, as Native girls had no other options for education at the time. It ultimately opened up to boys as well, serving as a boarding school for mostly Native children through the 1980s when the residential side closed and it became the day school it is now.

Pierre Merrick was a student at the school in the 1960s, residing on campus despite the fact his family lived a mere 10 miles away at the Omaha Reservation in Macy. He was sent to St. Augustine not just to get the quality education it provided, but the faith-based foundation it was built upon. "My mother had me baptized when I was a baby and she wanted me to know about God and Christianity," he said. His mother died when he was young.

Today, Merrick is back at St. Augustine, serving as the school's Omaha culture teacher. He instructs the children, all of them, on the history, culture, and language of the Omaha people, infusing all of those lessons with the spiritual gifts inherent to both Catholicism and Native life.

"If we're going to survive and our language is going to survive, we have to talk about prayer," he said.

Preserving the language and culture of both tribes has become a part of the mission for the school. In some ways, it's doing so to atone for past mistakes.

"The tribes are struggling to hold onto their culture and we're part of the reason. So we see it as part of our responsibility," Father Mark said.

Over time, after Saint Katharine founded the school, lay and church leaders believe it was the school's objective to rid the Natives of their language and traditions, to hasten their assimilation into the dominant U.S. culture. And, in many ways, it worked.

"You hear stories about children punished for speaking their language, told their language was the devil," Pierre Merrick said. "That probably happened in the 1920s and 1930s."

By the 1960s, when Merrick was a student, it wasn't necessary. English was the language spoken in most homes of both the Omaha and Winnebago tribes.

People such as Merrick and Vinetta Snow were the exception, Natives who grew up understanding the language of their ancestors. The rest were part of the "lost generation," said Vinetta Snow, who serves as the Ho-Chunk cultural teacher at the school. Ho-Chunk is the language spoken by the Winnebago Tribe, who arrived in the community after their forced relocation from Wisconsin in the 1800s.

Vinetta Snow grew up learning the language from her grandfather, and her fluency far exceeds her mother's. She put her skills to work immediately upon her graduation working for the Ho-Chunk Renaissance program, an effort begun in 2001 to revive the language on the reservation.

Her work there provided a natural segue to St. Augustine, where she can begin the process with the youngest tribe members at an age when language retention is easiest. She's seen results already. "My eighth graders were only in sixth grade when they started, and now they can read Ho-Chunk pretty easily."

But to truly flourish, she knows the language must exist outside the classroom. Children have to speak it at home, with encouragement from families. In some cases, the children may be doing some of the teaching. "If we don't have speakers, what will happen? I can only take it so far. These kids need to take it into their own hands and learn it themselves."

Embracing the Native culture, spirituality, and language does not detract from the Catholic education the young people are experiencing. Rather, such lessons enhance it, Deacon Don Blackbird said.

"What St. Augustine has been trying to do, and a lot of other Native American Catholic institutions have been trying to do, is show you can be Native American and keep your culture, keep your language, and you can have your Catholic faith. The two do not conflict; they complement each other," he explained. "The Native spirituality and way of living can flow into your Catholic identity. It brings beauty to the Church."

Getting the larger Catholic world to understand and accept this idea is not a finished process. Some still see the use of Native practices as a threat to the sanctity of the Eucharist. Reassuring those who object remains a dialogue the Church and indigenous peoples of all kinds must continue to have, he said.

Fortunately, the Archdiocese of Omaha is a strong ally of the Native peoples of Nebraska. All deacons and men in formation come to Winnebago to see the uniqueness of the culture. "The Archdiocese of Omaha has done a really good job of being open and respecting the spirituality God has given Native people," Deacon Don said.

The spirituality is reflected in the school and the church itself. The building is designed in a shape reminiscent of a tipi. The stained glass windows feature Native peoples ministering to other Natives. And over time, many other elements of Ho-Chunk and Omaha design and art, such as Winnebago applique, have been incorporated into the artwork and iconography. The students themselves have even contributed to the church. "We try to incorporate things as we go," Deacon Don said.

Since I was writing about the parish school, my Mass visit occurred on a Wednesday, when the students of St. Augustine were worshipping. The young people, less than half of whom are Catholic, were engaged and alert, which isn't the case in every school Mass setting.

If history is an indication, over time some of the young people who aren't Catholics will join the faith, often bringing their whole families with them, a testament to the commitment the St. Augustine staff has to the full Catholic education of its students.

"Parents are choosing to send their kids here because they want a faith-based education. They understand Catholic values and teachings and want their kids to have those, even if they themselves are not Catholic," Deacon Don said. "As a Catholic school we try to provide those things, the positive values, the virtues of the Catholic faith, how we treat each other and walk with each other."

Our Lady of the Fields

Millersville, Maryland

St. Vincent de Paul

Baltimore, Maryland

Jesus said to his disciples: "When the Son of Man comes in his glory, and all the angels with him, he will sit upon his glorious throne, and all the nations will be assembled before him. And he will separate them one from another, as a shepherd separates the sheep from the goats.
He will place the sheep on his right and the goats on his left.
Then the king will say to those on his right, "Come, you who are blessed by my Father. Inherit the kingdom prepared for you from the foundation of the world.
For I was hungry and you gave me food, I was thirsty and you gave me drink, a stranger and you welcomed me,
naked and you clothed me, ill and you cared for me, in prison and you visited me.'
Then the righteous will answer him and say, 'Lord, when did we see you hungry and feed you, or thirsty and give you drink?
When did we see you a stranger and welcome you, or naked and clothe you?
When did we see you ill or in prison, and visit you?'
And the king will say to them in reply, 'Amen, I say to you, whatever you did for one of these least brothers of mine, you did for me.'
Then he will say to those on his left, 'Depart from me, you accursed, into the eternal fire prepared for the devil and his angels.
For I was hungry and you gave me no food, I was thirsty and you gave me no drink, a stranger and you gave me no welcome, naked and you gave me no clothing, ill and in prison, and you did not care for me.'
Then they will answer and say, 'Lord, when did we see you hungry or thirsty or a stranger or naked or ill or in prison, and not minister to your needs?'
He will answer them, 'Amen, I say to you, what you did not do for one of these least ones, you did not do for me.'
And these will go off to eternal punishment, but the righteous to eternal life."
Matthew 25: 31-46

Breaking Bread with the Hungry, Deacon Ed Stoops' long-running ministry, began with a stockpile of good intentions and an equal amount of naïveté. Interestingly, it also began with his daughter.

In 1991, Kate Snyder was watching the television news when the anchors warned that evening was expected to be the coldest day of the year in the Baltimore area. The frigid conditions would be particularly challenging for the city's homeless population, so City Hall was collecting blankets and other goods to help gird the men and women against the plunging temperatures.

Kate Snyder, a perpetual do-gooder like all in the Stoops family, rounded up some blankets from her home, then called some friends for more. Then she took off for downtown Baltimore to drop off her collection.

Her arrival was met with the kind of cartoonish bureaucracy that too often plagues well-meaning efforts. The sole individual she found at City Hall had no idea what to do with the materials, suggesting they could be passed out the following day or so. She was aghast. "'That doesn't make any sense if tonight is the coldest night of the year,'" she recalled saying. "'They need them tonight.'"

Rather than rebuff her completely, the employee allowed her access to the room where other blankets had been collected and welcomed her to deliver them herself. Which is just what she did, loading up her Ford Escort station wagon with as many blankets as she could and circling the downtown area, passing them out to anyone she saw on the streets. "I had no clue what I was doing, just driving around the city handing out blankets. I had no idea where to go."

She repeated the process a few more nights, adding hot coffee and some sandwiches to the mix, the better to aid the impoverished through the rough winter conditions. She continued to drive through the city, learning where she was most likely to find Baltimore's poor. Eventually, one of the beneficiaries of her efforts told her if she picked a single spot, the community would come to her. She didn't have to spend the evenings navigating the downtown streets.

By then, with some prodding by wife Francine, Deacon Ed had joined his daughter on her trips into Baltimore from his home in Millersville, where he served at Our Lady of the Fields. Francine didn't really need to do any arm twisting, however. "I said, 'Katie, you're having far too much fun. I'm going to start helping,'" Deacon Ed recalled.

Slowly, the ministry took shape, the Stoops family settling into fixed locations from which to provide assistance. Francine also joined the ministry, making the food at home for Deacon Ed and Kate Snyder to deliver.

Deacon Ed's wife passed away in 2012. Her contributions to the ministry are remembered each year on the Friday after Thanksgiving, when Francine's Feast is held in her honor.

Eventually, his daughter's other commitments, most notably her own family, kept her from making the weekly trips up north. But her dad was more than ready to take the ministry's reins.

In the 30 years since that initial trip, Deacon Ed has barely missed a Friday. When protests over the death of Freddie Gray while in police custody descended into riots, the chaos wasn't enough to keep Deacon Ed from his weekly mission. "He's so passionate about this ministry," Kate Snyder said admiringly. "These are his people."

For several years, the ministry moved around Baltimore. It spent time serving outside the War Memorial, then relocated in front of City Hall. Another move was required after the terrorist attacks of Sept. 11, as our collective caution pushed any gatherings away from public spaces.

Enter St. Vincent de Paul, a parish fully committed to the mission of its namesake. A deacon from the nearby church had been volunteering with the Breaking Bread ministry and offered the parish as a convenient location from which to serve. The guests could enjoy a leisurely meal in the church basement, free from the elements that had often made the nights quite taxing for all involved.

Breaking Bread with the Hungry would no longer be forced to find other accommodations. The ministry had found its perfect home.

Over time, the ministry also began to expand in Millersville beyond the extended Stoops family. Today, parishioners from Our Lady of the Fields prepare the meals at home, then take them to the parish to be heated before being hauled a half-hour north to St. Vincent de Paul, which does not have a kitchen. "Our Lady of the Fields supports it very generously," said Deacon Ed, who has retired from most of his duties except the Breaking Bread ministry. "It's grown far beyond my family."

For St. Vincent de Paul, these Fridays are, in many ways, just another night. The downtown parish is one that is fully dedicated to serving its neighbors in all ways. It operates a food pantry on Monday nights, runs a men's clothing program twice a month, and participates in numerous social justice ministries.

One of the more innovative programs the parish is involved with in service of the poor is the Resource Exchange. Through the ministry, those area residents who are transitioning from the streets to residential housing are provided with furniture and other basic necessities to help their ability to thrive in their new surroundings. As these tireless volunteers know all too well, neither living in nor escaping poverty comes cheap.

Parishioner Peggy Meyer oversees Breaking Bread with the Hungry from the St. Vincent de Paul side of the program and she's also involved with the Resource Exchange. It's a gratifying ministry, seeing the people they've met through the years achieve their dream of returning to a life with four walls and a roof. She recalled one man who was inside an apartment for a full month before the Resource Exchange could stock his home. "I said, 'It must really feel like home now.' He said, 'It felt like home when I got the key and closed the door.'"

Her participation in multiple ministries is common for the parishioners at St. Vincent de Paul, the typical inner city parish with not a lot of names on the rolls but a lot of desire to contribute. "Service is very big in our parish."

It was that chance to serve, with an assist from her son, that pulled in Anne Asquino, who had been looking for a new parish home after relocating from New England. Her son had battled drug addiction for many years, and came across St. Vincent de Paul when he was taken there by a peer in the early days of his sobriety. "He told me he had found the place for me. He said, 'You'll love this church. It's filled with old hippies.'" She and her son attended Mass that Sunday, and she's been a fixture ever since. Her work schedule initially prevented her from participating in many ministries when she joined, but she was able to volunteer with Breaking Bread with the Hungry.

As with virtually everything else, the ministry was upended by the onset of the coronavirus pandemic. The parish could no longer host the meals in the basement, given various state, local, and archdiocesan guidelines. But that didn't mean the ministry would close up shop altogether. Regardless of how the world was hunkering down, poverty wasn't taking a break. "At the beginning of the pandemic, when things were so uncertain, things shut down for a minute. But we had to figure out how we could do this. The need didn't go away," Anne Asquino said.

Their solution was to use the breezeway, a tunnel-like path that runs underneath the church, opening on either side. The volunteers erect several tables, the first filled with food and drinks, the next offering any other necessities their guests might require. On the day I was there, during the first week of Advent, gloves, hats, and socks were distributed, a reminder that the coming of our Savior also means the arrival of those cold winter nights that served as the launching pad for this 30-year ministry.

The guests are allowed inside one at a time, to walk through and obtain what they need. Peggy Meyer soon realized the meals shouldn't be prepackaged, so the volunteers could inquire about the guest and what was needed. "Maybe some people want to breeze through, and that's fine. But a lot of people are more engaged this way," she reasoned.

Standing just outside the breezeway, occupying his regular post, is where Deacon Ed can be found. He is, quite literally, the face of the operation these days. As the guests line up to take part in the ministry, Deacon Ed is there to greet them. His commitment and good cheer earn him admiration from all involved. "He does a wonderful job," Peggy Meyer said. "They all love to see him and not just because he has tokens in his pocket he hands out."

"He's always there," said James, who has known Deacon Ed since 2013 and visits St. Vincent de Paul on Fridays now and again. "That first impression is a good one."

Before the event began, Deacon Ed led the assembled guests in prayer. But just as important as the spiritual and corporal needs he's meeting, he is also addressing their emotional well-being. He takes the time to speak to each and every visitor, men and women who have become more than people he's serving, but friends.

Wendell had only known Deacon Ed for about a year when we met, but it was enough time to recognize the clergyman's quality character. "When he walks by, everyone runs at him. He's a good man."

What makes him good? "He treats us well. He doesn't judge us."

After each Friday night's service wraps up, Deacon Ed summarizes how it went for Our Lady of the Fields' weekly bulletin. His accounts are not simply a dry retelling of the number of meals served and guests who came by. Rather, he updates the parish on the lives of the Baltimore residents he has come to know. Their highs and lows, triumphs and setbacks, detailed for the parishioners of his home church.

On the weekend after I was privileged to experience Breaking Bread with the Hungry, he filed this report for the parishioners back home:

Dear Companions,

We served 33 guests.

Mr. L. just got out of the hospital. He suffers from arthritis, especially in his shoulders, but really all his joints – possibly from sleeping on cold surfaces. The pills the hospital gave him help some.

Miss B. spoke of how she enjoys meeting with us every Friday; seeing friends is the best.

Miss K thought the slouchy beanie cap I wore because without hair my head gets cold, to be hilarious. She couldn't stop laughing.

My little hatch-back was loaded with sleeping bags, tents, blankets, quilts, coats, hats, gloves and socks from many generous people. My car is empty now, but many hearts are full of gratitude for the gift of warmth.

As we approach Christmas more and more of you are donating Christmas candy and cookies. Please keep them coming. They can be brought to the kitchen at Our Lady of the Fields, especially on Thursday before Christmas eve.

Our friends gathered from the West Side and from the East side rejoicing that they are remembered by God who is leading them in joy by the light of his glory, with his mercy and justice for company. (Paraphrase of Baruch, 5, the first reading for the 2nd Sunday of Advent.)

Ed

His decades-long service to the hungry is not perfunctory. He doesn't just punch the clock on another two-hour shift.

No, he's reconnecting with friends, engaging in a mutually respectful relationship that recognizes the inherent, God-given dignity each one of us is bestowed with. That is his legacy, and it's a beautiful one.

Catedral Basilica Menor de San Juan Bautista

San Juan, Puerto Rico

"And I saw the river over which every soul must pass to reach the Kingdom of Heaven, and the name of the river was Suffering. And I saw the boat which carries souls across that river, and the name of the boat was Love."
Saint John of the Cross

MARIA.

There are few names more sacred on the island of Puerto Rico than the Spanish, and Latin, for the Blessed Mother. Thus, it is a cruel irony that in this most Catholic of locations, a place that's experienced more cruelty and irony than any population deserves, the name has taken on an entirely different and tragic meaning.

It was the late summer of 2020. The 3.4 million people of the territory were still cleaning up the wreckage caused by Hurricane Irma two weeks earlier when they were dealt an even bigger blow. On Sept. 20, shortly after daybreak, Hurricane Maria made landfall in Puerto Rico, bringing with it the most devastating storm in the island's history.

Over the course of a single day, the Caribbean isle was battered by unimaginable rainfall, brutal flooding, and 150-mile per hour winds. The destruction, both during the storm and in its unimaginably long wake, was profound. More than $90 billion in property damage. Power lost for months for most of the island. And, most tragically of all, close to 3,000 people dead from a variety of storm-related causes. On an island that defines itself chronologically by its tropical storms, Maria became the tempest that would serve as the ultimate timeline reference point.

Yet two days after the storm ripped through the archipelago and swirled back off into the Atlantic, the first sign of hope emerged. The people of this resilient island who could make their way into Old San Juan would find one bedrock there for them in this most difficult of times – the doors to the Catedral Basilica Menor de San Juan Bautista would be open. Mass would be said. As always, Christ would be there to guide us through the darkness.

"The archbishop asked, 'Please keep the Cathedral open?'" recalled Rev. Ernesto Gonzalez, then and now the vicar for San Juan Bautista. "And the Saturday after the storm, we did that."

Like the rest of the island, the Cathedral had no power and wouldn't get it back for three to four months. Even places that you never want to see without electricity were no match for Maria's wrath. Father Ernesto anointed three people right there on the steps to the Cathedral, patients awaiting surgery but taken out of the hospital because it was simply too hot for them inside.

The sun, which poured in from over the water just west of the Cathedral, provided the main source of illumination. The voices of Father Ernesto and the pastor, Rev. Benjamin A. Perez Cruz, got no amplification from a sound system rendered useless. Yet the men were there to offer Mass all the same, a testament to the fact no storm is a match for the faith that unites us.

But the Church was not just there for the people of the island to receive the sacraments. It was also instrumental in aiding the population's immediate physical needs.

Caritas, the Puerto Rican arm of Catholic Charities, was the driving force in assisting the people across the island, not just in the Archdiocese of San Juan. Founded in 1969 to aid the transition of people to and from the mainland, it has become the primary charitable organization for the Church in the territory. The organization has been through its share of brutal storms, including previous major hurricanes George and Hugo, but none was as ruinous as the 2017 tragedy.

"We've been working for a long time in disasters. When Hurricane Maria came, we were already organized. It was not something very different from what we were doing for years, except for the gravity of the situation," said Rev. Enrique Camacho, who was appointed to head up the organization a few years before the storms.

In the aftermath of Maria, Caritas worked with the parishes across the island, distributing food vouchers and other necessities. The organization's ability to provide immediate help was aided by the strong groundwork laid in advance of the storm, building solid relationships with the Catholic churches that are found everywhere on Puerto Rico. In fact, it's what made Caritas such an ideal source of aid to the population.

Unlike any of the 50 states, Puerto Rico is majority Catholic, with estimates running anywhere from 55 to 75 percent of the population identifying that way. Most of the rest of the people are also Christian. Thus, Caritas and the long-established Salvation Army were perfectly positioned to reach the people under conditions where access and communication were so limited.

Caritas also benefited from its relationship with Catholic Charities USA and other organizations based on the mainland. Their responses to the catastrophe were thorough and generous. "We were blessed with the help of a lot of organizations, communities, families," Father Camacho said. Among the givers were many people in the Puerto Rican diaspora spread out across the United States, men and women who had relocated to the mainland but never forgot about their homeland during the crisis.

Donations of food, money, and other essentials came pouring in from around the country and world and Caritas served as the distribution arm, relaying it to the people in each of Puerto Rico's six dioceses.

But, Father Camacho is quick to point out, aid comes in many forms, not just the tangible. That's where an organization such as Caritas distinguishes itself from other nonprofits and service organizations. "It was our moment to be present," he related. "Our purpose is not just giving aid; our purpose is deeper. It is to be the love of Christ among our people, especially those most in need."

In the weeks and months after Maria's devastation, long after TV news crews and other organizations hightailed it out of Puerto Rico in pursuit of a more recent event, Caritas remained on the ground, addressing the ongoing needs of its communities.

The organization transitioned from direct aid of food and water and money to longer term demands, such as establishing clinics with doctors, nurses, psychologists. Homes were rebuilt, communities strengthened. And Caritas continued to act not just with the people of the island, but as the clearinghouse for those from elsewhere who still wanted to help. For example, Caritas has partnered with Catholic Charities of Omaha, using the Nebraska organization's Microbusiness and Asset Development Program to help people at home who wanted to create their own businesses. "We are still working in helping the victims of Maria because we are still recovering," Father Camacho said.

The past five years and counting have been anything but easy for Caritas and the people it serves. Yet, there have been blessings to be found throughout the ordeal. "It has been a journey, full of hope and good things," he said.

The recovery from Maria is ongoing and will take years to complete. But there are signs of progress, small gains among the hardships. The Cathedral is just one such example.

The year of my visit, 2021, represented the 500th anniversary of Catedral Basilica Menor de San Juan Bautista, making it the oldest Catholic Church in the United States and the second oldest in the Western Hemisphere. A new round of renovations had just been wrapped up in advance of the milestone, a process Maria played an accidental part in completing.

There was once a series of doors at the top of the Cathedral that would be opened and closed periodically. Stained glass had replaced the doors at the start of the 20th century, but Hurricane Hugo blew out all of the glass in 1989. The fix, if it could be called such a thing, was to simply board up the windows, a solution that led to mold and other forms of deterioration.

About 10 years back, a new remedy was devised, installing vented windows where the doors and stained glass used to sit. The first one was put in place right before Maria. "It was great. It actually held, which proved the concept," Father Ernesto explained. By 2021, the remaining windows were installed, righting one of the design wrongs that tend to plague long-standing church buildings.

Another unorthodox decision by past well-meaning leaders will be a little more difficult to rectify. Underneath the altar are the tombs of 17 of the 58 bishops who have served the archdiocese. During a previous attempt to prevent against ransacking – many of the bishops having been buried with rings and other valuables – the crypts were whitewashed. Then, in a decision that perplexes Father Ernesto, they were sealed, incapable of being accessed through the Cathedral. "Now, the only way to get to the crypts is to move the altar, which is never going to happen. We have to find a way around it," he said.

In some ways, the inaccessible tombs only add to the story of this wonderful site, a Cathedral awash in history, art, and peculiarities. Few know that better than Luis Jay Rivera Marcano, the young man who serves as treasurer of the art, of the Cathedral.

The custodian took me on a tour of San Juan Bautista, explaining the stories behind each of the Cathedral's chapels and where many of its gifts came from. Its relics include the display of the body of St. Pius, the only pope whose remains are kept in the United States. And as many statues and sculptures and paintings are showcased at the glorious worship space, even more are part of a collection in a city museum, all of them under his curation. He treasures his role and the location where he serves.

"This is a very special place for Puerto Ricans, not just for Catholics, but for all Puerto Ricans. Here is their house," he said.

That the population is protective of the Cathedral is not surprising, as the faith has such an integral part in the island's history.

"Catholicism has played an important and significant role in forming the culture of Puerto Rico. I remember many years ago when the late William Cardinal Levada visited Puerto Rico, he mentioned to me, 'I can tell this is a Catholic country,' related Most Rev. Roberto Octavio Gonzalez Nieves, the archbishop of San Juan. "I presume that he detected the subtleties of Catholicism present in the daily social life in the country that distinguishes it from the religious climate, for example, in the United States."

It is not just island natives drawn to Old San Juan and its many churches, including the Cathedral. Daily Mass is typically a tourist affair, as it was on the day I attended. But visitors aren't limited to devout Catholics such as Justin and Karlene Hibbard, attending Mass on their trip to the island from Utah. The Cathedral is also descended upon by simple gawkers, though the area's many tour guides try to keep them from interfering when Mass is being said or from entering the presbytery when it's not, an infrequent but occasional violation.

The four Sunday Masses are more local, though oddly they're typically populated by former residents of Old San Juan who have relocated, while the people who live nearby worship elsewhere. "It happens a lot with parishes in Puerto Rico. People just go where they are happiest," Father Ernesto said.

It's all part of the unique charm of the island, where influences from many cultures, including the Spanish, Dutch, French, and its stateside neighbors have created a delightful mix of Catholic traditions and rituals.

"We have a hodgepodge here," Father Ernesto said. "But it's great."

Or, as the leader of the Church on the island noted. "The greatest strength of the Catholic Church in Puerto Rico is the weight of its historical presence and cultural influence. So many of Puerto Rico's thinkers, poets, political leaders, and artists have rooted their views within the Catholic 'weltanschauung,'" said Archbishop Nieves.

St. John Paul II Catholic Mission

Rutledge, Tennessee

"It is not the soul alone that should be healthy; if the mind is healthy in a healthy body, all will be healthy and much better prepared to give God greater service."
Saint Ignatius of Loyola

It is a match most fitting. In the early morning hours on May 12, 2022, the St. Mary's Legacy Clinic set out from Knoxville en route to St. John Paul II Catholic Mission. The trip to Rutledge was part of the clinic's normal monthly rotation, one of six sites the mobile clinic visits where its volunteer brigade serves the healthcare needs of the underserved rural south.

And St. John Paul II is the ideal choice to see their wondrous work in action. The young church was founded by the Glenmary Home Missioners, the 83-year-old society of priests and brothers formed to serve the spiritual needs of underserved rural America.

The body and the soul are both being cared for in a single location in East Tennessee.

St. Mary's Legacy Clinic is the spiritual heir of St. Mary's Hospital, the Knoxville medical center opened in 1930 by the Sisters of Mercy. Following decades of the kind of mergers and acquisitions that have defined modern healthcare, the hospital became part of a for-profit healthcare operation, whose mission is vastly different than the one established by the women religious.

However, with help of money negotiated in the final sale, the Diocese of Knoxville established the St. Mary's Legacy Foundation, which ultimately launched the clinic under the leadership of Sister Mariana Koonce. From its humble beginnings in January 2014, the clinic now travels approximately 100 miles per week, seeing more than 800 of the working poor in East Tennessee.

Martin Vargas serves as executive director of the clinic, though he acknowledges Sister Mariana's fingerprints remain all over the organization. "She did everything a founder does. She built the building. She got the bus. She incorporated. She recruited the first volunteers. So we have her legacy to build on and the legacy of the Sisters of Mercy before her from the 1930s forward," he said.

The clinic provides the full range of primary care services to its clients, the uninsured or underinsured of places such as Grainger County. Its services include chronic disease management, preventive care, annual physicals, screenings pap smears, and some outpatient procedures. "Anything you can do in a family medicine doctor's office, we can do here," said Sister Mary Lisa Renfer, RSM DO.

Sister Mary Lisa speaks with authority. The young sister is not just a member of the religious community, but also a medical doctor. She serves as the clinic's medical director, one of only three full-time employees at the clinic along with Martin Vargas and Beth Ann Arrigo, the nurse manager.

St. Mary's very existence has become particularly important in recent years as changes in healthcare economics have resulted in many rural hospitals and other care facilities shuttering. That makes proper health management even more difficult for the less fortunate in communities such as Rutledge, as the men and women must often take time out of work to drive long distances simply to see a physician.

Not surprising, many of these people have responded to these hostile conditions by simply ignoring their bodies' needs. "A lot of them haven't seen a physician in years. It takes a lot of courage to step out and say, 'I want to do something to better myself,'" Sister Mary Lisa said.

In addition to the costs and inaccessibility, previous sour experiences with the for-profit health system have only increased St. Mary's patients' dissatisfaction with the process. "A lot of them have not been treated well, especially in emergency rooms," Sister Mary Lisa said. "If you don't have insurance, people make assumptions."

The parishioners don't encounter that attitude with the clinic. "Many people are in tears by the end of their visit. Even if I can't give them everything they're looking for, they've been treated so well it gives them that little bit of boost to keep them moving forward," she said.

Patti Pemberton has seen how the clinic's positive approach pays remarkable dividends. The nurse works in triage with Mary Ann Tonniesson, reviewing medical histories of the clients before they board the bus to see one of the two physicians on duty. Thus, she's able to chronicle the changes that take place with the men and women they have treated regularly. It's immensely gratifying, she said, to see patients returning with their blood pressure under control or the smoking habit having been kicked.

"There's a lot of teaching that goes on in the bus. That's why we're here," she said.

The two women are a part of a full team of care givers. That ranges from the doctors such as Sister Mary Lisa to a bevy of nurses. But it also includes people without any background in medicine such as Susan Lawlor, who welcomes each patient into the clinic and gets the process started. "My only requirement of a volunteer is a good smile," Martin Vargas said.

And that's easy to find at St. Mary's. "The joy of a volunteer-run health clinic is people are here because they want to be here. They love what they do and they give 110 percent to help our patients," said Sister Mary Lisa.

All of St. Mary's services are provided at no cost, which can include medication. That's obviously an incredible benefit given the astronomical costs of some pharmaceuticals. Mary Ann Tonnieson recalled an instance where the clinic was able to provide free medicine to a man with diabetes, who then walked out of his visit and beamed to his wife, "They gave me all my medicine. I don't have to worry about it anymore."

Securing that medicine and other donations is one of the many functions Sister Mary Lisa performs. The habit doesn't hurt, said her fellow physician, Dr. Charles Groves.

"She does a great job of getting free drugs and other things. It's a little harder to say 'No' to her than it would be to you or I," said Dr. Groves, who has a full-time job working for an insurance company in addition to his extensive volunteer work with the clinic.

"It's great working with people of faith, especially the nuns," he added.

The team's day begins well before the first patient arrives, as it takes time to both set up the bus in the parking lot and the clerical side of the operation inside St. John Paul II where patients are received.

The clinic now has ample room to operate at the church, though that wasn't always the case. The mission recently left its storefront operations across the highway to its newly built facility on Bryan Road. So new, in fact, that two weeks after I was there, Bishop Richard F. Stika of the Diocese of Knoxville was in Rutledge to dedicate St. John Paul II.

And the church was designed with further expansion in mind. As the community continues to grow, the current worship space will be converted into a church hall and a new sanctuary will be constructed. Church leaders hope to do so in the same way the first building project was done, almost entirely with volunteer labor and with no mortgage on the property.

The establishment of a permanent worship space is a big step forward for the mission church, which began operations in Rutledge in 2011, part of the Glenmary Home Missioners' ongoing commitment to bring the Church to places it's never been before. It has 13 active missions at the moment, all in the Southeast.

"Our goal as Glenmarys, we come to an area where there's no Catholic presence or minimal Catholic presence and we help build up the community," said Rev. Neil Pezzulo, pastor. "We build up their spiritual life."

That has to be done a little differently in a mission church. As the people in the area have little experience with the Church, Father Neil must be visible in the community, whether that's through ecumenism or simple acts of mercy. "Many diocesan priests view the parish as a destination. The difference for me and most missionaries is we view this as a launching pad to the community."

The local church's growth to date has not yet been the result of converting native Tennesseans to the Catholic faith, but serving the influx of Catholics to the area. They are represented by relocating or retiring people from up north, drawn to the country comfort of Grainger County, or immigrants from Mexico and elsewhere in Latin America, a cohort that makes up the bulk of the congregation. St. John

Paul II offers an English language vigil Mass on Saturday followed by a Spanish Mass on Sunday.

Over time, the hope is that growth will continue until the mission can become a full parish, at which point the missioners will turn it over to the diocese. That transition typically follows hitting such goals as reaching economic stability, offering religious education, and creating outreach efforts, a few of the benchmarks of a traditional parish. But it's the road to get there that energizes Father Neil.

"Most diocesan churches are well established. They've got their programs, their schools," he said. "We're not plugged into something that's already established. I'm co-creating our future with the people of God here."

Likewise, the professionals and volunteers alike of St. Mary's Legacy Clinic are continuing to create their future. That includes the recent introduction of an Electric Medical Record system. The EMR allows for much more efficient tracking of patients' medical records.

Additionally, the clinic began expanding into telehealth during the pandemic, which it continues to offer as an option. Such an alternative has allowed St. Mary's to double the number of patients it can care for.

Looking ahead, Martin Vargas envisions a day when each of the rural counties in the Diocese of Knoxville is served by St. Mary's. And he's always interested in expanding the services provided, including the ability to add gastrointestinal care and improve its mental health-care capabilities.

But that's then. For now, the team of volunteers will continue to focus on the patients in front of them, men and women in all parts of their health journey. The desire for each of the patients they serve is to set them on a path where they won't need St. Mary's any longer. "Our goal is to get them to health to wellness to wealth. When you become insured, you graduate," Martin Vargas said.

Of course, that isn't possible for everyone they see. Some will continue to need their services. And some, the St. Mary's team knows, will die, death being the natural outcome of life. But just as there is profound joy to be found in healing, there can also be beauty in the passing from this life to the next.

"We are an active participant in helping people find comfort as they move on to their end," the executive director said.

All of life's mysteries are present in the clinic. "As a physician, it's very gratifying because it's a group of people who really need care, who desire to be well and often we can help and make a difference," Sister Mary Lisa said. "And as a religious sister, it's very rewarding because you encounter Jesus Christ every day in these people in a very real way."

Nativity of Our Savior

Portage, Indiana

*"Christ be with me, Christ within me, Christ behind me, Christ before me,
Christ beside me, Christ to win me, Christ to comfort me and restore me,
Christ beneath me, Christ above me, Christ in quiet, Christ in danger,
Christ in hearts of all that love me, Christ in mouth of friend and stranger."*
Saint Patrick

LET'S START THIS FINAL CHAPTER RIGHT – WITH A CONFESSION. This book's title is a lie. *52 Masses* is both too many Masses and too few.

It was too many because the services at the Eastern churches are not formally called Masses. At the Melkite Church, the congregation celebrates the Divine Liturgy. At the Syro-Malabar Church, it is Holy Qurbana. These are just two of the innumerable lessons about the Catholic Church I learned over the course of the past year and a few months.

Yet, even with those subtractions, 52 is still far too few. There were vigil Masses on Saturdays followed by another Mass on Sunday. There were two or three Sunday Masses in a single day. There were untold daily Masses and even a few Masses back at my home parish when I wasn't on the road.

I only wish it would have been more.

Now I'm back where everything, to an extent, began, which serves as a reminder of the foolhardiness of man's carefully constructed "plans." When this idea was first given to me, Nativity of Our Savior was, in so many ways, my home. It was where my wife worked for 10 years and where my kids all went to school. And it was where I served as a Eucharistic minister, joined the Knights of Columbus and became a member of the Society of St. Vincent de Paul. For 15 years, our lives revolved around Nativity in every way. And I fully expected it to be my home when I completed this trip. Alas, life often intervenes in ways we cannot predict, and we moved from Indiana to Illinois in 2020, a year before I took off.

Still, it felt appropriate to finish here, where so much of my Catholic life began to take shape. And here, where I've spent so many Sundays, is an ideal spot to reflect on how much the trip has molded me even further.

Put simply, the past year and a few months have been a revelation. Before heading out on my first Mass visit, I knew I was embarking on a life-changing pilgrimage. Still, it managed to exceed even my ridiculously lofty expectations.

The experience was remarkably enriching in so many ways. Obviously, and most prominently, my spiritual life grew exponentially. I feel closer to Christ than I ever have, and my connection to my Catholic faith has never been stronger. Frankly, I'd be profoundly disappointed if I didn't feel that way.

But the growth didn't end there. I was also stimulated emotionally and intellectually. I heard stories of pain and joy in equal measures, from men and women of devout faith. I saw in their faces and heard in their voices how blessings exist in both tragedy and triumph. They took strength from their faith in Christ, and in turn inspired me to do likewise in all my life's occurrences.

My understanding of the faith and its history and all that surrounds it exploded. As a lay Catholic who, unlike his children, never had the privilege of a Catholic school education, I had ample room to grow my knowledge. I was a pretty lumpy piece of clay, catechistically speaking.

From late night conversations at the rectory with Father Bernie at St. Peter the Apostle in Kansas, to sitting in on a fascinating Adult Faith Formation classes taught by Rev. Randall Rentner, CSC at Sacred Heart in Colorado Springs, and so many others, I was blessed to soak up the wisdom of learned men and women in vocations. Yet lay people were also sources of great insight, whether that was Josephine Belloso's work in Catholic art or Susan Treacy's intimate understanding of sacred music or Dr. Carole Brown's profound acuity on discipleship. I felt I was getting a master's level education in all things Catholic, only without the crippling student debt.

And wisdom didn't just come from scholars. At Holy Name in Providence, Nigerian-born Paschal Aguocha outlined the list of three things every Catholic should do, including my favorite: Three times a year, upon the completion of Mass, each Catholic man and woman should go to the cemetery and pray the Rosary for those who have passed before us. Listen to him.

Even at the Mass itself, surrounded by hundreds of other parishioners, the readings, the Gospels, and homilies took on greater meaning, had more relevance in my day-to-day life than I ever noticed before.

The first time I felt like a homily was directed at me, but certainly not the last, was at Extreme Faith Camp in Minnesota. The congregation at EFC, teenagers almost all, is quite a bit different than the norm, a bit more energetic, a little more spirit filled. Rev. Brian Park was feeding that spirit, encouraging them to chant a response. He instructed one section of the worship space to say, "Do not." Another was told to say, "To God." And the perpetual adoration gang above was instructed to declare, "Say no."

I dutifully did my part, and it quickly reminded me of my brief crisis just a week earlier. As I was driving out on my very first visit, watching the gas prices skyrocket and worrying about how I would keep pace with my work duties and obligations to my wife and children, doubt began to creep in. But the following day, as I was on my way to my first Mass, a sense of calm came over me. It was the Holy Spirit, reminding me not to worry, that this was what I was supposed to be doing. God would take care of me.

I was being told, quite clearly, "Do Not Say No To God." I could only smile when Father Park reminded me.

In Mississippi, after having spent the night in a hotel room most charitably described as "lacking," I listened as Rev. Guy Wilson zeroed in on the part of the day's Gospel reading from Mark where the Pharisees mocked the disciples for eating with their hands. "Nothing that enters one from outside can defile that person; but the things that come out from within are what defile," Jesus instructed us, a pointed reminder I absolutely needed to hear.

It was still ringing true in the very last Mass at Nativity. During this latest of Rev. Kevin McCarthy's always-engaging homilies, he mentioned how the Eucharist quenches our thirst and satisfies our hunger. This idea was proved again and again on the road, as I drove hundreds of miles without stopping for food or drink or rest, the Eucharist amply sustaining me on my mission.

In retrospect, it's obvious the Gospel readings and homilies during my trip were not more laser-pointed at me than the ones I hear at home. Rather, I was simply more open to the wisdom and universality of the message being delivered.

The helpful instructions from the clergy could come from anywhere. In November 2021, in between trips, I came across a message from Pope Francis directed at the journalists who cover the Vatican and other Church matters. During a ceremony awarding the ranks of Knight and Dame of the Grand Cross of the Order of Pope Pius to Philip Pullella and Valentina Alazraki, the pope said:

"For a journalist, listening means having the patience to meet face to face with the people to be interviewed, the protagonists of the stories being told, the sources from which to receive news. Listening always goes hand in hand with seeing, with being present: certain nuances, sensations, and well-rounded descriptions can only be conveyed to readers, listeners, and spectators if the journalist has listened and seen for him – or herself. This means escaping – and I know how difficult this is in your work – escaping from the tyranny of always being online, on social networks, on the web. The journalism of listening and seeing well requires time. Not everything can be told through email, the telephone, or a screen."

He was, it goes without saying, absolutely right.

Much of the material for this book was gathered through phone interviews, set up by email exchanges. It was practical and considerate, allowing me to speak to people on their schedules, rather than mine. It allowed me to spread my work over a longer period, not rushed upon return. It made sense.

Yet without attending those Masses, without meeting face to face and receiving that news, I would have missed so many wonderful conversations, so many encounters. I loved every suggestion, every recommendation how I needed to visit this parish when I go to Arizona, or this shrine in Ohio, or just this special aspect of the parish I had just visited.

Many times, fulfilling those requests was not feasible, having already been to a state or knowing I was going to be writing about that particular topic somewhere else. But it was the passion these devout Catholics had for so many elements of the faith that stuck with me, that cemented a smile on my face as I ambled out of Mass each Sunday and stayed with me on the long drive home.

And sometimes, those tips even worked. At Notre Dame of Bethlehem in Pennsylvania, I was struck by the sign of Bethlehem Catholic's baseball team filing in to the 10:30 a.m. Mass as a unit, each young man wearing his BECAHI pullover shirt and taking a seat in one of the first few pews.

I learned from a parishioner this was a requirement of the team and Matt Corsi, its second-year coach. If the team has a Sunday game or obligation, as they did that evening against rival Allentown Central Catholic, then the team must attend Mass together at one of the three main parishes that feed into BECA – Notre Dame, St. Anne, or Our Lady of Perpetual Help.

"To me, there's no better way to get close as a team than attending Sunday Mass together," said Coach Corsi, who attended Bethlehem Catholic and played for the equally devout Mike Grasso. "We're going to show them that you want to go to Mass. You want to get closer to God."

I think it's a wonderful practice, one that other coaches – whether those heading up CYO teams up through Catholic college programs – should consider following. I'm not alone in that sentiment.

"That's what you should put in your book. That's a coach who understands what his role is and how the Catholic faith comes first," implored my wife, a longtime Catholic school principal, when I related this story to her that evening. It turns out that the best way to spur the author to follow through on your suggestion is to be married to him, to be the woman who graciously supported her husband while he spent so many weekends on the road over the course of a year-plus. Who knew?

All of the most memorable experiences, the most impressionable events, took place around the parishes, when I was engaged with these unforgettable Catholic men and women. I heard stories that could only be told in the intimacy of a personal setting, not shared on a conference call. I experienced evening prayers in the friary with Father Joseph and Brother Nick, marveled at the tireless but joyful work of the volunteer medical professionals with St. Mary's Legacy Clinic, flew with Father Scott, and laughed with too many great people to count. Yes, laughed. On top of everything else, it was simply great fun.

To paraphrase Pope Francis, I wore out the soles of my shoes. I did so figuratively and, as when I logged about 2.5 miles with the Sacred Encounters Ministry in Seattle, literally.

I know I've been blessed beyond belief, over the course of those 52 Saturdays, Sundays, and more, to be introduced to the most inspiring group of men and women. I hope these stories that preceded do their incredible work justice. When I set out on this trek, I never expected to be gifted with so many amazing accounts to share, so many blessings. There were, as Bakersfield's Gary Ridgeway so colorfully put it, graces all over the place. There was also, I must acknowledge, one instance of total gracelessness.

In San Juan, Puerto Rico, I was on a behind-the-scenes tour of the Catedral Basilica Menor de San Juan Bautista, descending the marvelous spiral staircase. I stepped improperly on the final stair, precipitating an awkward tumble.

As I brushed off 500 years and approximately 30 pounds of limestone dust from my pants while trying to ignore the searing pain in my rapidly ballooning left ankle and the even greater injury to my pride, my tour guide decided to give me a helpful bit of free narration to be used in these pages.

"On the oldest spiral staircase in The Americas, I decided to dive down," Luis Jay Rivera Marcano said, providing the laugh the situation called for and I so desperately needed.

One of the most common questions I was posed during the course of my trip is how I decided to do this at all. Initially, my response was something about coming up with the idea after dropping my youngest son off at high school soccer practice. But that answer, time and experience demonstrated, was incorrect.

It wasn't me who came up with the idea. At parish after parish, as blessing after blessing, grace after grave revealed themselves to me, it was clear this was not my doing. Rather, it was the Holy Spirit, planting the seed and pointing me in this particular direction or calling on me to speak with this man or woman. And it was that knowledge that aided me. Many times, when I was weak, I wondered if this was appropriate. Should I, the very definition of a lay Catholic, be doing this? Or was this better suited to someone else, a Catholic scholar perhaps, or someone closer to holiness than an ordinary sinner such as me? And those doubts could have doomed me if not for that sense that I was called to do this. Why? I don't know. I'll never know why I was chosen, but I'm supremely grateful I was.

The guiding hand of the Holy Spirit was never more clear to me than when I visited St. Gianna's Maternity Home in Warsaw, North Dakota. While the entire weekend was wonderful, as I knew it would be, one thoroughly unanticipated moment will stay with me forever.

I was in the parlor room, interviewing Ke, the young mother staying at the home. She was telling me about her upbringing before St. Gianna's, a childhood bereft of the love and kindness that should be the rule in every house. During the course of our conversation we were interrupted, and I took that as the natural time to end our conversation. "No, no, no," she said. "We have to keep talking," an insistence I rarely experience from the people I'm interviewing.

She closed the door and proceeded to spend the next 20 minutes asking me questions: "How do you stay married? How do you trust your spouse? How do you keep from getting bored?"

The queries kept coming and I did the best to answer them truthfully.

Whatever else I expected from my pilgrimage, I never thought I would ever be in the position where I was uniquely qualified to help. But this young woman saw in me a man blessed with a loving wife and three great children, which is what she desperately wanted out of her life. She wasn't going to pass up the opportunity presented to her.

I knew then the Holy Spirit had placed me right there, at the very moment in time, to be the resource this young woman so richly deserved. And whatever else happened over the next 45 weeks or so of my trip, no matter what inconveniences large or small befell me, that chance to be a fount of help and hope to that young mom validated every last mile of my journey.

When I started, it was my dearest hope I would paint a picture of life in the Catholic Church and all that makes it special, all that makes it the universal church. And that I would do my part to glorify God. I hope I've done that, at least to the absolute best of the ability the Lord granted me.

My other hope, the personal one, was to come home a better Catholic, a better person. Now, I can't be the judge of that. That is a question only my wife, my children, my friends, co-workers, and even strangers I meet along the way can speak to. I will say, however, that I feel different. I feel more at peace. I feel more patient, more compassionate. I feel less inclined to temptation. These are really great feelings to have.

I pray it lasts. I pray I never lose this. But the beauty of my experience is if I do start to backslide, to suffer some loss of that fulfillment that can only come from a meaningful relationship with Christ, I won't have to travel thousands of miles to find it again.

It's here.

In our Church.